Effective Strategies for Helping Couples and Families

John S. Carpenter

PESI, LLC
PO Box 1000
200 Spring Street
Eau Claire, Wisconsin 54702

Printed in the United States of America

ISBN: 1-9722147-0-4

**For information on this and other PESI manuals
and audio recordings, please call 800-843-7763
or visit our website at www.pesi.com**

Dedication

To Debra, an intelligent, gifted, and beautiful woman whom I love and enjoy as my best friend and fun-loving partner in life. She is the inspiration and loving support behind this work.

About the Author

John S. Carpenter has been a Licensed Clinical Social Worker in the field of Psychiatry for over 23 years. Having obtained a BA in Psychology from DePauw University in Indiana and a Masters in Social Work from Washington University in St. Louis, John began his practice in Springfield, Missouri, in 1979. John has worked in a variety of settings including outpatient clinics, in-patient hospital units, day treatment programs, and private offices. John has offered therapy services to individuals, couples, families, and groups for a wide assortment of mental health disorders, behavioral problems, and relationship issues. His therapeutic approach was influenced by a mixture of Psychodynamic Theory, Transactional Analysis, Gestalt Therapy, Family Systems, and Psychodrama.

John was also trained in Clinical Hypnosis at the Menninger Clinic which led to a greater interest in the power of imagery, sensory experiences, attitudes, and beliefs. His willingness to conduct professional research into paranormal phenomenon led to international recognition as a responsible hypnotherapist, researcher, writer, and speaker worldwide.

John combines this interest in how the mind perceives, learns, and remembers with his desire to explore relationship issues in couples and families. Having worked with hundreds of couples and families over the years, John has found the approaches and techniques which seem to yield the best results. Presently, he has offices in both Branson and Springfield, Missouri. John lectures to other professionals nationwide every month for a few days on working with couples and families.

John also has enjoyed volunteer activities such as working with Parents Anonymous and several adoption agencies. He helped to found Worldwide Love for Children, Inc. in Springfield, Missouri.

John's father was a well-respected and well-known Methodist minister in the state of Indiana. John's mother was dedicated toward the family and her husband when he suffered many years of disability from Multiple Sclerosis. John's brother has worked for years in New York City as an attorney. John's sister and her husband gave up careers in the medical field to pursue wilderness photography in northern Michigan and the Great Lakes region.

John enjoys music, playing piano, photography, traveling, writing, computers, water sports, and family activities. He and his soul mate Debra share so many common interests, activities, and beliefs. He is a proud father to Josh and Bobby in Springfield and to Megan, Katie, and Ben in Dallas.

Contents

Preface

This is a book about helping people in relationships. Although couples and families represent the most intimate, emotional, and satisfying kinds of relationships, these effective strategies will help all kinds of relationships in all kinds of situations. These techniques are visual, metaphoric, and experiential—all of which promote clear understanding, efficient learning, and a lasting memory. This book is a challenge for therapists to begin trusting their own eyes, intuition, and creativity. These approaches will lure therapists from their chairs and into a more experiential and revealing form of therapy.

Solutions are developed from emotional positions and perceptions —not from verbal contracts. Changes occur from *feeling* the correct directions rather than guessing at them. Images stay in our minds for a very long time; words are forgotten tomorrow. Words are misleading, misunderstood, misrepresenting, and mistaken for other meanings. An image can capture a perspective in one unforgettable moment. An experiential exercise may stay with us the rest of our lives. Every person can *know* what feels comfortable or *feels right* for him. As professional counselors helping people, we need to use whatever is going to be the best teacher, best experience, and best help for those troubled in relationships.

The original title of this book was going to be:

Smart Eyes, Silent Mouths, Knowing Hearts, Wiser Paths

However, this title—being just a bunch of words—could have confused, misled, or repelled potential readers. These words do not acquire their true meaning until *after* the reader has completed this book. Readers may *assume* that they might know what this book may be about, but they would likely guess wrong from these words alone. Meaning is acquired with the *experience* of absorbing the contents of this book. Then, these words finally gain the full meaning that was intended for their selection and use as a title.

Until the reader has completed this book, the title shall remain *Effective Strategies for Helping Couples and Families*. At that time the reader can return to his world, using his eyes more wisely, listening more than speaking, trusting his intuitive and creative directions that *feel right*, and, as a result, choosing wiser paths for helping his clients.

Effective and Experiential Therapy

The Endless Search For New, More Effective Interventions (Somewhere Over the Rainbow)

Life would seem a whole lot easier if therapists could find that "silver bullet" or one fantastic technique which would solve many difficult situations that couples and families face. Despite reading countless books on various approaches, studying the published research, and attending numerous workshops, we often keep looking for that magical solution. Sometimes, after attending a professional conference, we arrive home feeling disappointed, disillusioned, or even angry because we did not find what we were looking for or needing. Many seminars focus on philosophy, research patterns, and statistics. Although this may be interesting information, it does not really serve the therapist in the trenches with the difficult families. The therapist feels ill-equipped and not confident in tackling these families. And because he or she obtained a professional degree, it may be difficult to admit that he or she does not know what to do with a particular family. It certainly was different from the role-play situations rehearsed in graduate school. One may have marveled at the videotapes of the masters in the field, displaying their best work—not their hair-pulling errors. Therapists often expect their clients to *want* to change and are baffled when they seem to be content with not making any recommended changes. Families who are non-verbal, resistant, less motivated, less intellectual, or of a different ethnic/cultural background may find many therapists unprepared and inexperienced in recognizing or meeting their needs.

Does the therapist "burn out," quit, or move on to a different job position when tired of being unable to effectively meet the needs of couples and families? Is the search for the new and improved technique merely a hope toward feeling more adequate and confident? Are therapists working too hard to solve the family's issues while the family seems to just be waiting for answers? Do all of the therapist's techniques make sense intellectually but fail in actual practice? Or do the therapeutic approaches *only* work for the "right kind" of family? What *do* we need as therapists to feel confident and effective in *all* therapeutic situations?

Perhaps these answers are *not* beyond our own backyards in the next book published or *over the rainbow* at the next professional seminar. Perhaps we need not look any farther than within ourselves and what is available to us in *every* couple or family with *every* session. Perhaps we need to look at the invisible elements, influences, and tools which are constantly available to us if we only knew how to see them and make use of them. Some therapists will recognize these tools but may quietly admit that they let go of them—or traded them in for more comfortable, less risky, cognitive approaches. Some of the famous family therapists like Peggy Papp and Virginia Satir emphasized in their workshops to focus on the simple basics that exist right in front of you in every session. By stating less, listening more, and watching how a family or couple operates, the therapist begins working at the "feeling level." These action-oriented therapists were less

2

conventional but frequently more effective because they were working directly on the emotional level with couples and families. All that a therapist needs—even without a history—exists right before your eyes.

However, the therapist has to be *willing to look* and step outside of his or her comfort zone by performing tasks which help to elicit and illuminate these hidden family dynamics, emotions, and powerful influences. Therapists are no different than any other human beings who seek security, "comfort zones," predictable routines, safety, and emotional stability. Therapists who venture daily into the unpredictable jungles of various family networks truly seek to survive emotionally as well as succeed professionally. The offices of therapists often become that "safe" territory which offers constancy, stability, predictability, and security to the therapist who dares to enter endless tangled webs of family dynamics all day long. Therefore, therapists like to have their offices arranged predictably—perhaps with a certain number of chairs, a desk for the professional, and favorite locations for that coffee mug, pad of paper, and client file. Though the family may squeeze themselves into the safe domain of the therapist's office, it may innocently serve to "hide" the family from the hard-working therapist. Even though the therapist may have learned some of these "risky," action-oriented techniques, he or she may choose to "play it safe" by *just talking* about their issues and stated problems. Even active therapists often become less so with the passing of years and settle into "sit and talk" approaches again as they become complacent and secure with an office routine.

This entire book is dedicated to the belief that therapists can be more effective with making use of many creative ideas, invisible tools, and imaginative techniques which work within the emotional level that couples and families operate from. Many of these approaches will bypass intellectual defenses and sidestep resistance. Some of these approaches enable non-verbal families to *show* their emotional positions in a loud and unmistakable manner. Whereas some couples have spent years trying to comprehend each other's views, some of these techniques help them to *see* each other's perspective clearly *for the very first time.* These approaches also offer a great deal of safety in that clients are often speaking indirectly or one step removed from painful realities.

Therapists need not look any further than their own back yard. Everything you have needed is right there in front of you, ready to be discovered and utilized. Sessions without any written history or referral data may be some of your best sessions ever because you *had to* depend upon your eyes, ears, and instincts rather than someone else's opinion or perceived goals. What is lacking to achieve this glorious success may simply be your own resistance or complacency. You must be willing to do things differently. You must be willing to get out of your chair with confidence and purpose. You must be willing to trust your eyes and feelings so that you can follow your intuitions without fear. You must be willing to be creative and fun so that your clients can *see* their issues safely. You must be willing to *act* rather than talk in order to create a "family portrait" for all to see. You must be willing to take risks and do things in a different manner with each hour—like an talented artist who never will paint the same painting twice. And if all of this sounds too hard, you have come face to face with your own resistance. (We can work with that! Put your resistance in a chair and talk to it . . . if you dare.)

It has been said that the *only* way to change another person is to change what *we* do. If you are engaged in a game of chess, you will force your opponent to make different moves if you begin to make unpredictable and uncharacteristic moves with your game pieces. Nobody can do the same dance with us if we change our style of dancing. If we want our clients to change, we should worry less about their resistance and more about our own. When we start saying that "our clients seem boring or uninteresting," perhaps that is a reflection of ourselves as therapists—similarly becoming uninspiring or not interesting. Being content, organized, and secure as a therapist does not necessarily mean that one is effective or interesting. Going outside of our "comfort zone" and creating memorable sessions by being effectively different may go a long way toward instilling true change in our clients.

For those who cling to clever cognitive techniques, it is important to remember that it is always *an experience* which leads to our subsequent thoughts, feelings, and reactions. Although cognitive behavioral therapy focuses successfully on identifying the negative or non-productive thoughts, this book's emphasis on action-oriented, visual, experiential, and emotional level changes will clearly demonstrate how this form of therapy *does encompass* cognitive therapy as well. People will develop different ways of thinking based on the experiences the therapist initiates during the sessions. What they are able to visualize and *feel* will be much more memorable and, therefore, more likely to alter old habits and ways of thinking. Albert Ellis, founder of Rational Emotive Therapy (R.E.T.), concentrated on identifying irrational thoughts and then consciously challenging them. However, in his four-step model that consists of (1) Event, (2) Thought, (3) Feeling, (4) Reaction, it is the initial *event* or life experience which triggers this important chain reaction. If clients can experience something emotionally significant or have their awareness enhanced in a visually memorable fashion, cognitive changes are more likely to naturally occur because of the therapeutic *experience*. Just sitting and discussing such changes has less of an impact and often does not connect them emotionally to this need for change.

The exciting news is that a therapist already has everything he or she needs for any and all therapy sessions by just working to bring these hidden or invisible components to light so that everyone can see and/or experience them. If there is emotional distance, let's see and feel it. If there are attachments or alliances, let's experience them. We can make visible all of the powerful influences, hidden emotions, bad habits, and childhood scars so that we can recognize them, *see* their effect, and deal with them openly and directly. Not only is this very revealing and helpful for the therapist, but it may be the *first time* that the couple or family understands each other's views, perspectives, and positions as well. Awareness for all of those involved can be greatly enhanced by simply being part of the process and *feeling* their situation rather than just talking about it.

Illustrate your therapy! A session just full of words is like a book with no pictures. Illustrate your therapy sessions, and your clients will take home memorable insights that may last for years.

How We Learn

We have often heard it said that children learn from what they observe rather than from what they hear. A father can preach about the bad habit and harmful effects of smoking cigarettes while he takes another puff on his own cigarette. The child may simply learn that *anything* that his Daddy does *must* be okay—*despite what he says.* Parents may insist on their children not hitting each other or talking with foul language. Yet, when they, themselves, are upset, they may cuss at their children and spank them hard. And therefore, the children learn that the way to parent kids is to cuss at them and hit them. In fact, most parenting skills are absorbed from our experiences with our own parents from when we were children—not from reading books or attending lectures. We either decide to parent young ones just like we observed our own parents doing, or we decide to *not* act like they did—making that decision also because of what we observed and experienced as children. If they were abusive, we may decide to never resemble that behavior in any fashion whatsoever. But, again, this decision is based upon what we observed and experienced—not from any verbal discussion about what is right or wrong.

We *know* what *feels right* to us. Call it intuition—call it a "gut feeling"—but this intuitive feeling often guides us directly against what we have been told. Why would we ignore parental warnings and verbal preachings about the evils of drinking, smoking, and touching each other's "privates?" Because we have to experiment and *experience* for ourselves in order to learn the real truths in our lives. If two teenagers experiment with sexual relations and decide that it *feels good* and is not at all harmful or evil, then they tend to trust their own *feelings* and *experiences* much more often than what they will hear from others. In fact, they may develop a deeper distrust of what parents or other authorities may tell them.

We can tell the three-year old repeatedly not to touch the hot stove only to see his curiosity lead him to touch it. Once he *experiences* the awful pain associated with touching a sizzling hot burner on the stove, he will probably never try that again in his whole life. Or *watching* his sister do this and scream bloody murder for the next hour may be compelling enough to *not* ever try it himself. Indeed, "Experience is *the best teacher.*"

We *experience* right and wrong. A teenager may playfully shoplift items from stores until the security guards catch him and call his parents. He may be suddenly shocked by the serious actions of the guards. This *experience* with all of its consequences will probably teach the teenager that this is no "game" at all. Those children who rarely experience meaningful consequences learn very little—except, perhaps, how to manipulate others to avoid consequences. Similarly, adults often don't *feel* the need to wear their seat belts—until a deadly accident claims their best friend or their own family members. Despite years of warnings and educational efforts, this *experience* makes the biggest difference toward actual learning.

A young woman who naively disregarded warnings about walking alone at night may become traumatized for years after an *experience* with assault, robbery, or rape. Not only has she learned from her encounter with an *experience* that she will never forget, but she may be overly sensitized and reactive to any cues which are reminiscent of the upsetting event. This is certainly an example of how memorable and unforgettable experiential learning can become. Emotional experiences carry more weight and influence than verbal warnings or endless speeches—from burning a finger on a hot stove to being assaulted at night in the park.

Another familiar statement is, "Actions speak louder than words." A woman could be dating a boyfriend who promises her many things, raising her hopes, building her dreams, and creating false expectations. Although he may lead her on with that gleaming carrot dangling just ahead of her, a close look at his actual behavior and actions would reveal that he has not fulfilled one single promise. Sometimes we allow words to mesmerize us into following our hopes and happy fantasies, only to find empty promises when actions fail to reflect those wishes.

A young mother with her young children in the grocery store may find herself wrestling with their demanding behaviors. She threatens to spank them if they do not quit throwing their loud and embarrassing tantrums. Although she keeps threatening them out of frustration, she never actually spanks them. Therefore, the children have already been taught to *ignore her words* and pay more attention to her *actions*. And since she never ever spanks them, they have no consequences with which to be concerned. The mother is always amazed at how well they behave for their father—who (they have learned *from experience*) will quickly spank them at the first sign of disobedience. In fact, *just a glance* from their father, may be all that is needed with time as the children learn what his actions shall be—without any words even needed!

Observations, experiences, and actions. If we indeed *believe* what we have been saying for years about how people learn, then why do we spend so much time as therapists focusing on the *right way* to say our words, present the issues, or problem-solve verbally? If we want *genuine learning* to occur, then it would seem that therapeutic experiences, visualizations, observations, and active exercises would indeed succeed more often. When we work on that level of emotional experiencing, we shall find access to lasting changes more easily.

How We Remember

If I were to ask anybody what they remember about the terrorist attack upon the World Trade Center towers in New York City, what do you think they would say? Are they likely to describe what a particular newscaster stated? Or are they more likely to describe the graphic and visually-stunning images of two jet airliners crashing into the towers with an explosive and terrifying cloud of fire and smoke? Images of people fleeing, buildings collapsing, and blinding, suffocating smoke stay etched into our minds forever. No verbal description is ever likely to be as powerful or more memorable.

On a less dramatic scale and on a more personal level, that "first kiss," "favorite family vacation," "best birthday," or "most exciting trip" evoke fond images probably before any words related to those events. That is not to say that unique phrases, loving comments, harsh criticisms, or verbal reactions may not be memorable. It seems that memorable images frequently accompany any such words and tend to come to our minds more readily. If I were to ask you what you *said* to a friend on March 22, 1985, you probably would not have any idea at all. But if I asked you to describe what that friend *looked like* around that time, you could probably do so. Furthermore, if I asked you to recall your first sexual encounter, some vivid images would probably come to your mind. But, could you remember the calendar date or day of the week that it occurred? Most people would not recall such non-visual information.

Which do you find easier to recall—a person's name or his/her face? How many times have you looked at a schedule and failed to remember a client by just reading his name? Then when you see him in your waiting room, you suddenly can recall his whole situation, character, and other details. How many times have you seen a client in public, recognized his/her face but forgot his/her name? (Recall that phrase: "I never forget a face.") These are just more examples of how visual memory is much more effective than verbal memory. Why do we make notes in patient charts? To help recall what we discussed?

That may help the therapist, but if a client does not make similar notes, will they recall anything easily?

Likewise, flashbacks and recent dream imagery can pop into our minds during our waking hours—jolting us and eliciting emotional responses before we even have a specific cognitive thought. Our environment is constantly full of visual stimuli which can trigger emotional reactions. Of course, so can sounds, smells, textures, and weather conditions! These are some of the reasons why clinical hypnosis and hypnotherapy are very successful. Within a hypnotic trance, a client is relaxed and focused on sensory experiences—what they can visualize or imagine smelling, touching, tasting, or hearing. Clients under hypnosis are also more aware of temperature, body sensations, movement, color, and other sensory details. They are *much less focused* upon words. A talented hypnotherapist will make good use of each and every word he chooses in order to elicit emotional, visual, and sensory experiences. This is why hypnosis works well with resolving flashbacks and traumatic imagery through processing these images and emotions finally as adults. And, in a positive sense, this is why certain influential images and physical sensations experienced in hypnosis help other clients deal with smoking cessation and weight management. In the hypnotic process of systematic desensitization to help clients with fears and phobias, the client *experiences* a calm and successful encounter as a visual rehearsal toward successful coping. This sensory experiential series of rehearsals goes much further toward challenging their fears with more confidence than any words of reassurance could accomplish.

How many times do we as parents give our children verbal instructions or important spoken information—only to later learn that all they remembered was that we were angry or excited or sad. They *observed* the emotional condition, remembered *that*, and essentially ignored the words spoken. This suggests that human beings will sift through all incoming stimuli and process what is most relevant for their own coping and survival. Words don't rank very high when the brain is taking in all other kinds of important sensory information.

Therefore, if we learn more deeply from what we observe and experience—and we remember most successfully from our sensory and emotional experiences, then why do we place such an emphasis on talking and listening in therapy? We *assume* that talking with clients can be intelligent, clever, insightful, and useful. We also *assume* that they are listening!

Why Words Fail Us

Thus far, I have been emphasizing the effects of visual imagery and emotional experiences upon genuine learning and lasting memory. I have implied that spoken words are both less influential and less memorable in general. And if they *are* recalled well, it may be that they are *visually observable* as contained in a slogan on a poster, or as a *written* reminder on a posted note in the home. As a therapist I have found that if I really want a client to absorb the ideas that we have discussed, I will write down some of the key points on post-it notes for him/her to place at home on their refrigerator, bathroom mirror, or bulletin board. Then, my therapeutic words become a *visual* cue which can be *viewed* repeatedly in a daily and hypnotic fashion for maximum benefit. These clients report more success and have added that they have kept their notes posted—often for years! But these key words were more memorable when they became visual.

Common spoken words seem to be less of an impact in general upon our minds—that is, *if we are even listening!* Because we take in so many kinds of sensory input constantly, words can be taken in numerous ways depending upon various associations with other stimuli—such as a facial expression, a type of eye contact, an accompanying gesture, intonation of the spoken words, body posture, or eve a subtle emphasis on certain words. Meaning can change all too easily depending on how all these signals are received, processed, and sorted. For example, the following seven words take on seven different meanings based *solely* on emphasizing each of the seven words, one at a time.

"**I** never said that you stole money."

"I **never** said that you stole money."

"I never **said** that you stole money."

"I never said **that** you stole money."

"I never said that **you** stole money."

"I never said that you **stole** money."

"I never said that you stole **money**."

Despite using the exact same seven words, seven different interpretations emerge simply from the addition of—and *only* the addition of—a simple emphasis. Imagine how many more interpretations would occur with the addition of other perceived stimuli. And because we do not communicate like robots in a monotone, emotionless, expressionless void, countless distortions, misperceptions, and misinterpretations *are* going to happen!

So, when I feel as if I have communicated clearly to my spouse, my child, or my client, what *have* they actually heard?—that is, *assuming* that they were listening! It is for this obvious problem in communicating words that we have to resort to time-consuming techniques such as, "What did you hear me say?" and "Repeat back to me what you think I said." Although this takes effort and time, it certainly does help clear up distortions immediately. However, most people do not verify the way words are perceived in every conversation that they undertake!

Recall that wonderful therapy session that you had with a client in which you felt that you had clearly and eloquently related some clever insights and ingenious words of wisdom which they undoubtedly could never forget. You shared with colleagues about that rewarding session and went home that day really satisfied with your efforts. Two weeks later, when you interview the same client again, you are shocked to learn that he does not seem to recall any of your brilliant remarks—also admitting that he was distracted by a headache and unable to focus well that day. Yes, he had nodded his head, smiled at you, and appeared to have been absorbing the remarks. He had even confirmed several of your perceptions—yet the discussion was not memorable, the words became lost, and nothing has changed.

Often we assume that our clients will hear our comments with the same meaning that we intend. But our very own excitement, energy, intensity, facial expressions, emphasis, and intonation may create a different result. One client stated that he had not listened well because of the way I looked while I was talking reminded him of his father's behavior, causing him to get lost in those thoughts and feelings for a few minutes. While talking with another client I learned that my facial expressions reminded her of her mother's emotions, and she completely blocked out what we had been discussing. The intensity and energy behind some comments can be reminiscent of potential anger about to erupt. We can never be certain how any client is going to hear our words—even if they *are* listening.

Even if the client is listening and perceiving well, that does not mean that we as therapists will react appropriately to the gestures, reactions, facial expressions, emotional tone, etc. of our client. We are only human and have all of our own childhoods, background experiences, life traumas, and personal biases that will automatically color *how* we listen and process what is stated—that is, if we are truly listening. No therapist can honestly claim that he or she *always* listens with 100% attentiveness. Some clients speak in a monotone—almost hypnotizing—tone which lures us into drifting off into our thoughts. Some topic or remark may trigger a personal feeling or recollection which distracts us momentarily. Or our own mental or physical fatigue may cause us to daydream or escape momentarily into our private worlds. This is human nature and naturally expected to occur.

A study from about 20 years ago indicated that only about seven percent of communication is comprised of spoken words, while ninety-three percent consists of various forms of non-verbal elements: body posture, body "language," gestures, facial expressions, intonation, stance, emotional distance, verbal emphasis, emotional tone, type of eye contact, attitude, breathing behavior (sighs, gasps), etc. People pay much more attention to all of these other elements while deciding how to process any spoken words just uttered. It is not surprising that people frequently get frustrated over feeling "not heard" by loved ones—family members who are used to "reading" all the other signals given in a communicative interaction. This, of course, does not guarantee that anybody actually interprets the intended message correctly! Some couples think they know each other so well (and they often do!) that from just a certain glance, muffled groan, or sigh, one will fully interpret what the other is thinking well before any words are ever spoken. Nevertheless, this *still* does not guarantee a correct perception. All of the non-verbal cues certainly add meaning and color to each effort to communicate—often beyond the conscious awareness of the communicators. Sometimes, it is rather amusing when one member of a couple insists that the other is quite angry, and the accused stands in a defiant posture with arms crossed, reacting with a hateful stare, sharpness in his/her tone, and yet denies (while looking away) such a claim. We are quick to doubt or ignore the words!

"You sure seem angry right now."
"*#@&! I AM NOT ANGRY!!!!!"

Therefore, when individuals, couples, and families are guarded, defensive, cautious, scared, or resistant, why would we ever believe just what is stated or presented verbally? Many fine schools teach therapy students to recognize all of the non-verbal cues, but the emphasis remains on verbal discussions, cognitive approaches, and problem-solving with the stated issues. This may work just fine with many situations if it is truly reaching down to the more political and emotional levels from which behavior usually originates. But if we focus only on words—talking and listening, listening and talking—therapy may never deal with the real emotional issues or genuine change at the emotional level.

Many clients have proven to us over the years that it is very easy to lead therapists away from difficult emotions, scary issues, and situations that create insecurity. We can be lured into "talk contracts" for years which never actually produce real change. The client may still gain a sense of support from his therapist but prefers to keep it at this safe kind of "talk level" to avoid facing tougher issues, bigger decisions, or difficult emotions. Often that therapist may come to realize that the client's goals have become vague or absent, and sessions seem more like social visits. This subconscious preference to avoid tough feelings may be present in *both* the client and the therapist; therefore, "talk therapy" continues indefinitely.

Other clients with personality disorders (i.e. Borderline Personality Disorder) can hold our attention for months with dramatic, intriguing, and upsetting tales from their past in order to avoid dealing with an emotional (yet minimized) roadblock in the present. This is another form of avoiding healthy changes and maintaining "talk therapy" and therapist support. Sometimes, the attention, contact, and concern of the therapist *is* that client's primary goal—instead of healthy growth, overcoming fears, and facing tough emotional decisions as confident and assertive individuals. The approaches in this book help with bypassing resistance while creating safe, more indirect methods of facing those tough emotions more easily. As therapists we also have to examine our own reluctance, hesitation, and avoidance in regard to certain issues and deeper emotions which we are still not comfortable with. We might learn that we also *prefer* "talk contracts" with those particular clients or sensitive issues that trigger our own feelings and personal backgrounds.

How Imagery, Fantasy, and Metaphors Safely Bypass Defenses and Resistance

Therapists are constantly bombarded by the clever and well-practiced verbal manipulations of clients. Numerous defense mechanisms are activated to mislead therapists or put them on the wrong track to avoid scary changes, emotional issues, traumatic feelings, or embarrassing topics. Most of these defensive maneuvers are protective for the insecure and distrusting client. If the client could only discuss such difficult issues or scary feelings without feeling so uneasy, anxious, vulnerable, or fearful, therapy would be more enticing. Until therapy can feel safe, secure, and reassuring, much resistance and avoidance may occur. If the therapist could find another way in which clients could feel safe *sooner* and work on their issues *indirectly*, yet productively, successful results could happen effectively in less time with little if any resistance.

Fantasy, imagery, and metaphors take people into a safer, imaginary realm that is one big step removed from the painful reality of the clients' everyday world. Yet, the same emotions that are experienced in these painful, difficult, and stressful situations travel with us into the realm of fantasy and metaphoric imagery. As we create imaginary scenarios and characters, our feelings color and influence the direction and nature of the fantasy. The same themes and types of characters resurface in our fantasies and metaphoric images, yet, somehow, it is now safe and okay to deal with them. The same process occurs nearly every night in the realm of our dreams while we are asleep. Here we take our emotions and stresses from daytime reality into a fantasy world of escape. Yet, our current and perhaps unresolved emotional issues color the dream world with similar characters, themes, and behavior that will essentially match and represent what we are still dealing with, emotionally. We may not find an easy solution, even in our dreams—and may awaken from such nightmares feeling anxious, panicked, or scared. Yet, we often comfort ourselves with the misleading claim that "it was *only* a dream."

In a similar fashion, fantasy and metaphoric images enable couples and families to work in a playful and safe fashion with difficult emotions and sensitive issues. This indirect method is often *preferred* once they become accustomed to this safer mode of therapy. When words have failed numerous times by being confusing, misleading, suggestive, defensive, or falling on deaf ears, metaphoric fantasy may be a welcome method to represent feelings, visualize each other's position more clearly, and to successfully characterize potential solutions or changes without feeling the pain or anxiety of dealing *directly* with reality.

Clinical Case Example

A 28 year-old married female was being seen in individual therapy when it became clear that marriage counseling would be necessary. However, her husband still believed that she "just needed to be fixed," and that he did not have any significant issues. After all, *she* was the one with depression—not him. Using one of my favorite approaches with resistant people, I phoned him, telling him that I really needed his expertise and years of experience with her. Only with his "unique knowledge" could I possibly "fix" her. Flattered and ready to tell me all about her problems and flaws, he arrived at the next session with her. However, this reluctant mate had been accused by her of being mean and abusive, so he sat, quite guarded, glaring at me, with his arms crossed in front of his chest. I knew that he would be defensive and resistant, so I proposed to do "something for fun" before we would begin working. He would not expect that "something for fun" would be a threat to him; therefore, he was open to participation in the exercise.

I asked both of them to imagine for a moment that each partner had become an animal. What animal comes to mind? What type of animal would make sense or *feel right*? And what kind of animal would *each* become in relation to the first image that was thought of for the other partner? This fantasy exercise removed them from the present sense of reality of marriage counseling and into a quiet and distant realm of make-believe. The wife described that he was a barking dog, and that she was a scared kittycat that would run and hide. He then proudly took his turn, announcing that she was a soft, cute bunny-rabbit while he was a snarling German Shepherd dog with sharp teeth and claws which could rip and tear the fur from her little body anytime that he wished. Suddenly, his mouth fell open and he then realized what he had revealed, metaphorically. While momentarily stunned, I quickly asked him to go ahead and find animal images for his Family of Origin. He thought for a moment, and then he stated with some sense of relief that he now realized that he had come from a long line of snarling German Shepherd dogs. Although still talking on an indirect fantasy level, this helped him to realize that there were good reasons, historically, for his hostile behavior, and he did not stand out like a sore thumb. We connected to work with the imagery and how it could be better, different, or reversed at times. Because I kept this discussion *one step removed* on a fantasy level, this couple was able to discuss some very difficult feelings and scary situations.

The use of fantasy and metaphoric imagery in this simple exercise produced powerful results in a less threatening manner. This technique successfully sidestepped intellectual and psychological defenses as well as conscious resistance. By remaining in the metaphoric realm, this couple could safely explore difficult feelings indirectly—avoiding the scary intensity and insecurity produced by painful reality.

Why Hypnosis Works So Well

I never wanted to be trained in clinical hypnosis. I had thought of it as an archaic, mysterious, and forbidden intrusion into a client's mind. I associated it with entertainment and hype—not meaningful therapy.

The psychiatrist who insisted that I learn about it also strongly advocated psychoanalysis—an expensive, non-directive, and less used process in modern psychiatry. I did not know why or how I would actually use it with any of my clients. But I was willing to attend the four-day training seminar at the prestigious Menninger Clinic in Topeka, Kansas because that same psychiatrist offered to pay for it!

I was surprised and impressed by the effectiveness of the technique in our practice sessions. I soon realized that it was merely an intensive form of therapy based less upon words and more upon visualization, imagery, experience, and emotions. By either reliving or anticipating particular life situations, one could visualize any moment in time and experience all the feelings and thoughts related to that situation. With the emphasis on emotion and experience instead of words, I found the hypnotic imagery, metaphors, and visualizations to be extremely memorable and therefore effective and lasting. The similarity to sculpting and other visualization techniques added credibility to the idea that dealing less with words and more with experiential processes to elicit emotions is extremely helpful.

Clinical Case Examples

Gladys had been to every doctor to try to find a solution for her intense migraine headaches. Typical medications had not worked effectively. There was no obvious life situation or relationship problem to examine. She described her headaches as feeling like "one hundred little Leprechauns beating on drums" in her head. Given this particular image to connect directly with her emotions, I used hypnotic relaxation and suggested that these one hundred Leprechauns were also becoming very relaxed and sleepy. One by one each Leprechaun would fall asleep. Each drum would become softer—from a sharp banging to a very dull, "squishy plop." She began to monitor her progress by how many Leprechauns would fall asleep until she succeeded at all one hundred becoming quiet. She would experience the imagined peacefulness and treasure the serenity. She felt such wonderful relief with each session. By practicing at home with a tape-recording of our therapy session, she extended her success at eliminating the migraines.

Teresa came into our clinic, hobbling with leg, abdominal, and stomach pain. She had been thoroughly examined and tested by medical specialists who could not find anything physically wrong with her. Teresa was a simple-minded, somewhat backward, country girl who tearfully described her ongoing pains, tingling, and numbness throughout her body. As I explored recent stresses or losses with her I learned that her Grandfather had died in the past few months. She became choked-up and quite emotional, indicating a strong need for grief resolution therapy. Because of her lack of sophistication and articulation, I chose a visual method through hypnosis to access her unresolved emotions. After having relaxed her deeply, I had her visualize a beautiful place in nature where she could feel safe and secure. Then I suggested that her Grandfather had appeared and could talk with her. She experienced his presence and all the wonderful feelings of being with this man who had been more of a father to her than her own father had been. Not only did she express what she wanted to say to him, but she imagined how he would probably respond to her comments or questions. And he told her that she needed to go on with her life while he watched over her from heaven. After each reassuring visualization, she would say her good-byes and sadly watch him leave. By having a chance to be with him again, she could express her feelings, experience or "hear" his loving responses, and learn to say good-bye each time and move on. All of her physical symptoms seemed to magically melt away after this series of sessions. In fact, she never focused on her original physical complaints ever again. The visual and emotional experience under hypnosis brought sufficient relief to this client who was unconsciously more willing to feel physical pain as opposed to emotional pain.

Joe, a salesman, had entered the hospital with the unusual problem of his eyes involuntarily shutting, which especially caused a dangerous predicament while driving his car. Originally diagnosed as a

Bluffer Spasm, certain medications did not alleviate the tension. Antidepressants and sedatives did not help suspected anxiety. Eyedrops and even a form of surgery to release tension in the muscles around the eyes and eyelids did not help. However, I noted that when he anticipated that the surgery may really help, his symptoms began improving in the days *before* that surgery. I proposed an approach with imagery while under clinical hypnosis. We learned that there was a life situation regarding his sales work which angered him greatly. He was reluctant to "see" or face this issue directly, so his unexpressed anger literally led him to "shutting his eyes" to the problem. I suggested that his anger was indeed important but that it should move to a location in his body where it could be expressed more effectively—his fists. Under hypnosis he visualized moving that anger from his eyes, down his body, into his arms, and finally into his hands—allowing them to *feel* that rage and clench into fists. After the session the hospital staff was stunned by his ability to walk around with his eyes wide open for the first time in weeks. I continued to help him focus his anger by pounding pillows with his newly-clenched fists, and *openly looking at* or problem-solving his work situation.

Elaine was diagnosed as having a Panic Disorder with Agoraphobia. In other words, this housewife was too disabled by intense anxiety to leave her house, drive a car, or go shopping. In fact, in order to retrieve her mail from her own mailbox out by the street, she had to walk backwards going out to the street so that she could see her house at all times. Using hypnosis, imagery, and a classic desensitization procedure, she rehearsed *visually* and *experientially* these anxiety-producing situations. Because she was able to mentally and emotionally *experience* these events through visual and sensory imagery under the relaxed conditions of hypnosis, she learned that nothing disastrous ever happened and that she could control her anxieties through certain relaxation techniques. The powerful effect of visual rehearsals enabled her to approach her fears with confidence and experience actual success.

Emotional Distance as a Therapeutic Tool

2

A Free, Easy, Exciting, Powerful, Omnipresent (but Invisible) Resource

Wow. A free resource that is easy and powerful to use—which is always available to us *anywhere* we perform a therapy session! We *know* about it yet *rarely* take advantage of its significant use as both an assessment and therapeutic tool. It is always there if we give it the opportunity to be seen and felt. I am talking about *emotional space*.

Often referred to as "personal space," this dynamic occurs in our environment without any planning, conscious effort, or particular awareness. When we go to a movie theater, we enter the auditorium and seat ourselves at a "safe" distance from all strangers without much conscious thought about doing so. We find ourselves evenly spaced around the theater—yet, we never planned this strategy in the parking lot prior to entering the theater. If we find the theater rather crowded, we may note that our anxiety increases when there is less opportunity to preserve our "personal space." This "lack of safety" may enter our conscious awareness if someone sits right next to us, behind us, or directly in front of us. Our personal space feels violated, intruded upon, or unsafe. Different people have different boundaries and different needs regarding the amount of space desired to maintain emotional security. At such a moment we often make the conscious choice to get up and move until we locate a more comfortable space in the theater. One can note that most people will attempt to always leave at least one seat between themselves and others until they *absolutely have to* sit next to a stranger. The anxiety may increase to a panic attack level for some individuals if they do not maintain enough personal space in public areas.

This dynamic of emotional space creates the same kind of reaction as when one brings two repelling magnets toward each other. The repelling magnetic forces intensify as they are brought closer in physical proximity to each other. The emotional intensity of the urge to avoid other human beings also increases significantly as boundaries are crossed and personal space is infringed upon. As couples or family members feel safer with each other, they allow those "safe people" to enter their personal space and exist emotionally closer to them. Another example of this occurs when one asks two strangers to walk toward each other, stopping only when each begins to feel uncomfortable. Neither knows exactly where or when that will occur, but his or her feelings will alert them from a deeper emotional level. In sharp contrast, asking a newly-wed couple to perform the same exercise will most likely demonstrate that there is very little if any distance keeping them apart!

This suggests that each of us makes private, subconscious, emotional decisions about every person that comes into our lives. We *just know* at an emotional level what kind of personal space we prefer with each human being whom we know—or don't know! This emotional space can and will change with the passage of time in nearly every kind of relationship. Within couples the marital relations will ebb and flow over time due to various life situations, challenging stresses, and demands upon each other's time for togetherness. Similarly, members of a family will feel closer or farther apart at different times in their lives. As therapists we can get a "reading" on this emotional distance within couples and families at any point in time—just like using a thermometer to obtain the air temperature.

However, to take advantage of this invisible yet revealing dynamic, therapists must arrange their offices differently in order to make it visible. Normally, therapists arrange a certain number of chairs in their office according to how many people are expected for any scheduled session. If a family of five members is expected, therapists logically set up five chairs. With the logical and exact number of chairs pre-arranged, family members will simply sit down and reveal practically nothing in terms of emotional distance. But if therapists really wish to observe the emotional spacing among family members, they need to set up eight to ten chairs. The family of five now *has to* choose where to sit and will make choices subconsciously based upon emotional feelings. It is not unusual for a family to stop and ponder the extra chairs—even asking, "Where should we sit?" or "Does it matter where we sit?" And the therapist simply replies, "Sit wherever you feel most comfortable."

family

therapist

Clinical Case Example

The identified patient, a 13 year-old female diagnosed with the beginning symptoms of schizophrenia, demonstrated troubling, unpredictable moods along with irrational and tangential remarks. At times she was hysterical; at other times she was withdrawn and resistant. Her family "seemed normal" by comparison but was rather quiet themselves. Having had one session at the hospital in a small room with limited seating, the patient seemed restless and defiant. Having the next session at our office with twelve chairs arranged in a group therapy room for the family of six revealed a much different picture of this family. Despite all the seating options, the 13 year-old identified patient sat directly on her mother's lap in the middle of the semi-circle of twelve chairs. The two younger female siblings sat directly next to the mother on either side of her. Four chairs away to the left sat a quiet father all by himself. Three chairs away to the right of mother sat an angry, aloof, teenage brother. Every now and then, the identified patient would leave Mom's lap and move around the room to visit other family members. As the therapist I began to feel that she was the glue that was stretching to try to tie everyone to each other in the room. She obviously was working the hardest and, as a result, feeling the most frustration. In fact, her words and actions seemed more rational and purposeful in this session. It seemed as if she was literally trying to "save the family" from drifting away from each other. Yet, none of this had been visible previously. And, *because* it was now quite visible, the identified patient could *feel* this distance again and react to it in the session, thus depicting her overwhelming private struggle with hidden family dynamics.

A number of therapists complain that they either do not have the office space to add chairs, or they do not have a group therapy room with more seating space. If one has removable chairs, one can create more space by eliminating all chairs from the room. Or the therapist can simply ask the couple or family to stand up for a few minutes. Instead of inviting the family members to sit wherever they feel comfortable, one asks them to "stand wherever you feel most comfortable," or "stand next to whomever you want to be near." Again, the family will know what *feels right*, and emotional space will become visible and thereby a useful and workable dynamic.

When dealing with an individual's family issues, a therapist can have play therapy dolls represent the family members. The client can place them on a table or on the floor in an arrangement which will represent their emotional distance from each other. *Be certain to include a figure for the therapist and where he/she is involved or entering the picture.*

Mom, young sons

Teenage brother

Daughter

Therapist   Dad

Example of family emotional positioning with removal of chairs or with representation by play therapy dolls

Some therapists have found great success with their clients simply using coffee mugs, playing cards, ink pens, or even paper clips to represent family members and their emotional space from each other. Each family member could present his/her "picture" individually.

A deck of cards can be interesting because it offers four adult males (kings), four younger males (jacks), four females (queens), two "wilder" characters (jokers), four babies (aces), and children from ages two through ten (four of each age). Also, the symbolism gained from the colors black or red as well as implications from the four suits of diamonds (money-oriented), hearts (empathic, nurturing), clubs (powerful-abusive), or spades (laboring, hard-working) could be quite interesting. Placement of cards is easy for showing emotional spacing in a limited physical space.

Because therapists have found much success using objects as simple as paper clips, this demonstrates that clients can project their emotional impressions into just about *anything*. When a therapist states that he cannot perform such exercises for various reasons to make emotional space become visible, then *therapist resistance* must be the real issue since the creative possibilities for easily revealing such ever-present dynamics are endless.

Utilizing Personal Space to Work On an Emotional Level

Emotional Experiments With Families

Having provided an exercise or seating arrangement which elicits visibility of the emotional space among people, a therapist can begin assessing rather quickly which relationships are strained, distant, dependent, overinvolved, or missing. There are a number of therapeutic directions one can pursue with this obvious and visible information—which *all* of the family members are now *seeing* and *feeling*.

1. **Explore with all family members, <u>one at a time</u>, how they feel about the position in which they find themselves.**

   Does it evoke a particular emotion—sadness? anger? loneliness? comfort? security? anxiety? grief? fear? confusion? abandonment? joy?

   Is this position a *familiar* one?

   How *often* do they find themselves in this position?

   How long have they been in this position?

   Are they "stuck" or can they move out of it?

   Despite their feelings, do they *prefer* this position?

Why have they *not* made a change?

How long can they imagine it staying like this?

How do they possibly keep themselves from making changes?

Who *seems* to hold them in this position?

Do they have a sense of being in control—or not?

Who has the control over them?

Ask them to recall a time when it was better or different. What position were they in at that point in time? What led to their present position?

2. **Explore what kind of changes are needed before each family member would want to move from his or her position.**

   What do you need to *hear* from someone before you would consider moving closer? What do you need to *see happen* before you would consider changing your position?

   What has happened in the past to make you want to move to or from this position?

   What does the family need to do before you would change your stance?

   What kind of emotions do you need to experience from someone before you could move closer to them?

   Take on the role of another family member and express or show what you want to see them say or do in order for you to feel like changing your position.

   What would somebody else in the family need to say or do to get another member to want to be closer/farther from you?

3. **Instead of *discussing* changes, have each family member take a turn at *showing* these ideas by rearranging the emotional positions into what that family member has decided would *feel right* or work better.**

Show us how you would like this family to be and where you would be in that picture.

Place each family member where you would like him/her to be.

(Check the results with each family member—with the kind of questions as in #1.)

(As you get reactions allow each family member to then rearrange it his/her way.)

4. **Allow each family member to dream up his version of this family becoming "perfect," and then position everyone in those ideal (not realistic) roles to fit this fantasy.**

This encourages freedom of expression and the revealing of secret wishes and needs.

Each family member indirectly learns what everybody else really wants to see happen.

Again, check the reactions of each member to the resulting "family sculptures."

Find out how impossible/possible, realistic/unrealistic each result actually is.

Note who shares similar dreams as well as whose fantasies are in conflict.

Discuss whether any of the fantasized ideas are at all possible.

5. **The therapist can exercise his right to place the family in any emotional arrangement he wishes to see or experiment with.**

BEST GUESS: The therapist tries to place the family accurately in their emotional positions with each other based upon his perceptions and gathered information. What is nice about this approach is that it will be okay to be wrong. The family can quickly tell the therapist what does not *feel right* about his version of the "family sculpture," thus enabling the therapist's "best guess" to be adjusted to a more accurate portrayal.

DELIBERATELY WRONG: The therapist deliberately places family members in unlikely emotional positions with each other, knowing all too well that this is like placing repelling magnets next to each other. This action is often more effective as it elicits emotional responses and quicker reactions to "correct" the therapist by moving to where each family member *knows* they feel more comfortable. Repelling magnets will move with more speed and accuracy to safe places of least resistance.

NEW OPTIONS: The therapist exercises his right to place the family members in emotional positions they have not yet experienced or been unwilling to explore. The therapist can explore various ideas, options, and symbolic changes in the family's network of relations to see what kinds of emotional reactions, resistance, or positive feelings may occur. The way each family member reacts gives the therapist a great deal of information regarding treatment goals and therapeutic directions. The manner in which the therapist attempts various changes may stimulate ideas within the family as well as they begin to *see other possibilities*.

ROLE OF REALITY: Sometimes the therapist may need to play the necessary role of reality when families attempt to make changes unrealistically, too quickly, or without enough cognitive comprehension. If the therapist simply does not believe such a change would happen as easily as the family portrays it, he can "play the Devil's advocate" and challenge their sculpting arrangement. This makes the family either work harder to prove the therapist wrong, or it allows less active members the opportunity to reveal hidden feelings or resistance that may validate the therapist's intuitive reaction.

PARADOXES: For the family that is reluctant to attempt any changes, the therapist may need to stimulate action by encouraging them to *never change* and to keep everything emotionally just the way it is right now. The dislike for that idea of *never having anything ever change* may create more energy and willingness to take some risks when weighing these options. People may be afraid of change, but they may also be more afraid of having things remain the same! This approach is more effective than similar verbal discussions because of the physical apartness and emotional spacing within emotional sculpting—*seeing and feeling* the dilemma stirs more reactions!

RESISTANCE: Despite the energy and engaging spirit of many confident therapists, there will be family members who adamantly refuse to participate—through criticism, silence, arrogance, or denial of the therapist's authority or control. What every therapist needs to remember is that their "*acting out*" is already demonstrating their position(s) in the "family sculpture." Resistant adolescents may ignore a therapist's request and sit in defiance off to the side. *Great!* They are already *showing* the therapist their position in the family picture. Do not waste time giving them negative attention and allowing them to control the moment and derail the family sculpting exercise. Often, they become curious about the emotional spacing and visual depiction of the family and *want* to join in later—especially with their own opinions, reactions, and chance to *show* everybody how they want it.

"STUCK" FAMILY MEMBERS: Occasionally, a family member will become confused, lost, or unable to express a solution. That person may seem "blank"—void of thought, feeling, or action. At such moments, the therapist can either take charge and move them to another emotional position to see if that stirs a response, or the therapist can seek an idea from other family members—one of whom *usually* knows what that family member may be needing. Later, it may become more apparent why that particular emotional space led to their "numbing out." When working on an emotional level, it is not unusual for family members to become overwhelmed with more feelings than they can have time to process and understand cognitively. Some family members may not be regularly in touch with their emotions, so integrating what they are experiencing may take longer.

Clinical Case Example

A 20 year-old, single, female, college student became hospitalized with a diagnosis of Anorexia Nervosa, weighing only 83 pounds. Family dynamics seem strongly involved in cases with this kind of diagnosis. I arranged a family therapy session and decided upon an emotional sculpting approach as they seemed non-verbal and passive. I began the session by simply asking them to get up from their chairs and stand wherever they felt most comfortable. The parents simply stood side-by-side in front of their chairs. A younger daughter moved closer to stand right next to Mom. The teenage brother moved toward the door, standing away from the parents, and remained aloof. The identified patient, the 20 year-old female, walked away from the family, crouched down into a fetal position with her back to the family and her head lowered into that farthest corner of the room. Immediately, the parents could feel the emotional distance and loss of contact with their daughter.

I gently challenged the parents to find words that may entice their daughter to come closer to them. Mom tried to say a number of pleasant, caring things about the patient while Dad stood silently next to his wife like a statue. Only when Mom cried softly from the frustration of being unable to connect with her daughter, did the daughter turn around to gaze at her briefly. I congratulated Mom on getting a response and asked her to think about how that had happened while

33

I asked Dad to now try to connect with his daughter. He did not know really what to say or do, so I asked the aloof brother for his opinion. It was at this moment that the aloof brother revealed more information about Dad's general lack of connection with this family.

"I can tell you exactly what is wrong here. Our father never did *anything* with us. When we would go on a family picnic, he would never even get out of the car—simply waiting there for us until we were all done. I bet she's pissed at not knowing how he feels about her."

Dad fumbled with a few words, attempting to tell his daughter that he does care about her, but she showed no response to his efforts at all. Dad began to feel the physical distance, emotional space, and utter frustration at his inability to reach his *starving* daughter. He became restless and choked up with tears. He blubbered out a tearful, "I do love you," which was more than the family had *ever* heard in many years. The daughter turned around, stood up straight, faced him, and took five steps toward him—stopping about seven feet away. She said nothing, but continued to stand there as if waiting to hear or *feel* more from her father.

I congratulated Dad on finding a way to connect with his *starving* daughter, and asked him to reflect upon that experience over the next week. Very few words were needed in this powerfully emotional therapy session. Yet, the whole family understood much more about the daughter's silent cry for connection with them—literally *starved* for her parents' love. So much more had been felt and experienced than a discussion of words could ever have revealed.

Emotional Experiments With Couples

Working with couples is really not very different. However, the therapist must remember to include and represent all influential forces (relatives, employers, addictions, etc.) that have an emotional pull or impact upon the couple. A close connection to a mother may be more of a bond than that which is within the couple. Visibly seeing and experiencing this hidden connection is much more effective than just talking about that perception. In other words, the emotional space just between mates may not be the *only* emotional space that needs to be explored.

EMOTIONAL MAGNETISM: Have the couple stand at opposite ends of the room (or a hallway if the room is too small) and walk slowly toward each other, stopping when each decides he or she is becoming uncomfortable. That amount of distance between them will probably vary from week to week depending upon moods and situations. Then, as a regular discussion of issues begins, either one can take a step *backward* at any time he or she *dislikes* what is happening between them. In the same manner, when either one *likes* the progress or remarks made, that one can take a step *toward* the other partner. Like two magnets attracting or repelling each other, their emotional distance is constantly monitored and displayed throughout the entire session.

Everyone can witness the progress or lack of productivity at any given moment—without the couple ever having to be asked. And the couple, itself, is receiving immediate feedback, visually, regarding its own process. Being able to *watch* the process of communication fail may serve to help abort a destructive direction before it continues for too long or goes too far. By the same token, steps taken toward each other will reinforce the efforts which are succeeding. If one of the mates is more passive or non-verbal, this exercise gives him an easy way to *show* his reactions.

ROLE-REVERSAL: A unique technique to assist each partner with seeing the other's perspective is reversing roles. In other words, the man portrays how the woman "looks and sounds" from his perspective while the woman portrays her version of how he comes across to her. Of course, there will be distortions and exaggerations to emphasize various traits, communication styles, and emotional issues. Yet, each partner gets the chance to *see and hear* how the other views him. Each can depict his or her sense of emotional spacing as well. Each partner can also *experience* how his manner of arguing *feels* as portrayed by his partner. This exercise provides a visual, active, and experiential encounter—which both will remember more readily.

TIES AND BONDS: Other strong influences that exert an emotional tug or push upon the couple can be represented by nylon ropes, children's jumpropes, plastic chains, or a strand of scarves tied together. These visible "bonds" can illustrate the types of influences that are *pulling* upon the couple. These could be emotional forces exerted by families of origin, interfering friends, children, ex-spouses, deceased persons, hired helpers, co-workers, employers, addictions, obsessions, or habitual behaviors. This enhances the couple's awareness of how many influences impact upon them. It also allows them to physically experience and emotionally react to such interfering forces.

SPACE EXPLORATION: Once the couple has visually displayed the amount of emotional distance between them, the therapist can begin experimenting with changes in that spacing. One can ask a distant couple to sit very close to each other in order to gather their emotional reactions and subsequent reasons for desiring some distance. A couple sitting closely together could be asked to sit far apart—again, to assess emotional reactions and subsequent preferences. What gets in the way? Dependency? Anger? Fear of being controlled? Feeling suffocated? Loneliness? Resentments? Guilt? Hidden loyalties to others? Anxiety? Independence? Fear of intimacy? Fear of being hurt? Projections of other feelings? Displacement of other emotions?

POWER POSTURES: Having the couple assume certain postures that depict power positions can (1) validate certain client feelings, (2) confirm therapeutic impressions, (3) serve as a method for experiencing new positions of power or helplessness, and (4) visually reveal the couple's dilemma and enhance awareness. For example, if the husband is dictatorial or judgmental, he may be asked to assume a standing position which towers over his seated mate. He is also asked to point a finger at her or pull her shoulders back from behind her. Either will create a visual and emotional experience of being controlled. The therapist asks each partner if this is *how it feels* for them, and they will either confirm this emotional arrangement or direct how it needs to be altered in order for it to "feel right" emotionally. The therapist may add a symbolic rope to match any metaphoric phrase such as "feeling tied down," "feeling tied up," "feeling tied to my husband," or "feeling held back." It is especially important in this exercise to use role reversals so that *each* can experience the *other's* sense of control or feelings of frustration. The therapist could also uncover two victims or two mates trying to gain power over the other. One can make use of the basic egostate stances from Transactional Analysis:

Critical Parent:	standing over, pointing finger, disapproving
Strong Parent:	standing behind, holding partner by shoulders, arms
Nurturing Parent:	standing beside or behind, arms hugging, supporting
Adult:	sitting "on the level," direct eye contact, open hands
Free Child:	sitting on the floor, looking away, arms crossed

| Little Professor: | sitting on the floor, head cocked, eyes direct at partner |
| Adapted Child: | sitting on floor, head down, submissive, knees to chest |

Role reversals are extremely effective in shifting positions of power around as well as *experiencing* and *feeling* these changes. One partner can more easily become aware of how any situation must feel for his mate after experiencing such a role reversal.

Finding Solutions That *"Feel Right"*

Therapists need to learn to trust that their clients will *know* what emotionally *feels right* for them as they get the opportunity to experience various emotional exercises. Many therapists claim that this is "unreliable intuition" rather than meaningful change. Yet, emotions are the very source of powerful subconscious decision-making that directly determines our reactions and behavior. Often what we *expect* to feel in certain emotional situations may be quite different from what we *actually* experience. It is true that many clients *think* they know how they will feel in different situations, but, actually, they may experience a surprise once they "rehearse" a new position in this kind of emotional therapy.

Perhaps, this is more of a comfort issue for the therapist. There may be more security for the therapist in sticking with predictable and organized strategies of cognitive therapy—regardless of their outcome or effectiveness. Some therapists may prefer to stick with set procedures with more predictable results. The more open and unpredictable directions that emotional exercises may lead to could be too anxiety-producing for some therapists. Other therapists may be clever at concealing or controlling *their own* emotions, and they may not wish to work on such a potentially intensive level of emotional therapy that could stir up their own sensitivities or unresolved issues.

A number of therapists admit to being very uncomfortable and even guilt-ridden if too many intense emotions arise too quickly from their clients due to these encounters which elicit feelings. This suggests to me that they are uneasy about truly allowing their clients to *feel* their own emotions. It is an issue *for the therapist,* himself. Therapists do not *cause* or *create* the emotions that our clients express. These feelings have often been carefully hidden or suppressed for long periods of time. When a therapist has discovered a safe manner in which these important feelings can be released openly, that should be a time for celebration—*not* a time to to back away, clamp down, or feel guilty because our clients are emotionally expressive! Protecting the client from *feeling* important emotions may be the reason that the client has not made much progress. Explosive or dramatic releases of feelings (unless this is a regular, habitual pattern) occur because the client is ready to do so. The therapist does not *make him* do this—therapists just do not have that kind of power! The therapist should be the facilitator or catalyst which provides the safe place and therapeutic opportunity for emotional release to occur.

One family therapist was highly criticized by another therapist for "re-traumatizing my client" when a sculpting exercise revealed genuine feelings from family members which had been unspoken and well-hidden previously. The protective therapist, who had been providing individual counseling, was mortified at the emotions his client experienced. However, the exercise helped break through an impasse and led to some needed changes which probably prevented the client from worse troubles which would have kept brewing silently in the family over many more years. The therapist who "protects" his client from the release or expression of intense feelings may be actually *protecting himself* from similar unresolved emotional expression—and projecting that need onto the client. The client does not need another Mommy—he needs an assistant to facilitate and support his own growth.

Even if the therapist is willing and ready to handle intense feelings that could arise from emotional exercises, he may still not trust that his clients actually *know* what they need. I have yet to find one client who has trouble knowing where he or she feels comfortable or uncomfortable in any given situation or relationship. Even ambivalence will be represented by a visual "bouncing back and forth" between two emotional positions. The client who doesn't know where to move in an emotional exercise . . . is *already there!* The defiant adolescent who refuses to participate . . . is *already showing* the therapist his emotional position—and should maintain his defiant stance.

That is the wonderful magic about this kind of work—the couple or family will be *showing* you how they *really* feel about each other *before they know they are doing so.* And just like powerful magnets, each family member *just knows* where each one feels attracted or repelled, pulled or pushed, loved or disliked, accepted or rejected, close or distant in an emotional sense. Their *stance* and their *actions* shall reflect this political arrangement before they even utter one word. And . . . they can continue to *show* their responses and reactions by way of these exercises rather than find some form of verbal expression. The family may often surprise itself when it has the opportunity to finally *see* how each member feels by what is *shown* through visual displays. What is observed may also contradict all that the family *had been saying in words*—until now! Words are so frequently used to cover-up issues, mislead the therapist, detour from needed changes, minimize situations, blame others, and simply avoid various emotions. But a visual depiction of emotional distance can betray the most verbally convincing family member!

Common phrases used to elicit the visibility of emotional spacing are simple in nature. In fact, the less said, the better may be the results. Here are some examples:

"Everyone stand wherever you *feel* most comfortable."

"Each of you move to a position that *feels right* for the stressful situation you are in presently."

"Each family member can now move to a position that would *feel right* in regard to where you would *prefer* and want to be."

"If this does not *feel right*, then move to the position that does."

"*Show* me what would need to change in this family picture for it to *feel right* to you?"

"Each of you can sit next to whomever you *feel* most comfortable."

"Each of you take a look at this family sculpture. *Show* me what does *not feel right*."

Therapists get caught in standing and discussing certain situations, when they should spend as much time as possible getting the family to *show* what it would change rather than talk about it. Words can distort or mislead; actions and reactions are more genuine and heartfelt.

Therapist Resistance and Excuses

The first reaction one may have in reading the title to this section could be, "This does not apply to me." If that is your reaction, then please read this section anyway! As therapists we often do not like to examine our own dynamics, ironically. And if we do not do so, then we are missing nearly half the equation for successful therapy. Many times throughout this book I shall suggest strongly that the therapist include himself in the exercise, metaphor, imagery, or mapping of the family. We are part of the picture and can become entrenched with certain family system dynamics as therapy moves forward. We always need to see where we are in the therapy picture as that just might explain the couple's or family's recent behavior as well. As I travel around the country providing professional seminars, I always invite a clinician to present a case in which he or she "feels stuck." As we create a picture, map, or living sculpture of his couple or family, I invite the clinician to place himself in that scene. It is often at that moment that it becomes very clear how he became "stuck." Not only can he see his position, but he can also *feel* it quite well—often *knowing* what needs to change.

As therapists we need our own sense of safety and security as we work with many challenging families and couples over many years. We may make our office space quite predictable and comfortable. We latch onto our favorite chair, favorite corner, favorite coffee mug, and predictable placement of notepads, client files, family photos, and schedule book. More recently we may have added a computer system or laptop to our beloved desk space. And we probably have a set number of chairs or seats in our office to accommodate most if not all kinds of sessions. Likewise, our preference may be to stay with therapeutic approaches which are simple, clear, and easiest for our clients to understand and work with. We may have printed handouts and suggestions for books to read. Cognitive behavioral therapy may serve us well along with other problem-solving strategies, assertiveness training, communication skills training, and an assortment of stress reduction techniques. All of this preparation and organization may serve us well in feeling ready for a variety of clients. Yet, it is not enough for many families and perhaps not working as well as we had thought with a number of couples. We sit there at times feeling frustrated, uncertain, unclear, and ready to refer them to somebody else. Nothing we have *talked* about seems to be working.

There are many therapists still around who did receive excellent training back in the 1970's and 1980's from programs with worldly masters such as Virginia Satir, Salvador Minuchin, Carl Whitaker, Peggy Papp, and Jay Haley. Many social workers and psychologists being trained today do not even know who they are—and are even less likely to have found a book or seen a videotape of their work. One colleague told me that "sculpting a family" must be a play therapy technique using modeling clay to make each of the family members. Another colleague told me that she does not use emotional sculpting any more because she doubts that her clients would do well with that approach. Another therapist claimed that he just does not have enough physical space in his office to perform such exercises. Other clinicians give me a more credible response, "We just became complacent and lazy."

Complacency probably is one of the main culprits. Sitting, listening, and talking take the least energy and often the least effort on our part. If we can be successful without being more active, creative, spontaneous, and imaginative, then we will probably choose the approach which will conserve the most energy and yield the easiest results. There is little doubt that we can become quite comfortable and secure in our organized little offices.

"Why get out of my chair if I don't have to?"

"Why be creative and imaginative if I don't have to be?"

"Why be active and spontaneous if I don't have to be?"

"Why risk taking a chance on appearing foolish or silly if that exercise or sculpting does not produce any results?"

"Why risk being different and possibly losing clients because these approaches may make them uncomfortable?"

"After all, I am not that sure of how to introduce this or make it work right."

"It's just easier to sit here and discuss their issues."

"I am afraid I would not know what to do after I sculpted them."

"My clients just wouldn't go for this kind of stuff."

"It would just be too much work and take too much time."

"I'm not sure what that family would think about me if I started to do this stuff now."

Despite being trained in these wonderful techniques, therapists tend to get lazy, complacent, burned-out, and tired over many years.

Others never felt they could be as successful as the worldly masters they had observed, so low self-confidence and self-doubt derailed their efforts. As I travel around the country meeting with professionals at seminars, I usually ask these groups how many know about these techniques and used to use them. As many as 50% will respond, but that percent drops dramatically when I ask how many clinicians are still using these approaches. Only a handful (around 5%) indicate they are still actively using such strategies. Quite a few therapists indicate that these seminars are a useful and motivating revival for them as they cannot find hardly any other workshops training therapists in this manner. Therefore, the "old-timers" from the golden era of family therapy return to become revitalized, and the more recently-trained therapists are now exposed to new ways of *seeing* their couples and families.

I have heard from a number of therapists who have practiced for years that they feel that they do not get as interesting clients as they used to get in earlier years. Their clients just seem monotonous and boring. I often smile to myself and think, "I wonder if this is a projection of their own complacent or monotonous style." Perhaps their clients find *them* uninteresting and boring as well! Perhaps their clients would respond better to more activity and interesting therapeutic experiences.

Making the Invisible Visible

3

Listening for Metaphors and Somatic Imagery

Because visual images are more memorable and very effective in producing emotional reactions, people often use such imagery in their communications to vividly illustrate their present predicaments and feelings. If one doubts that imagery can be that influential, consider these suggestions and note whether you feel anything or have a reaction.

"Imagine a fresh cut slice of lemon resting on your tongue while you close your lips."

"Listen closely as I scrape my fingernails slowly across this chalk board."

"Close your eyes. You are standing at the edge of a cliff with your toes just over the edge. As you hear the ocean waves crashing on the jagged rocks a thousand feet below, a sudden, strong gust of wind blows you from behind . . ."

"As you drive down the street, you suddenly see the flashing lights of a police car in your rear view mirror and a policeman waving you over to the side of the road."

"You feel a tickle on your leg. You glance down and see a large, hairy spider slowly creeping up your thigh."

People often talk in a metaphoric fashion to add color and imagery to their remarks. Remember these familiar examples?

"I feel like a *huge weight* is finally off my shoulders."

"She *stabbed me in the back* by telling others about what I did."

"Trying to find that book will be like looking for a *needle in a haystack*."

"She is just frantic—running around like a *chicken with its head cut off*."

"My pain is so great that it feels like somebody *took a knife and twisted it* inside me."

"She is so forgetful that she would *lose her head if it weren't attached* to her neck."

"My depression feels like *a deep black hole* that I cannot climb out of."

"I was so mad that *all I could see was red*—I was *spitting nails!*"

"I am so nervous that I have *butterflies fluttering* in my stomach."

"You are so restless that you must have *ants in your pants!*"

"My husband is so controlling that I feel like I *wear a collar and leash*."

"I'm as happy as a *pig in a puddle*."

As clients describe their problems and use vivid imagery, take note of the phrases, descriptive adjectives, and image-producing words that

46

they use. This is another way in which they are telling the therapist *how they feel*. To connect quickly and efficiently with their frame of reference, use their own imagery to create therapeutic metaphors. Act out the metaphors whenever possible. Develop visual sculptures to illustrate their emotional state. Continue to talk in the language of this imagery to develop the metaphors into more detail and deeper meaning. It is often much easier, less stressful, and safer to capture meaning and emotion with such imagery. Clients find it more comfortable to work in this visual, creative, and *indirect* method of exploring issues and emotions.

Clinical Case Example

Andrea was a 22-year old college student who had been raped by a stranger near her apartment building in St. Louis. Although the rapist had attacked others and finally been apprehended, she found herself still reacting with fear whenever she walks anywhere by herself. Suffering from Post Traumatic Stress Disorder, Andrea sought therapy to reduce her fears. In that process she explored her fears, focusing on issues of "feeling controlled." At one point she compared it to being "led like a dog on a leash" instead of feeling a freedom to do as she pleases without fear. I invited her to experience that "being on a leash" to get more in touch with those particular feelings. Using my belt, I fastened it around her neck (with her approval) and began to lead her around the room—*like a dog on a leash*.

> "I hate it! I *hate* it! I hate being led—I feel stupid . . . Damn it, let go! People shouldn't do this to me. I don't *want* to be led. I want to be able to do what I *want* to do!"

However, she began to accept that *she allows* others to control her at times to "avoid hassles." She allowed me to place the "leash" upon her as—only to immediately regret that decision. We explored how and why she lets others "take the lead" in her life.

"I don't like being led, but I'm gonna do it . . . um . . . it'll make things a lot easier for me. *It won't be a hassle.* I dislike a hassle if it's caused by something *I have* to do. This is just the easiest way to get along. I don't want to always do exactly what *I* want to do 'cause then I lose some of the benefits of being led. But I don't want to be led *too much* and lose myself. I want a combination."

After further exploration the present-day trigger for her fears and issues surrounding "control" was realized. This self-proclaimed feminist had recently agreed to get married.

"What's flashing for me right now is really big—the marriage plans . . . I'm getting married to *avoid hassles.* I feel like—Okay, I'll give in, but I'm gonna have it my way still! I'll play by the rules, but I'll have it *my* way in the end."

Andrea made a reference to being "like Superwoman," so I had her stand up, place her hands on her hips, and give me a speech *as Superwoman.* Although she briefly enjoyed that sense of power and control, she also decided that it was "lonely at the top" and that she *did* need other people. She admitted that she had always had trouble asking for help and had stubbornly always tried to do everything by herself. Working within *her own* metaphors by acting them out, she connected very quickly with her innermost emotions and needs.

"For years and years and years that's been a big thing of mine. I never admitted to any problems, and I never asked anyone for help . . . I'm working on that now."

Many clients present physical complaints and somatic symptoms such as headaches, back pain, irritable bowels, constipation, diarrhea, unexplained numbing sensations, muscle soreness, shortness of breath, panic, heart pounding, sweating, and eyelid spasms. Although there may be a real physical cause for such reported symptoms, there is little doubt that anxiety and stress intensify such pain and discomfort. In many cases anxiety, stress, and ambivalence are the *only* cause for these symptoms. Several cardiologists have reported that they have much difficulty determining whether the reason for reported heart attack symptoms is due to either genuine heart problems or a case of intense anxiety—at least until proper tests can be run. It would not be surprising to learn that a client experiences back pain when he is reciting metaphors like "a *huge weight* on my shoulders," "feeling *stabbed* in the back," discussing "*back-breaking* issues," or having "too many worries *weighing me down.*"

Constipation is frequently correlated with *holding in* important emotions. Diarrhea, likewise, is associated with feeling emotionally *out of control.* Headaches and muscle tension are most commonly connected with stress, tension, and situational pressures. Anorexia is often linked with "feeling *starved* for emotional attention" from some distant or controlling parent. Many symptoms of anxiety such as heart-pounding and sweating stem from a perceived, *visualized* threat or imagined danger. Therefore, it is not a surprise that *visual* techniques provide such an effective and successful relief. People simply relate their feelings through familiar images that best depict, symbolize, or describe their issues.

Clinical Case Example

One therapist shared that when he decided that a patient was intensifying or even creating his back pain by *not* dealing with important emotional issues, he gave the client a pillowcase filled with rocks. On each rock was written a word or phrase that represented a specific emotional issue that the client had avoided, denied, or minimized—essentially, a "piece of unfinished business." The therapist had that client hold his bag of rocks out in front of himself so that the client could physically feel the weight and strain upon his back. The therapist insisted that this client actually carry his bag of rocks with him everywhere—even into his shower at home—to make the point that these unresolved issues are *weighing heavily* upon him at all times, no matter where he goes or what he is doing. To lighten that "load" or reduce that emotional burden, the client would need to choose a rock (and respective issue) to deal with during therapy. Once that issue had been faced and reasonably resolved, the client could remove that rock from his bag. Thus, in a visual and symbolic fashion, that client could actually comprehend the effect of unresolved feelings upon the physical body.

Clinical Case Example

A 20-year old married female was admitted to the hospital with severe constipation. Having not had a bowel movement for many weeks, she was given medications and laxatives yet without any significant relief. Because an abusive marital relationship and two small children in the home, she was referred to me for therapy. It did not take long to understand that she had taken a safe and passive position in trying to deal with this violent spouse—while holding in many intense feelings of anger, resentment, frustration, and hurt within herself. She was scared of letting those emotions out—both in terms of how she might lose control and attack him and how he might behave violently in return toward her. So she had been *holding everything in*—literally! With the benefit of ego-strengthening therapy, support from group therapy, and appropriate assertiveness training, she began to share her feelings safely and productively while taking any necessary precautions for herself. I will never forget the day in the hospital when she ran up to me and exclaimed with excitement about finally having a wonderful bowel movement. She then added that she had told her husband the night before how she had been feeling, that she was filing for a divorce, and that her family was moving her things and her kids out and into safe hands. Her bowels finally emptied as her emotions flowed well.

Making the Invisible Visible and Useful

There are so many kinds of influences which impact any family or couple. These pressures remain rather invisible as the family comes for therapy. **Stresses** from an intruding mother-in-law, demanding grandfather, hectic business situation, flirtatious secretary, jealous coworker, or irritating ex-spouse will exert pressure upon the couple or family members. There are numerous **situations** which also add an influence to how a family copes or conducts its business: a surprise pregnancy, death of a close friend, disability, psychiatric label, alcoholism, drug abuse, religious cult, obsession with a job, hobby, or outside activity, weight problem, learning disability, gambling addiction, etc. Many **emotions** also lie hidden or suppressed and would add certain "color" to a visual family "picture" if they could be portrayed for all to see. **Burdens** such as unresolved grief, emotional baggage from childhood or prior relationships, depression, held-in resentments, shame, and guilt need to be represented for their effects upon the couple or family. Once these numerous influences and pressures are properly represented, the clients will *see* and *feel* their presence—no longer being able to minimize or deny their impact. Sometimes a family does not realize how many pressures are pulling on them, creating weight and a lopsided burden until they can see all of these forces represented visually and accurately (until it *feels right*).

Emotional ties, bonds, and connections must all be represented in such a manner that one can *feel* that tie or bond through something like a rope, cloth, scarf, chain, or pair of handcuffs! Hands, arms, and legs can also be used to restrain, hold back, connect, support, cling, or repel. Body position can also represent which family members prefer to face each other, communicate, avoid, or ignore each other.

Burdens must be represented by something *heavy* like a stack of books, bag of rocks, bowling ball, or large furniture. By physically experiencing the *weight* of the situation, the client is more likely to want to make a change more quickly. Caring for everyone else's feelings is a different kind of burden—and could be represented by carrying a carton of raw eggs, a fragile load with which one would be fearful of becoming careless or insensitive.

Emotions can be depicted through drawings of faces with a variety of emotional expressions to select from. Each family member could select one for how he has been feeling and hold it on his lap or have it pinned to his chest. As the family looks around at each other, they can easily *see* each other's inner emotions. Scarves of various colors could also be utilized to represent the emotional *color* of each family member: red for angry, blue for cold or distant, etc. Each person would wear his selected scarf throughout the session, changing colors as appropriate. Family members may even begin to "trade or borrow emotions" for various therapeutic reasons.

Psychiatric labels, medical diagnoses, stereotypes, and disabilities can become visible by simply writing the particular "label" with a black marker on a sheet of white paper. Then this label can be attached to that person in some fashion. The person might have the option to remove his label, hang on to it, or draw attention to it for secondary gains. He might be *seen* as a different person *without* his label on. Or perhaps the label is *only thing* the family has *ever seen* about that person.

Many props can be used to make other influences become visible. Alcoholism can be depicted by beer cans or wine bottles while drug addiction can similarly be seen through pill bottles and syringes (toy ones preferred). Religious preoccupation could be depicted by a cross or small religious statue. A deceased person could be *seen* as an empty chair. A stack of play money could represent preoccupation with wealth, materialism, or the obsession of a "workaholic." A toy computer can symbolize an overinvolvement with the Internet or computer games, etc.

Halloween masks and props are also very useful. An angel's halo, devil's horns, witch's hat, or hostile monster mask can add appropriate effects. A ghost mask may symbolize how that family member seems absent or invisible.

Communication problems can also be nicely enhanced into a tangible and visible number of techniques. "Mixed messages" can be *seen* more clearly by writing each conflicting message on separate pieces of paper so that they can be passed back and forth between family members or from Families of Origin to partners in a couple relationship. It becomes clear rather quickly who is sending and re-sending certain messages, who is receiving or refusing them, and who is becoming confused or stressed by them. If this problem is in regards to a parenting issue, perhaps the couple may see how their mixed messages are causing problems among the children. The children's reactions may also help the couple see how these conflicting signals are splitting the parental dyad and causing tension and conflict in the couple's relationship.

Between marital partners, it may be useful to have each mate write down his or her main point or most important message for his mate on a sheet of paper—summarized or stated succinctly. They can then trade messages and discuss reactions. Making it tangible allows it to be held, shredded, discarded, ripped, or treasured. Making it visible and *to the point* on each piece of paper helps focus and clarify marital communication. Posting those main points at home in a highly *visible* location helps the couple remember and stay focused.

When parents suspect their children are giving them different stories or conflicting messages, each parent can make a sign with a piece of paper that represents what each parent *thinks* he or she is hearing from that child. The child could also make a sign to represent what his or her message actually was. If that child *has* been giving two different messages to the parents, it will force him to have to make a choice, blend them, or revamp his original message. It should aid in clearing up the confusion.

Examples of Ideas for Props

Relationship connections	Jumpropes, plastic chains, string of scarves, soft ropes
Overinvolvement	Really tied to that person with several bonds
Dependency	Hanging on to that rope and having it encircle him
Underinvolvement	Loose rope with much slack
Detachment	No connection at all; rope could be lying on the floor
Attention-seeking	Jerking and pulling on the rope with that person
Co-dependency	Each has own rope connecting with the other (2 ropes)
Keeping in touch	One finger placed on a rope between two others
Having an influence	Grabbing firmly the rope between two others
Domination, control	Person is roped from behind, led like a dog on a leash
Passive, dominated	Person sits on floor with ropes tight with dominator
Influence from others	Scarf, towel, or rope draped over one shoulder
Alcoholism	Beer can, wine bottle, brandy fifth, six-pack
Drug addiction, abuse	Pill bottles, toy or real syringe, M&M's, Tic-Tac's
Gambling addiction	Pair of dice, toy slot machine, deck of cards, play money
Physical disability	Crutches, cane, wheelchair
Religious obsession	Religious statue or figurine, cross, Rosary beads
Puts everyone else first	Must hold carton(s) of raw eggs the whole session
Workaholic	Stack of play money, toy cell phone, heavy bag of coins
Somatic complaints	Must hold bag of rocks (issues), causing physical strain
Busy school schedule	Must hold pile of books, notebooks, papers, and pens
Psychiatric label (diagnosis)	Label written on a sign which can be held, pinned, taped
Death	Empty chair, photo of deceased on chair
Depression, Guilt	Must hold a bowling ball, bag of rocks, heavy object
Religious Conflict	Wooden or cardboard **block** with religious label
Abortion, miscarriage	Baby doll
Sexually abused	Completely covered up into a fetal position on the floor
Abusive, severely critical	Point toy gun at each "wounded, damaged" person

Internet overinvolvement	Both hands placed on a toy computer, TV set, keyboard
Sexual Addiction	Naked Barbie or Ken doll, Playboy magazine
Self-Mutilation, Cutting	Rubber knife (Who is it *really* intended for?)
Affective/Emotional Colors	Scarves, towels, hats of various colors, i.e.: Angry, frustrated = Red; Sad, depressed = Black; Happy, content = Blue; Jealous, anxious = Green; Loving, nurturing, dependent = Yellow; Cold, distant, scared = White; Hyper, out of control = Orange; Controlling, in power = Purple, or a king's crown
Feeling Suffocated/Trapped	Blanket placed over person's head and body
Not Allowed to Have a Voice	Scarf or towel used as a gag for mouth
Needs to be Nurtured	Give them a big Teddy bear or pillow to hug and hold
Rescuer	Nurse's cap, Red Cross badge, Hero medallion

Using Bodies to Sculpt the Picture

BODY POSITION: In any relationship would the two people be facing each other, side by side, back to back, front to back, perpendicular, or completely detached?

facing each other
direct and loving

back to back
mad, at odds

front to back
one happy, one not

side by side
focused as team
but not on selves

perpendicular
as two individuals
acting independently

completely detached
unhappy, empty

↓☺☺↑   →☺ ☺←   ←☺ ☺→

| together but going two different directions | pulled apart by others, facing but held distant | involved with distractions back to back, self focused |

It is one matter to display emotional space and distance, but positioning of each body is crucial to accurately depict the emotional stance in each relationship. Is there direct communication? Is each person focused appropriately on his/her own needs as well as those of others? Just because a couple *feels* together emotionally does not mean that they are focused in the same directions. Do they have good eye contact? What are they actually spending their time doing? Are they involved with each other, the kids, their jobs, their parents, or their friends?

EXPRESSIVE GESTURES: Along with positioning and distance comes some kind of depiction of each person's attitude, personality, mood, and quality of relations with each other. Hand gestures can capture much of this.

Defiance = hands on hips, head turned

Control = hands on shoulders

Loving = holding or hugging

Blaming = pointing a finger

Rejecting = one hand out to block

Withdrawal = fetal position

Open = hands held out, palms up

Not listening = hands cover ears

Afraid to speak = hands cover mouth

Frustrated = hands on top of head

Blocking = one hand held palm out

In touch = one finger on the situation

Resistance = arms crossed on chest

Support = arm around or hand on back

Clinging = wrapped around leg or neck

Threatening = raising a clenched fist

Rejection = head lowered, looking at floor

Angry = standing with fists clenched

Depression = head held in hands

Not willing to look = hands cover eyes

Confused = hands raised outward & upward

Helpful = an open hand held outwardly

Scared = both hands blocking, crossed over face

Connected = holding hands, hand on shoulder

There are, of course, slang or obscene gestures that could be used or chosen by a family to depict their feelings, but the therapist can usually assist with ideas for less graphic and more acceptable forms of expression. However, sometimes, it *may* be the best representation of that family member's emotional stance.

FACIAL EXPRESSION: This is self-explanatory, of course, in depicting feelings by using familiar, accepted facial expressions. However, it is difficult for a family member to maintain a particular expression, grimace, scowl, frown, or even smile for very long without becoming weary—or simply forgetting to maintain it. Props may be more practical—such as the emotional "colors" represented by scarves, or drawings and photographs of facial expressions which can be selected, assigned, or chosen by each family member to hold or wear pinned to their shirts.

DEGREE OF TOUCH: This is vital in accurately depicting the finer aspects of their emotional space and distance from each other. Are they only connected through a third person? Are they connected only by a rope, chain, or scarf? Is there any *real touch* that occurs between them? Is it *mutual* touching? One-sided? Controlling? Is it just one finger, a hand, an arm, or an embrace? Is it a kind of motherly, fatherly, or brotherly touch? Do they wish to touch but find that something has come in between them? Be sure to explore these finer aspects of connection among relationships. Does the particular touch evoke any particular feeling or unexpected reaction? Is the touching accepted, condoned, appreciated, dreaded, disliked, optional, or essential? Does one person love the contact while the other only pretends to like it? Has the degree, extent, or quality of touch/contact changed over time? What event(s) or other people have had an effect which somehow altered the quality and degree of contact? What would it take for the degree of touch to improve? If the connection is "hanging by a thread," be sure to tie a thread between these two people!

EMOTIONAL AGE: There is often a dramatic difference between a family member's actual, chronological age and the emotional age that his mood and behavior reflect. A thirteen year-old may demonstrate advanced maturity and *seem thirty years old*. Often, adults are seen as acting immaturely like grade-school children. Emotional age may be a more accurate indicator in terms of one's ability to problem-solve, cope, love, or communicate. As therapists do we expect more out of our clients than they are reasonably or maturely able to handle? Are we missing the *real picture* by not depicting the perceived and reported emotional ages in a couple or family? Might this illustrate more accurately the frustrations in a couple or the role confusion in a family? When clients *see* and *feel* the emotional age their behavior suggests, it can be a power-ful, eye-opening awareness for them.

DEPICTING EMOTIONAL AGE: After an emotional age is suggested and assigned to each family member (either by the therapist or by a family survey), each person needs to assume a visual representation that befits that age. It may work simply by having "emotionally young" people sit on the floor like children while "emotionally mature" family mem-bers tower above in a parental manner. Everybody begins to really *feel* their positions in this respect. If an adult needs to be younger—but not as young as a child sitting on the floor—he can kneel to *appear* younger. In the same fashion, a child taking on a parental role may need to stand or kneel on a chair to *appear* bigger. Props can also depict these age roles. Anybody seen as a child may need toys to hold. Anybody viewed as an older adult may need a gray wig, a cane, or "granny glasses." By the time a family is accurately sculpted according to their emotional ages, dramatic and sometimes embarrassing revelations become unavoidably clear. Role confusion, crossed boundaries, and identity confusion may be quite obvious. Dependency, immaturity, and parental chil-dren may become clearly visible.

The family will always tell the therapist what *feels right* and what still needs to be depicted differently. Each family member may need his own turn at sculpting the family in this manner as there may be significant differences in perception. This will probably occur if family members are thinking about different situations, moods, or events in which behaviors may naturally change accordingly. This is just fine because it may serve to show how family members *can* act differently at var-ious times and in different circumstances—and are not *always* immature or bossy. This also underlines the idea that behavior *can* be controlled or changed by the individual given certain challenges and circumstances. It also reminds a family that a particular family member may not *always* behave in a certain way. And if the dysfunctional, age-inappropriate behavior *does* exist at all times in all situations, then that information also becomes very clear. By portraying these emotional ages *visually*, everybody can *see* and *feel* the family dynamics with greater clarity, awareness, comprehension, and lasting memory.

ROLE-REVERSALS: An added benefit with the Emotional Age sculpting is that family members can experience different roles, different ages, and what it would take to maintain such changes. It can then be learned what promotes or sustains certain dysfunctional behavior or age-inappropriate actions. If Families of Origin are also represented, certain behaviors may find their source or reason for existence. By having a parental child trade positions with an immature parent, we may learn the very reasons for the dysfunctional pattern that actually revealed an original role reversal.

Sculptures in Motion

Every therapist needs to remember that any physical sculpturing of a family or couple is simply "one snapshot in time." Like taking a person's body temperature with a thermometer or reading the barometer to recognize the status of present weather conditions, a family sculpture is just *one* reading at *one* moment in time. Relations in couples and families are constantly in motion—changing, developing, growing, altering, etc. Therapists can actually measure, visually, both progress and deterioration in relationships. Couples and families will display those changes naturally without even having to consciously think about it. As therapists we must constantly *allow* them to *show* us these changes in visual ways.

HOME MOVIE: A therapist can take any sculpted situation and move it backward or forward in time to acquire a sense of the flow of emotions over a period of months or years. By accumulating more "snapshots" of this family or couple, one begins to construct a "home movie" comprised of many "frames" from various points in time. It becomes quite clear what events, situations, or factors over time shaped various relationships, either enhancing or straining them. A therapist can observe emotional gaps developing, the formation of alliances, the effects of distractions, and the strain and stress from Families of Origin. A couple or family often forgets "how it used to be"—and reliving those moments in a physically sculpted scene can trigger old feelings and fond memories. Then a therapist can help them understand what changed or how they drifted away from such a good time in their lives. Often the couple or family spontaneously recognizes why it "was working then" and not now! The physical experience of *seeing* and *feeling* these spatial shifts in relations over time can enhance awareness toward genuine and insightful changes. The family or couple may literally stumble over what actions or behaviors made things work better over time.

This process of sculpting over time also emphasizes the fact that no situation or relationship is likely to escape change or "stay stuck" for very long. Therefore, if they are feeling hopelessly "stuck," this may help them to see how things *do* change and *have* changed over the years—and *probably* will again, eventually. This awareness may encourage them to seriously consider and reveal their inner hopes and wishes for the future. Then the therapist can assist them in viewing their own dreams for change by physically sculpting them—having them *come alive* so that they can experience how such changes might *feel*. Allowing each member to direct his own future sculpture can be rewarding to all involved as everyone comes to understand and experience each member's perspective and hopes in a visual fashion. Each family member will *experience* what every other family member expects, needs, or wants from him. By acting out everybody's hopes and wishes, each family member is more likely to remember what everybody else wants. It becomes psychologically reinforced when a number of family members desire the *same* changes from that person. A request seems *more valid* when most of the others agree on the desired changes.

KINETIC FAMILY SCULPTURE: Derived from Kinetic Family Drawings which many psychologists often administer to individuals along with the more familiar House-Tree-Person projective drawings, this type of sculpting is based on perceptions of how the family relates within types of activities rather than strictly upon emotional space among its members. As with Kinetic Family Drawings (KFD's) the instructions are very simple. Instead of requesting, "Draw your family *doing* something," the therapist asks each family member to "Position your family *doing* something." Although the implication suggests that the family *might* be doing this activity together, it is not unusual for family members to see themselves as detached and doing various individual activities simultaneously. Each family member gets his turn at sculpting the family into his own version of "family activity." Not only will this display what activities the family members engage in, but it shall also once again reveal another dynamic portrayal of emotional spacing and distance. Who joins in? Who have similar interests? Who is detached? Who is central? Who is controlled? Who is independent?

The therapist can move this Kinetic Family Sculpture back and forth over time to learn what kinds of activity linked more of the family members together as well as what kind of interests or events pulled them apart or left some members out.

TYPICAL EVENING AT HOME: A useful form of sculpting involves converting the therapy office or group room into the family's home. The therapist asks each family member, "What is a typical evening at home like? Where would everyone be? What would each family member typically be doing?" The therapist might suggest that each family member draw this arrangement or "at-home portrait" prior to the sculpting process. This helps each family member to focus and visualize how the family appears at home in its typical routine. The family can then agree upon what rooms of their home are involved or most important, designating different areas or corners of the therapy room as the living room, kitchen, dining area, bedrooms, etc. After the family agrees upon the imaginary layout of their home, each member has a turn at sculpting his/her family according to his or her opinion of a "typical evening."

(Example)

       tired Mom   helpful daughter   daughter doing
in kitchen   assisting Mom   homework

in bedroom

two sons fighting   Dad watching TV
over video games   in family room

Clinical Case Example

One family with an adolescent female as the "identified patient" inquired before their session about whether they should bring their four month-old baby or get a babysitter. Since the baby is a regular member of the family and certainly affects their home, I insisted they include her for at least one session. Then they asked about bringing the pet dog. I concluded that although the dog was part of their home, it might best be represented by a stuffed animal since a dog may react more to a different environment. The family continued to be concerned with the disruptions that the baby could cause. I assured them that we would just deal with any problems as they occurred.

We constructed the "typical evening at home" sculpture, having designated different parts of the group therapy room as different rooms of their home. Mother was holding the baby in the living room. Father was facing away from everyone and watching television. Teenage daughter (identified patient) was talking on a phone in her bedroom while two younger brothers were playing a game in their bedroom. Suddenly the baby began crying and mother appeared distressed. They all looked at me for my reaction. I simply asked them to handle this just like they would at home. Mother told her daughter to get off the phone. The daughter took the baby, patted it on the back, and began walking with the baby around the living room. The baby immediately calmed down, and Mother began watching television with Father. For the rest of the hour the daughter circled the living room, keeping the baby calm. The daughter commented, wearily, that, "This is just how it always goes."

Sensing that Mother frequently sought relief from childcare and that Father was completely uninvolved, I asked Father to relieve his daughter from her "parental duties" and take the baby. He began circling the room, patting the baby in the same manner that daughter had done. Daughter was delighted to be released from her Parental Child role. I processed with the family the role changes that had been acted out in this action sculpture, looking at how we could incorporate similar changes at home. The daughter's behavior changed dramatically once she felt less burdened by parental duties. Mother was glad to have Father's occasional help—as she had always been afraid to bother him with such requests. By bringing their home into my office, it became much easier to *see* and *experience* their dynamics and

64

roles. It became more obvious what changes were needed—and to be able to try them out in their "home" in my office. And it was more difficult for them to return to their usual routine at home without thinking about the rehearsed changes they had experienced in their family session in my office.

Families will show the therapist what they typically do at home without necessarily knowing how it will appear to an outsider to their system. This is the beauty in having them act out a scene from home. If some member tries to change, hide, or conceal a typical behavior, another family member will quite likely expose that discrepancy or different behavior in order for everything to look familiar and *feel right*.

Cycling Behavior Patterns

CIRCULAR: Occasionally, when the therapist may ask a family to stand where they feel most comfortable, a circular action may develop rather unexpectedly. One member (Susie) moves toward another (Paul) and finds that that member (Paul) is moving away in another direction toward a third member (Chris), who is actually chasing after the first member (Susie)! Because there literally is no end to this "chase," the therapist will have to "freeze the action" by telling everyone to stop in their tracks. Otherwise, the circular behavior will continue, build frustration, and possibly lead to aggression. This cycle of behavior—when acted out—can certainly enhance an awareness in everyone as to *why* and *how* they get so frustrated.

BACK AND FORTH: Often a family member will demonstrate either (1) ambivalence, or (2) an effort to please at least two other family members at the same time by drifting back and forth between them—not being able to settle into any one set position. That family member may also find themselves literally pulled apart in two different directions.

This is common with Parental Children, Identified Patients, and overinvolved mothers. This was demonstrated well in the clinical case (page 16) in which the 13 year-old identified patient moved constantly during the session to attempt to connect with all members of the family and become the only "glue" to hold the family together. This may often become visible in blended family scenarios as the children may resist and work back toward a more familiar but prior family arrangement while the parents strive for blending everyone into a new family unit. Court-ordered visitation back and forth between the divorced parents may need to be acted-out to reflect reality—despite emotional preferences.

DOMINO EFFECT: The "domino effect" may be seen as one family member makes a single move. A moment later, another family member *feels* that change and decides that he needs to move. That move may precipitate another family member to alter his or her position in another few seconds as each person *feels* each change and makes *emotional* decisions. A slow but ongoing chain reaction may be observed that may become perpetual until the therapist halts it and processes what is occurring. The family may be completely unaware that such an emotional "domino effect" or chain reaction is occurring until they *see* and *feel* it, themselves.

LIVE GRENADE: This effect is quickly and dramatically seen in a sculpture when a physical change in space by just one family member may send numerous other members of the family scattering simultaneously. This "explosive" emotional impact needs to be carefully processed and understood since its effect is so dramatic and pervasive. The nice benefit from sculpting is that everyone *sees* this reaction so clearly that it cannot be easily denied, ignored, minimized, excused, or forgotten. The physical move was experienced so immediately by everybody and reactions occurred spontaneously without any words having been spoken or exchanged.

Splitting Family Members Into Parts

Behavior-Altering Influences

Some family members may be more complex in their effects upon the family. This may require that this family member needs to be represented, visually, in more than one fashion. For example, the father may be a warm, wonderful parent and husband when sober. But when he is under the influence of alcohol, he is aggressive, abusive, and unpredictable. Because he *feels* like two different people, he should be represented in two different ways. Two chairs are probably the easiest manner in which to portray this effect. One chair would contain the kind, sober father while the other chair would hold the mean, alcoholic father. In this fashion, the family finds it much easier to focus their different emotions in the two separate directions rather than feel confused and uncertain how to talk or behave toward a single but complicated representation of the father. If the father is present, he may need to decide which chair to speak from or which chair he feels more comfortable in. The family can outline for him how they see the differences between the "two fathers." They may choose to *only* speak to the sober chair, thus reinforcing the need for him to be in that chair more often. The family may feel free to confront the empty chair that represents the alcoholic father—while the real father observes from the "sober chair." In the same manner, the family can praise him and appreciate him directly with loving remarks as long as he remains in the "sober chair." Hopefully, the father will gain insight concerning the family's different reactions to him depending upon which chair (and which behavior in life) he chooses. Splitting the father into the two distinct positions gives the family the opportunity to finally release both angry frustrations and fears as well as loving encouragement in a focused fashion.

Role Differentiation

The same process can work well for a family member who tries to maintain a number of roles—and perhaps *behaves differently* according to the demands and characteristics of each role. For example, Mom may take on the roles of (1) loving parent, (2) hectic businesswoman, (3) caretaking daughter for elderly father, (4) PTA chairperson, (5) Sunday school teacher, and (6) avid softball team member. Her mind-set, emotions, and behaviors may be quite different from role to role, thereby creating the need to set a chair for each of her six roles she participates in. Not only can she become more clear on how these varying roles affect her family, but she can also understand how it creates conflicting or exhausting struggles within herself. The other family members can help her see herself by describing what behaviors they observe for each of her six chairs (roles). They can also deal directly in a more focused manner with any of the six roles represented by the six chairs by sharing their own reactions and issues. This just makes it so much easier for the other family members to focus more clearly on Mom's various emotions and behaviors according to which "hat" she is wearing (One can also use *different hats*, of course, to symbolically represent her various roles that she assumes).

This "splitting" technique works well for couples also. Whether it is the wife dealing with an alcoholic husband or both partners heavily involved in many activities, the use of extra chairs helps to clarify their difficulties in relating or communicating effectively. For example, a couple may need to set up *five chairs each* to represent all the roles in which they are both involved. This will easily demonstrate in a visual fashion how their pattern of communication is affected according to which roles they are in at any given moment in time.

HIS ROLES				HER ROLES
prosecuting attorney	☐		☐	Sunday school teacher
bowling team member	☐	↙	☐	PTA chairperson
church deacon	☐		☐	caretaker for elderly Dad
Boy Scout leader	☐	↗	☐	loving wife
loving husband	☐		☐	hectic businesswoman

(five chairs each)

Past and Present

Another reason to utilize this splitting technique involves *past* and *present* behavior by a particular family member or partner in a couple. Perhaps that person is perceived as having changed significantly over the years—to the degree that a chair needs to represent a set of behaviors and emotions from years ago along with another chair for present feelings and actions. The other partner or family members can share their feelings about each chair—especially what they appreciate or miss in that person. Sometimes that particular person may deny, minimize, or disagree with the perceptions of others. Therefore, the reasons for this declared distinction between the past and present must be very clear and specific—not general or vague. When that person acknowledges the changes over time, a more honest exploration of how such changes came about will be more possible. It also gives the others an opportunity to openly focus on what is desired, cherished, and productive in that person. Much creativity and spontaneity can develop with this kind of technique.

Health Changes

Health conditions may create a need for more than one chair. A disabling condition, head injury from a car accident, chronic back pain, terminal cancer, or crippling disease may alter a person's outlook, attitude, emotions, and behavior. This observed change may make it seem

69

like he or she has become a different person. The therapist may set a chair for "before" and "after" this change took place to allow the family to focus their feelings properly and clearly either on *the person they have known* or *the person they now experience*. The therapist can also set a chair for the disease or injury itself, so that the others may speak *directly* to it.

Emotional Splitting

Some family members or couples may have so many intense feelings occurring at the same moment that extra chairs may help to illustrate and clarify these emotions for all persons involved. As the intense feelings of each participant are identified, a chair is set forth for each one of those feelings. For example, Susie may have three chairs for herself, representing her anger, hurt, and fear. Brian may have four chairs for himself to contain his joy, anxiety, fear, and emotional pain. Linda may have two chairs to symbolize her sadness and worry. Bill may also have three chairs for his rage, confusion, and scared feelings. As each person speaks from that particular emotion, he or she shall sit in the respective chair for that emotion. Then, as a discussion begins, each person realizes not only what each chair (emotion) has to say but what specific emotional mindset each person tends to gravitate toward or become stuck within. When each reacts to another person, he or she switches to the appropriate chair to represent that respective emotional reaction. Family members or couples soon learn how they interact with each other from various emotional states—how they may use certain feelings to manipulate others, control a situation, or hide from productive changes in behavior. They may also learn much more about how their own feelings interact and coordinate *within* themselves by having seen them so clearly represented by a number of chairs.

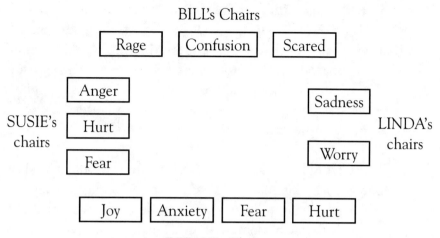

BILL's Chairs

| Rage | Confusion | Scared |

Anger

SUSIE's chairs

Hurt

Fear

Sadness

LINDA's chairs

Worry

| Joy | Anxiety | Fear | Hurt |

BRIAN's Chairs

When a certain feeling becomes resolved, relieved, or satisfactorily expressed, that chair can now become the "OKAY" chair or neutral position for that family member or partner in a couple. As other feelings become resolved, those extra chairs can simply be removed or turned around so that they cannot be used. Hopefully, everybody will eventually be sitting in just one "OKAY" chair, having worked through their various emotions. Some feelings may be important to retain—but at least that need and the reasons for that need should be very clear for everyone due to such a visual representation of family emotions.

Contraindications?

A number of professionals have queried about possible drawbacks or situations in which these techniques might be inadvisable to use. They have worried about clients with psychotic conditions, character disorders, explosive tempers, poor impulse control, or volatile resistance that might carry over to vengeful reprisals later in the home. They have also worried about their own lack of confidence, uncertainty, and insecurity in dealing with techniques which may elicit strong and unpredictable emotions from their clients. These techniques certainly have that potential, but that does not mean that this would necessarily be "bad" or unproductive for the clients. We all grow from pain and experience—not from pleasure and being sheltered. If we cannot bear to experience our clients' emotions, then we had better look more closely at our own insecurities.

PSYCHOTIC CONDITIONS: Often psychosis is characterized by fascinating imagery with symbolic or elaborate visions that may indirectly represent detached emotions. This suggests that schizophrenics are already in that visual frame of reference that can safely depict their troubles indirectly. They cannot deal with reality directly. In terms of emotional distance schizophrenics know very well where they feel comfortable. Wherever they sit, stand, or position themselves will accurately portray their emotional position. The therapist can listen to their imagery which is often based in some sense of reality. Imagery requested for various exercises may be relatively easy for the schizophrenic to connect with—even though the therapist may not fully understand the associations immediately.

CHARACTER DISORDERS: Because DSM-4 Axis II Personality Disorders are often difficult or unmanageable in forms of conventional "talk therapy," many therapists assume that these techniques will encounter similar resistance and difficulty. However, the nature of these techniques actually provides more potential for success because these techniques bypass resistance and conscious defenses. For example, Borderline Personality Disorders are already colorful, dramatic, and expressive. They often talk in metaphors, claiming that they have "raised walls" around themselves to protect themselves from more pain. A therapist could take sheets of cardboard and visually create those "walls" so that such a client would see that the walls do indeed protect them but also isolate them when they are emotionally needy. This same type of character disorder would also have little trouble sculpting emotional distance as they are keenly aware of such distance in all of their relationships.

The Narcissistic and Sociopathic characters would probably unknowingly reveal their perceptions of themselves (as well as others) rather easily with most of the metaphoric imagery exercises. They would also have difficulty knowing to defend against inadvertent and spontaneous displays of emotional spacing as with seating and sculpting arrangements. Resistance is a picture all of its own as it is a form of acting-out. Therefore, any occasion in which resistance rears its head has already begun the construction of an emotional "picture" for the therapist. Histrionic or Hysterical characters are also quite emotional, colorful, and expressive and would have little difficulty with any exercise. Paranoid characters may present the most resistance just because they trust the therapist the least and are less likely to take risks. However, they would be resistant to "talk therapy" as well. They might just feel safer with many of the indirect techniques as well as some traditional play therapy approaches that might seem less threatening. Just remember that any resistance begins the painting of an emotional portrait—perhaps, in this case, around a theme of fear and immobilization. Imagine the paranoid character with his back to the corner of the room while others show their attempts to lure him from his safe corner.

ANGRY CLIENTS: Clients generally become more irate and uncomfortable when the therapist moves too quickly from an indirect technique or safe image to a direct confrontation or painful return to reality. It may be advisable to work within the imagery or metaphors in order to maintain the level of safety and comfort. Continuing with an indirect approach can be an effective treatment strategy in that the clients understand at a subconscious level as in hypnosis. In other words, resolving the friction between a "grumpy bear" and a "shy lamb" becomes an easier exercise that leads to a deeper understanding of how these representative metaphors can suggest solutions for the actual relationship.

An outburst of rage, an attention-seeking tantrum, or a steamy retreat into silence can all create unique portraits which capture the emotional tone of each couple's or family's dynamics. It is the therapist who may be uncomfortable with the expression of anger—an emotion that may be routinely released in the client's home. Therefore, the clients may be quite accustomed to such angry releases but just now becoming more comfortable to show this style of interaction within the therapy arena—thanks to the therapist's selection of a safer approach. Since the therapist is often creating a stage for emotions to be played out, he should expect dramatic displays to occur. What the therapist may need to consider is whether or not this couple or family already is expressive and demonstrative enough—and does not need a technique to elicit even more.

UNCOMFORTABLE THERAPISTS: The greatest resistance to using these revealing approaches frequently comes from the therapist, himself. A lack of confidence, a fear of appearing foolish or "out of character," personal insecurities, and a great uncertainty as to "what to do next" are some of the more common reasons to avoid these techniques and find excuses why the clients cannot handle them! This is a common response from therapists who just have not had much practice or experience with this type of therapy in their training. The exercises are easy to implement but therapists doubt that they will know what to do next. They do not trust that their eyes will see many hidden dynamics and new ideas or that their hearts will provide keen intuition from being involved. What the therapist often forgets is that he, too, will be going through an experience which will provide more clues and emotional reactions than just talking about the problems would have ever accomplished. If a technique like sculpting actual people into an emotional portrait is too direct for the therapist, he may wish to use play therapy dollhouse figures with client(s) initially to provide an indirect approach while practicing and learning to become comfortable and experienced.

Helping Therapists Find Themselves

4

Mapping and Therapist Roles

First developed and popularized by Salvador Minuchin in the 1970's, the creation of a visual drawing of the family system became a very useful tool in "seeing" the family's relations, dynamics, structure, and emotional distance on paper. This family mapping procedure gives every therapist a structural plan for healthy change in the family system. A therapist now has a clearer idea of which relations need more time together and which ones could use some time apart from each other. It also provides a visual representation of the necessary boundaries and their relative strength in the family. Healthy boundaries should exist between parents and children, families of origin and parents, grandparents and grandchildren, etc. This mapping process can reveal when boundaries are crossed, weak, or absent. Various symbols are used to represent the strengths and weaknesses of relations and boundaries.

Relations   **Boundaries**

☹ // ☹	conflict, detached	. . . .	weak, unclear, confused
☺ – ☺	weak, strained		
☺ = ☺	normal, adequate	– – – – – –	normal, healthy
☺ : ☺	strong, healthy	———————	rigid, inaccessible
☺ ⇔ ☺	overinvolved, symbiotic		

---

parental child   mom   dad

☺ ⇔ 😐 / / ☹ ⇔ work

. . . .   – – – – – –   ———————

↑   ↑

☹   😐   / /   ☹

jealous   loyal   confused, detached,
sister   daughter   angry son
(identified patient)

Example of family map with marital conflict

This process of visually mapping out a family system on paper or a chalkboard can be useful not only for the therapist but also for the family as well. The family can look at the diagram and decide if it *feels right* or needs any adjustments. Each member could take a turn to verbalize his or her reaction to a posted "family map" on the wall of the therapy room. Are all relationships represented? Are natural boundaries distinct (i.e. parent/child), or are they unclear and confusing? How would any family member alter the diagram according to his or her own perspective of what *feels right?* Are detachments, alignments, conflicts, alliances, or symbiotic connections represented? Are strong outside influences such as supportive grandparents, nosy co-workers, close friends, involved teachers, charismatic clergy, abusive bosses, critical families of origin, assigned school counselors, intrusive neighbors, or interfering romances represented? Do these designated relations *feel* either appropriate and healthy or unusual and confusing?

As the therapist becomes involved with these clients in sessions, it becomes essential after a short time for a new map to be drawn. Not only does this help monitor the family's progress but **it must now include where the therapist *feels* his own position in this family "picture" has developed.** Many therapists may argue that they are not *truly* part of the family and do not need to be represented on a family map. However, because the professional clinician has engaged in a process with members of the family, relationships have developed which have a strength and a quality—as well as a few boundaries—that need to be recognized and reviewed. Although a number of clinicians are reluctant to examine their own position with a family—*simply assuming* that they are being appropriate and professional, a subsequent "blind spot" or "missing piece" in this therapeutic puzzle may actually be the therapist's role, itself.

As I travel around the country, providing professional seminars on my work in marriage and family therapy, I always ask if at least one of the therapists in the audience would like to *see* one of their frustrating cases from a new perspective. As that professional clinician maps his client's network, he *always* leaves himself out of the picture. When we create a visual sculpting of that same case presentation, it becomes much more apparent how the therapist may have become frustrated, based on the position in which he finds himself within that client's family network. Therapists often do not like to admit that they have been pulled into a family system to fill a void, satisfy a need, or take on a vacated role. As they *see* themselves in awkward or surprising roles in this visual display, it is not unusual to hear rationalizations, excuses, intellectualizing, minimizing, and denial that they could actually have fallen victim to such emotional influences. Did we forget that we are only human and inevitably going to feel such emotions? Can we completely and successfully block out the emotional learning and psychological effect of our childhoods? If—as therapists—we think it is possible to be completely objective and detached with *every* couple and family, then we had better *always* have another therapist sculpt our position within those clients' systems. When we minimize or avoid looking at our own position, then we are much more likely to blindly be an unhealthy or even dangerous influence within that client's family network. Until we comprehend *our own roles* and reactions, we cannot be healthy agents of change.

Examples of Therapist Involvement and Position

UNINTENTIONAL ALIGNMENT: The therapist is drawn to the more verbal, active, expressive, or charming partner in the couple and unintentionally ignoring the more passive, less articulate or silent partner.

husband   therapist wife

DELIBERATE ALIGNMENT: The therapist has decided at some level within himself which one in the couple is right and which one is wrong. The therapist then joins with a spouse to "fix" the other partner "for the good of everyone."

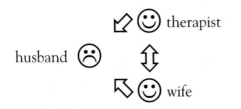

80

ADULTS vs. THE KIDS: The couple has convinced the therapist that one or more of their children is defective, guilty, sinful, bad or at least the Identified Patient. The therapist teams up with the parents to "fix" the problematic children.

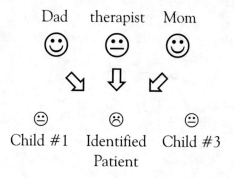

"BAD PARENTS": Either (1) the children have convinced the therapist that their parents are defective, immature, inappropriate, or dangerous, or (2) the therapist feels a strong need to save and protect these "unfortunate" kids and becomes their strong parent until or while the parents "get fixed."

☺   ☺   ☺ the children

↙😐↘ therapist

😐😐 the parents

FILLING A VOID: The therapist senses, subconsciously, where the family needs help with an absent or weakened role and fills in. This is often the case with one of the adult roles being physically or emotionally absent. The children may even look to the therapist for parental nurturing and support. The surviving adult partner may have seduced the therapist into this position while the distant adult partner feels abandoned or replaced.

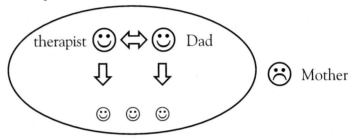

THERAPIST GLUE: This therapist attempts to be the "glue" that holds everyone together—and essentially is *working too hard* while the family basically sits back and waits for the therapist to "fix them."

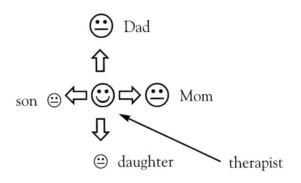

OVERWHELMED: The family makes it very clear to the therapist that they expect every issue to be dealt with *right now* and to meet *all* of their needs at once. They expect the therapist to lead the way, and they will *possibly* follow. With many issues and needs, other therapists/co-therapists are wisely needed.

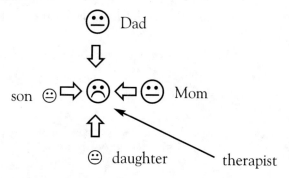

ALIGNMENT WITH PARENTAL CHILD: The therapist perceives the existence of a Parental Child role and chooses to align with that child at some level of emotion, sympathy, or pity—rather than helping the child "lose the role" gracefully and return across the boundary back to the subsystem of children. The parents may "pull rank" and end therapy to defeat this alignment.

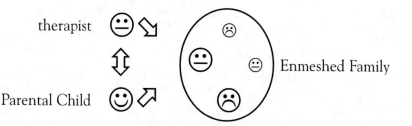

THE SIEGE OF SERVICES: The work with a family may become fragmented or disengaged itself due to the involvement of too many services, caseworkers, and therapists. Every worker has a piece of the puzzle but may not *"get the whole picture"* and may not communicate as often or as efficiently as needed in order to share his "puzzle piece" or opinion—or to receive valuable input from other members of the social services network. The conflict sometimes is reflected or mirrored in the behavior of each service which is aligned with a different family member.

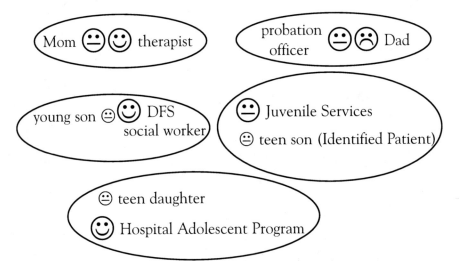

As the therapist, one may find that coordinating the various services and their work is almost as hard as getting the family, itself, to work together. Due to the different approaches, treatment models, and personalities involved, the extent of this problem may not be realized to its full degree of detriment until sculpted into a visual display and *seen*. Then a therapist can *feel* what is needed and *see* some new directions through sculpting the various options.

WOUNDED COUPLE: The therapist finds himself in a nurturing, strong parental role when he discovers that neither parent is "grown-up" or emotionally strong enough to act responsibly as an adult. The problem could develop that the therapist inadvertently fosters dependency and enjoys the idealization.

☺ therapist (parental role)

⇩

☺ ☺ parents (child-like role)

TRAFFIC COP IN THE WOODS: Many times a therapist is in the "thick of things,"directing interventions and "putting out fires." He finds himself right in the middle of all the action, but he is "too close to the trees to see the forest." He needs a chance to back out and see the whole system from a distance. Another therapist should help him sculpt this family picture with him in it as well.

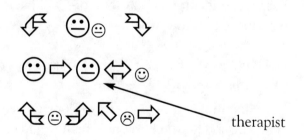

therapist

Despite all of the possible configurations and the few examples presented here, the greatest issue is simply convincing the therapist to actually take a look at himself with the couple or within the family system. Often the therapist waits to examine this dynamic until he is either overwhelmed and ready to quit or already blocking progress through his present role in the system. Therapists cannot wait to look at their own boundaries and degree of involvement until they are either frustrated, "burned out," or blinded by the client's emotional manipulations of their own personal vulnerabilities. Even each family member could sculpt where each one sees the entrance and present position of their therapist. This might be quite surprising to the therapist—who was probably denying or minimizing his own level of involvement. The family's positive and/or negative reactions to that perceived position of the therapist may also be *quite revealing* and useful. The therapist may then realize how the family is "stuck"—*because of the therapist's own position in the system!* It is a necessary experience for a therapist to truly understand his own vulnerabilities and emotional needs. Until he or she fully recognizes such tendencies and weaknesses, the therapist is very likely to end up playing a role in every family system—but probably not that of a therapist.

A Supervision Model

Utilizing mapping and sculpting techniques, any therapist can receive helpful feedback from his own co-workers or professional colleagues on his most difficult cases. A therapist will likely "feel stuck" with one of his counseling cases when:

(1) He has not explored enough aspects or directions regarding this case.

Example: He forgot to explore the Family of Origin background for the husband which would explain some influences and issues . . .

(2) He has developed an emotional involvement and cannot clearly see his own position and role within this family system.

Examples: See section entitled "Mapping and Therapist Roles"

(3) He has developed a dislike for a family member which paralyzes his objectivity.

Example: He cannot stand to be around Bill, who reminds the therapist of his own brother's cruel behavior.

(4) He has become swamped with too many emotional issues and needs within this family system but is too stubborn, naive, or embarrassed to ask for help.

Example: Sam has identified four family members who require individual therapy but figures that he will just get to them himself eventually.

(5) This family may have problems too similar to the therapist's own dysfunctional family, which make it difficult for him to know what to do.

Example: This family does not know what to do with an alcoholic father—which is exactly the same dilemma the therapist's family faced unsuccessfully.

In nearly every case "being stuck" has more to do with the therapist's own personality, unwillingness to admit that he is overwhelmed, or private issues of his own. Of course there are some couples or families that *most* therapists would have trouble dealing with and would react to them in similar ways. Nevertheless, it is the therapist's essential and critical responsibility to monitor his own role, position, and emotions when entering a family system or a couple's dynamics. However, this is very difficult to accomplish on one's own. This supervision model aids every therapist who is willing to look at himself and his own dynamics. Otherwise, a family may become stalled in their progress due to a therapist's own role and position *that actually blocks progress* because the therapist has been unwilling to examine his role and its emotional entanglements. Many therapists deny or minimize that they are actually part of the family picture once therapy has begun. They tend to map out *only* the family's roles and relations, excluding their own entrance and position in the system. They rarely think about where *they* might be in a family sculpture after the family has been in therapy for a while. This exercise helps them to *see the whole picture* much more easily.

Sample Scenario of a Supervision Model

1. A colleague has the therapist describe *how* he became involved and what his *goals* are for the family/couple.

2. The colleague interviews the therapist regarding what family members are involved in therapy and which other persons are *not* but are influencing the situation.

3. Using a dry erase board, the colleague maps out all the characters involved in this family system, including key roles and influences from Families of Origin, doctors, influential friends, co-workers, or other therapists/caseworkers.

4. The relationships are designated by mapping symbols (See section entitled "Mapping and Therapist Roles") to indicate the strength or weakness of the relations. This may take some time to draw lines between *every relationship possible* among the system's participants.

5. Other influences must be represented—including drugs, alcohol, sex flings, money, stereotype labels, disabilities, deaths, losses—because they play a role in this system. Draw relationship lines or mapping symbols to depict the strength of each influence.

6. Determine the "emotional age" of each key participant as perceived by the therapist or as reported by the family members to the therapist. Write the actual age under the designation for that key participant, followed by the emotional age in parentheses. This is an important aspect of *every* mapping and sculpting.

7. Have the therapist take a good look at the mapping of this family system to see if it *feels right* to him or if there is anybody or anything missing from the picture. Typically, the therapist will confirm that everything is accounted for—although he has usually left *himself out* of this family picture. Have the therapist place himself in the system map according to where

he *feels* that he is *right now*. He may have to admit that he is stuck between two key players or right in the middle of everything! Also indicate the strength of his own relations with the key players in the system.

8. Have the therapist and all other supervisory participants present examine the map and give their reactions, impressions, insights, and feedback.

9. Have the therapist select group members to play the various roles depicted in the map. Also make use of symbolic props to represent important influences. Ropes can represent the strength of relations; empty chairs can depict absent persons. Sculpt the family system into the picture suggested by the family map. The colleague can position them initially, and then, have the therapist adjust and correct them afterwards.

10. Position the key players according to their *emotional ages*. This can easily change the whole appearance and feeling of the family picture. A tall, strong-looking husband may appear as a providing man in control until his *emotional age* actually places him on the floor. The same ropes that appeared as "providing" now create the appearance of "dependency" and needing to be watched over.

11. Note what other influences or addictions become like other "members" of the family that cannot be ignored now. Their visual presence reminds everyone of the role they play and how they cannot be forgotten. Something *must* be done with them as they clearly get in the way of any progress.

12. Have the therapist play himself and be positioned right where he "feels stuck." It often becomes quite obvious in just a few minutes why this position may not work well.

13. Obtain reactions from each role-player as to what he experiences and feels in each role. Although fellow co-workers or colleagues are *not* these actual people, their reactions, feelings, and perceptions may be very similar and insightful

because of what this role and position create for anybody in such a situation.

14. Ask the therapist to position everyone in "better places" and make any desired changes to create a therapeutic solution. Then ask each participant what he believes that character might feel or how that character may react to any proposed changes. This feedback is very important and possibly invaluable in terms of insight.

15. Allow other colleagues or co-workers to take a turn at "improving relations" by moving people and props around to acquire a therapeutic balance. Gather feedback from all participants for each proposed experiential solution.

16. From any solution experienced in a positive manner by most participants, discuss how such a visual and emotional configuration could translate into positive changes in reality for the family/couple. What would it take at home for this to actually happen?

17. The colleague may wish to move the therapist around into different positions to allow the therapist to directly experience various solutions and his own feelings for each position he experiences.

Group Therapy Experience

This same approach and therapeutic steps could be translated into a helpful group therapy experience for one of its members. The rest of the group could role-play the parts and add appropriate props to help that group member gain valuable insight into his relationships. The group therapist would help direct and facilitate the action following the guidelines suggested above.

Couples: 5
The Core of
Family Systems

The Family as a System

No human being exists in a vacuum of isolation. Each person is greatly affected by the emotional climate—good, bad, or indifferent—among the members of his family. Even with great distance, separation, or even death, each member of a family feels the emotional impact in varying degrees. These emotional effects may create an imbalance or dysfunctional solution to re-establish a balance. A family is like a delicate mobile hanging in the air, trying to maintain a degree of balance while in motion. Take one part away or add an additional burden, and all parts of that system will feel the change. Families are no different in that every change to the system is experienced by each member with different degrees of stress. As an imbalance begins to occur this produces more stress on at least one member of the system. This additional stress may cause this part of the system to falter or "break," becoming the "identified patient." Mother may become overwhelmed and depressed. Son may start failing in school and stealing from stores.

Father may start working more late hours or hanging out more frequently at the bars.

To focus *only* on helping the stressed member of the system who has become the identified patient is to miss viewing the whole system and learning *how* it became burdened or out of balance. If a part in an engine keeps wearing out from stress placed upon it, replacing that part does not ultimately solve the overall problem. The part will keep wearing out and needing to be replaced until the reasons for it being under such stress within the engine is eventually understood. In the same fashion problems will keep reoccurring in the family until the true issues which cause this pressure are finally discovered and resolved. Mom may keep returning to the hospital year after year for individual therapy until somebody finally *experiences* the kind of emotional climate and political system she lives in at home. Hearing about it is never the same as experiencing it! Words can be so deceptive, misleading, and concealing rather than revealing. An identified patient never seems as "crazy" when finally viewed in the crazy system he or she lives in. Then, and perhaps only then, a clear and more meaningful solution becomes evident.

Often the family has created a new cohesion and balance through dysfunctional behavior as a means for survival. For example, when Mother became crippled from an automobile accident and could no longer meet her husband's high drive for sexual intimacy, the teenage daughter sensed Father's loneliness and sadness. He would not go beyond the boundaries of the family to have an affair because of his pride and religion. But the daughter—as part of the system—allowed Father to have intercourse with herself as a means of saving the family from divorce. In other words, sometimes families will do anything to stay together and re-balance even if it is in a dysfunctional mode and socially unacceptable to others outside the system. The drive for family cohesion and survival as a system can be incredibly strong. And to fully understand these dynamics one can *only* view the *whole* system in order to comprehend the *whole* picture, which then explains tı individual actions and behavior of each family member.

Couples: The Foundation of a Family

Couples face many challenges from the very beginning and through every phase and stage of family life. How they handle each challenge directly affects the emotional climate, stress level, and ability to suc-ceed and grow within the family. Here is a general list of challenges that each couple is likely to experience.

> **Separating from Family of Origin**
>
> **Establishing independence and identity as a couple**
>
> **Establishing power and roles within the couple**
>
> **Willingness to let go of learned patterns and negotiate new paths**
>
> **Adjusting to 1st child's entry into the system**
>
> **Accepting parents in new role as grandparents**
>
> **Adding children while preserving the couple**
>
> **Becoming victims of routines and schedules**
>
> **Grieving the deterioration or death of one's parents**
>
> **Emptying the beloved nest**
>
> **Re-discovering your spouse and yourself**
>
> **Becoming grandparents**

Problems develop when a couple gets stalled in any of these stages. Each one is a challenge with numerous pitfalls, but healthy couples tend to find a path through and around the various obstacles. A healthy couple helps each other with those challenges and communicates needs, wants, fears, doubts, and goals. However, this sounds much easier than it is to actually accomplish. It is easy to get lost along the way, distracted, or misled—thinking one is on the right track. A good therapist will help the couple examine what hurdles they have successfully surpassed and which ones they may be still stumbling over without fully recognizing it.

Awareness is the first key to any attempt to change a behavior. Without seeing and understanding what it is that needs to change, few are likely to navigate that dark maze by chance alone without some guiding light from insight. Playful strategies like metaphoric imagery exercises make it easier to see, comprehend, and envision the essential dynamics and necessary changes required to move effectively through those inevitable hurdles of the family life cycle. Because of its visual and experiential nature, imagery also makes those hurdles easier to comprehend than just words alone. With imagery it is no longer as much of an intellectual process as it is a visual and emotional process that becomes both genuine and enduring.

Troubles which are neither surpassed nor addressed tend to keep the couple bogged down in that problem area. Since the couple is the foundation of family life, these problem areas tend to directly affect, color, and characterize the quality of interactions, emotional expressions, and types of issues among family members. For example, if a couple is still caught up in selfish, competitive, immature power struggles, the children may either act-out (to elicit attention) or become parental themselves, sensing that nobody is really leading the family effectively.

Another example is the family whose parents do not communicate with each other or do not have much contact due to emotional distance. The children tend to choose sides and align themselves with either parent. Often the children will then openly wage the war between themselves on behalf of the side they have chosen to represent while the parents remain silent. Children can sense the emotions and frustrations of their parents and, therefore, may come to their defense or rescue. The warring children may appear to be the obvious problem initially while the quiet parents are aloof in the background.

Parents may frequently present their child as the problem or "identified patient" when, in fact, the couple has hidden troubles which are triggering their child's behavior. Only when the family is seen all together in therapy is the real picture likely to emerge. *Somebody* always knows the real story of what is happening in the family. Little children are often the quickest to tattle on their parents' behavior at home. When a therapist works carefully with the couple, many of the family problems begin to melt away if the therapeutic goals are on target. For example, in a family with four children, all four kids had been in trouble for various reasons all in the past week. The family session revealed that Mom was overworked at home and Dad was neither connected nor involved much. The children were trying to find ways to attract Dad's attention and involvement in order to bring him back into the heart of the family again. He agreed to participate in activities with each of the four children the next week. By the next session all the children were behaving wonderfully even though no attention had really been focused on each of their individual acting-out issues.

Sometimes the parent will find that they cannot deal with one of their children at a certain age. This may represent the fact that this parent, himself or herself, had trouble coping at that particular age. For example, the mother who simply cannot get along with her 13-year old daughter had much difficulty with her own parents at that same age and never dealt with those issues well nor progressed emotionally past that age successfully. Other parents are simply *emotionally younger* and cannot deal with children who are actually "older" than they are, emotionally. How can a "younger" child be expected to parent an "older" child?

When family therapy was being taught intensively in the 1970's, there were few if any courses on either marriage counseling or the dynamics within couples. As I travel around the country I ask groups of professionals if they have ever received much in the way of marriage counseling courses, and they consistently reply, "No." As I began working with families in the 1970's, I soon realized that a family's behavior is a direct result of the couple's unresolved emotional issues, absence, coping strength, or inability to handle either daily stress or the endless challenges in the family cycle of life's situations.

Nobody had ever presented a model that outlined the types of couples that commonly exist, resulting from various dynamics, pressures, and life situations. Eight types of couples are offered in this book to demonstrate the different degrees of difficulty in forming emotional bonds and an identity as a true couple. Each type of couple represents a different form of emotional distance and bonding. All couples exist on a continuum based upon the principles of emotional space. One extreme represents being pulled apart by many forces and the other extreme represents becoming too symbiotic and co-dependent. Somewhere toward the center is the "ideal" couple which seems to balance well the fulfillment of all needs. Each couple will be considered throughout the entire family life cycle in order to appreciate how each emotional configuration copes with each new challenge. The resulting systemic effects upon the children should become apparent as well.

Although many of these dynamics and challenges may be quite familiar to the reader, each type of couple is basic and simplified to illustrate how couples become entrenched in various struggles and either unable or unwilling to move forward. They usually have been lacking the knowledge or awareness of their own dynamics in order to effectively make wise and successful changes. As each type of couple is presented, the therapist will learn how to reveal the couple's emotional configuration and dynamics visually as well as how to work with each couple spatially and more effectively. The whole process becomes a more visible and memorable form of therapy for both the clients and the therapist alike.

Couple #1: "The Family Feud"

Family Map:

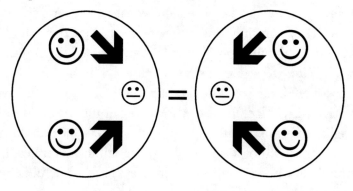

The "Family Feud" Family Life Cycle

One of the first hurdles any newly forming couple faces is the breaking away or letting go from each person's Family of Origin. This seems to be especially difficult the younger the couple is. As the couple attempts to carve out their own dreams, goals, and needs, they can be met with a contrary set of expectations and goals from each set of parents. The couple can quickly lose sight of *their own* desires as each partner is heavily pulled and influenced to follow the desires and traditions of his respective parents. Of course each set of parents believes that they "know best" and may actively campaign for their set of expectations for this couple. The couple may also begin to argue as each believes his/her parents are "probably right." This could cause further division and even permanent failure in the couple's quest to unite. The parents may launch verbal attacks both directly and indirectly at each other as well.

Assuming the couple does marry and begins their life together, arrival of the first child renews the intense interest from each Family of Origin regarding how the couple plans to raise "my new grandchild." Again, different views on parenting, discipline, health care, feeding, clothing, baby-sitters, baptisms, etc. all create the potential for another war to arise between the family camps. And once again, the couple could be torn apart as each side campaigns for its representative in the couple dyad to further its cause. The kids begin to take sides as well, depending upon what each "family camp" offers them! Grandparents can be especially vocal and interfering because they believe they certainly knew how to raise their own child—and, therefore, automatically *know* what is now best for their grandchild. Does anybody *dare* to argue this point? How can either member of the couple possibly disagree? The grandparents may be effective and manipulative with "blackmail" or threats regarding the couple's inheritance, rights to property, etc. if that grandchild is "not raised right!"

With each arrival of a new child to the family system each set of grandparents may make a move to win over that grandchild especially if they feel they "lost out" on the last one. This may continue to polarize and divide the couple between the family camps. Now the children may also be "taking sides" as well, knowing what each grandparent is promising or doing for them. The children then may fight among themselves, reflecting the bigger division that the two Families of Origin perpetuate. The couple has their hands full with battles breaking out all around them and eventually between themselves.

If the couple has survived all the previous challenges, then launching their children into the world may again be met with strong opinions and direct confrontation over what these kids should do with their lives. Topics of college, career choice, marriage, where to live, what kind of housing, money, etc. will all become potential battlegrounds. Even if a grandparent has died, their effect may still be felt strongly with the words, "This is how she would have wanted it" or, "How can we deny his deathbed wish?" or, "They willed this large sum of money for your college career—*only* if you attend UCLA!"

Basic Solutions

1. The couple must decide how they want to live their own lives in their own home.

2. Each member of the couple must stand up to his/her family and establish boundaries without fear.

3. The couple must learn how to support and give strength to each other.

4. The couple may need to live at a greater physical distance from families.

5. The couple must agree on plans for parenting children, finances, etc. while resisting clever bargains, influential manipulations, or threats from families.

What the Mouse in the Corner Hears . . .

(This is a 20 year-old couple announcing their engagement to both sets of parents.)

Sam:	"Hey, Mom and Dad—I asked her to marry me!"
Sam's Mom:	"Oh, honey! You are being too hasty—you can't be serious!"
Sam's Dad:	"You did *what?* But I haven't even met her yet."
Julie:	"Mom? Dad? I'm engaged!!"
Julie's Mom:	"Oh, no you're *not.* Just forget that silly idea right now!"
Julie's Dad:	"Over my dead body. My little girl is *not* going to marry *anyone* right now."
Julie:	"Oh!!! I just *knew* you were going to say that!"
Sam:	(to his parents) "But I really love her. I know what I am doing."
Sam's Mom:	"She just won't be able to keep house for you like I do."
Sam's Dad:	"I have heard stories about her and her family . . ."
Julie:	(to her parents) "Quit treating me like a little kid. I am a young woman now."

Julie's Mom:	"That's because we love you and know what's best for you, dear!"
Julie's Dad:	"You are *not* marrying *anybody* without *my* approval."
Julie's Mom:	"A young woman would use better judgment and wait for the right man."
Julie's Dad:	"He cannot provide for you, my dear princess, like he should."
Sam:	(to his parents) "You don't *really* know her like I do. She's great!!"
Sam's Mom:	"Honey, we are older, and we know what's best for you."
Sam's Dad:	"Besides, her Dad is a drunk, and her Mom is too stupid to leave the jerk."
	(to Julie's Dad:) "Hey—checked out the new pub downtown yet?!"
Julie:	(to his parents:) "Don't you dare judge me or my parents!!"
Sam's Mom:	(to Julie's Mom:) "You shouldn't let her act like this until she is older."
Julie's Dad:	(to Sam's Dad:) "You keep your pushy boy away from my little girl!"
Julie's Mom:	(to Sam:) "I am glad that you are friends, but she is just not all grown up yet."
Sam:	(to her parents:) "You both just *control every little thing* that she does!"
Sam's Mom:	(to Julie:) "Now, sweetie, you just go back home until you can grow up."
Sam's Dad:	(to Julie:) "You come from the wrong side of the tracks—GO HOME."
Julie's Mom:	(to Sam's Mom:) "You shouldn't let your boy put such ideas in her head."

Julie's Dad:	(to Sam:) "Don't you come near my girl. She *never* thought like this until *you* came along. You are a *bad* influence!!"
Sam:	(to Julie:) "Why don't you just tell them to go to hell, or I just might!"
Julie:	(to Sam:) "I don't think it's going to work with *your* parents acting like this!"

Wow . . . Confused? Frustrated? Tense? Angry?

Just listening to the pressures and manipulative statements surrounding this couple certainly explains the difficulty they would have in just making a simple decision *of their own*. Each partner's Family of Origin has strong ties and an overwhelming influence on any move the couple attempts to make. As this scenario began, the couple seemed excited and confident. By the end of the discussion, the couple is tense, doubtful, and argumentative. Both sets of parents are not only interfering with the couple but also fighting with each other. It is truly a family feud! Not only are the parents strong-willed and influential, but each partner in the couple is still rather dependent and non-assertive. Therefore, even though it may appear obvious that the parents are interfering, the couple actually may be too dependent and attached to their Families of Origin.

Clinical Case Example

Finding me in the phone book, Rick and Sue called to talk with me about having a joint therapy session. "We got a divorce, *but we're not sure why*," was their opening concern. There was a strong interest in reuniting, but they thought they ought to talk first about doing so. I agreed, and they made an appointment. On that day I opened the door to the waiting room and invited Rick and Sue to come in for their session. Six adults got up out of their chairs and walked toward me. (I wondered if by chance there had been three Rick's and three Sue's in the waiting room!) I soon learned that both sets of parents had come with Rick and Sue to *make sure that therapy went the way they thought it should!*

Knowing I was in trouble if both sets of parents were going to try to direct or influence the therapy process of this young couple, I had to think quickly about how to eliminate them gracefully from the therapy room. I complimented their constant and dedicated commitment toward overseeing this couple's progress—and emphasized how exhausting that *must* be for them every minute of the day. They agreed that they were all worn out from being so involved. When I suggested that they certainly deserved a break, they agreed. I then kindly offered them a one-hour "vacation" in the waiting room while I filled in and worked hard on their behalf. Surprisingly, they liked the sound of this offer and retreated to the waiting room.

At last the couple could talk and share some feelings without being interrupted or influenced by either set of parents. Now that they could be clear in their thinking, they quickly decided that they had never wanted a divorce—that it had never been *their* idea! Allowing them to make *their own* decisions based upon *their own* feelings was not so difficult now that all of the parental interference had been removed. They now wished to remarry and move far away from their families. However, I indicated that this physical distance would not resolve their lack of emotional distance. Families can still emotionally "pull your strings" and "push your buttons" from a distance by phone, by mail, and now by e-mail as well. Over the next few months we worked closely with each partner and each set of parents in various sessions. Rick's parents backed off rather quickly, not having realized before what an impact their actions had placed on the couple. Sue's mother clung to her relationship with her daughter to avoid having to deal with Sue's father. Sue had to learn and practice assertiveness in order to tactfully untangle herself from Mom's emotional grip. And she learned much more as well about her own "hanging on" to her parents for reassurance and security.

Visual Sculptures

(1) Position the couple facing each other with one hand reaching out toward the other partner. Each set of parents stands behind their child with at least one hand on each shoulder of their child. The other hand could connect the parents to each other or be used to represent additional influence upon their child (grabbing an arm, holding around the waist, etc.). Have each parent exert the amount of pressure, pull, or grip that he or she *feels* appropriate. Have each partner in the couple exert the amount of pull, resistance, or connection that *feels right* for each of them with their own parents. Ask every person involved if this is how it feels for them in this family—or how it could be represented more accurately.

(2) Position each partner of the couple sitting in chairs facing each other. Each set of parents stands behind their child's chair with one or two hands each pressing firmly down on their child's shoulders. The couple should feel trapped in their chairs and unable to move out of them. The parents remain in a controlling, superior position above and over their child, "putting them down."

(3) The addition of props are crucial toward enhancing the visual and experiential quality of the emotional sculpture. The parents can make use of jumpropes, plastic chains, or a string of scarves tied together to represent their "ties" that "bind" them to their child. Double or triple ropes may be utilized until the strength of that bond *feels right*. To speak for their child, interrupt, or silence him, a scarf, towel, or bandanna could be used as a gag for his mouth. If the parents do not wish for their child to see the other partner, a blindfold captures that feeling. One therapist suggested using a string of many neckties knotted together to metaphorically represent the "ties that bind."

(4) Missing members: Whether expected or unplanned, missing family members can be represented by empty chairs posi-

tioned at the same emotional distance. Ropes can be tied to the chairs just as easily so that the couple can feel the "weight", "resistance", or "emotional burden" upon them. A client can sculpt this same emotional configuration using play therapy dolls from a dollhouse and represent the same emotional distance, ties, and struggles. Other therapists claim success using coffee mugs, wooden blocks, or paper clips on a desktop to represent every family member and the distance between each of them. It just does not matter *what* is used to represent family members as much as *how* the relationships are represented in terms of emotional space.

Experiencing Dynamics and Changes

Once established in the initial formation of a visual sculpture, therapeutic work can begin. This couple's challenge within the "Family Feud" configuration is to somehow free themselves appropriately from their respective Families of Origin and form a clear identity as a couple with their own goals. Yet secret issues of loyalty, dependence, or insecurity may cause them to hesitate, doubt, or blame someone else. Denying, minimizing, avoiding, or rationalizing dynamics are much more difficult to accomplish within visual sculptures. Just stating that you are "rather close" to your parents can become a powerful emotional experience when you are sculpted into a submissive position in which you find yourself held back, tied up, gagged, and essentially powerless to move, speak, or act on your own! And, sheepishly, you may have to admit that this is *exactly* how it actually feels in this situation. Even if you try to deny such dynamics, all others may still place you in this position because *they* all agree that is exactly *how it feels* to them.

Of course, gathering everyone's perceptions, opinions, and unique perspective are essential toward closing in on a genuine and truthful consensus of the emotional realities. The therapist should also take a turn on how he or she views it—if differently than how anybody else may have visually portrayed it already. Please refer to the chapter on

"Utilizing Personal Space to Work on an Emotional Level" for many suggestions about working visually with this couple and their sets of parents.

Specifically, a therapist would want the partners in a couple to explore options for becoming less connected or entrenched while acquiring more power and assertiveness toward establishing appropriate distance with their Families of Origin. As a couple finds restricting hands on their shoulders or ropes binding them to their parents, the couple can experiment with actions that could reduce that pressure or create a healthier set of connections. Whatever sculpted solution they visually produce that *feels right* can then be processed and translated back into the reality of their lives. Clients often do not know *how* to change or *what* to change until they understand emotionally what would *feel right* or *feel better* for them. Then they can examine their situation to comprehend what it will take in their lives to produce this same particular emotional configuration and satisfactory solution.

Sample Scenario of Interventions

1. Bob and Julie find themselves sculpted into positions with their parents in which the parents have hands on their shoulders, around their waists—as well as a jumprope around each, tying them to their parents.

2. Julie finds a scarf being used as a gag for her mouth when she commented that she felt like they don't ever let her talk. She gets frustrated very quickly with this familiar feeling of powerlessness but does not know how to free herself.

3. The therapist explores how the gag got there, who claims responsibility, who benefits, and who will allow it to be removed. Perhaps Julie *assumed* how her parents felt and placed it in her mouth, herself. Perhaps Julie benefits from "not having a decisive voice."

4. The therapist allows her to remove the gag and speak so that she can assert her feelings and needs. The therapist notices that despite her verbal efforts she makes no real *physical* move to change her predicament. "Talk is cheap."

5. The therapist may employ a paradoxical approach, suggesting that Julie *stay tied* to her parents for at least the next five years as it "keeps her safe and secure."

6. Julie breaks free from the parental hands and jumprope out of frustration and faces her husband with her back to her parents. The therapist asks Julie if she now wonders how her parents are doing—behind her back, where she cannot see them. Julie admits she *does* worry about her Dad's health and how her Mom will handle things without her.

7. The therapist asks Julie if she would like to face her parents and "keep in touch" or "keep a finger on their situation" by taking hold of the rope (that they each hold one end of) with one hand or even just a finger.

8. The therapist notes that Julie faces her parents, grips the rope, but *now* has her back to her husband—still too focused on the welfare of her Family of Origin. Keeping one hand on the "ties to her parents," Julie turns halfway around so that she can grasp her husband's hand also. She now can see her husband and keep one eye on her parents as well. At least she no longer feels smothered, trapped, or controlled!

9. The therapist notes that when Julie removed herself from the "ties" of her parents and left them each holding one end of the jumprope, they became anxious. Mom let go of her end and took several steps away from Dad. At the same time Dad turned and looked away.

10. The therapist can comment on the quality of the connection between Julie's parents as represented by the jumprope. It could be asked as to why one of them let go or moved away when Julie left their grasp. Was Julie the necessary distraction

that actually connected her parents to each other? What kind of anxiety is created when Julie's parents are alone to face each other? Is Julie the "missing link?"

11. The therapist can experiment with the quality of space between Julie's parents. Was Dad always focused on his little girl more than on his own wife? What happens if Mom is asked to pick up her end of the rope again? What reaction occurs if the therapist asks Dad to "reel Mom in" with the jumprope? What do Julie's parents experience if the therapist insists that they try facing each other or standing right next to each other? Do they become like repelling magnets?

12. What is Julie's reaction or comment as she observes her parents' process? Does this help her understand why they clung to her constantly or why she felt so compelled to stay close to them? Did she *feel* at some level that they would not survive as a couple without her?

13. The same kinds of interventions can be used with Bob and his parents in another therapy session. Julie would probably be present as well—as the couple *needs* to be represented.

Couple #2: "Odd Man Out"

Family Map:

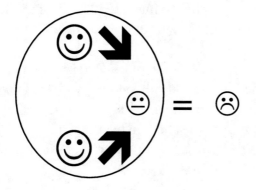

The "Odd-Man-Out" Family Life Cycle

The dilemma with this situation is that one member of the couple has successfully detached himself from his Family of Origin while the other half of the couple still remains strongly attached to theirs. This places a great deal of pressure on the "odd man out" as he/she becomes triangulated with the spouse and the attached family. The family continues to pull the strings of their child while minimizing or ignoring the wishes and opinions of the new spouse. The new spouse may directly confront the family which may embarrass or anger his partner, or, the new spouse may get frustrated at his own partner's passivity, dependency, or reluctance to be assertive with their own family. The family's puppet feels pulled intensely in two directions between the beloved spouse and the beloved parents. The family may ultimately insist that this new spouse is "just not the right person for you, sweetheart." The new spouse may also offer the unfortunate ultimatum of the partner having to choose between the marriage or the parents.

With the addition of children the dynamics of this triangulated situation essentially remain the same while the battlefield shifts to the topics of parenting, day care, baby-sitters, schooling, fad clothing, etc. The spouse grows weary of his partner's looking toward his own parents, who are "always knowing best," for guidance, ideas, and suggestions. The attached family may also begin brainwashing the children into disapproving of or doubting the words and actions of the "odd man out." Other children may adopt the opposing side, supporting the "odd parent out," thus creating battles among the children, reflecting all sides of the triangulated configuration. The children may also get blamed as the troublemakers while the grandparents look on "innocently."

If the couple has not divorced by the time of the children's natural departure from the home, then the likelihood for divorce may become greatest at the "empty nest" stage in the family life cycle. Many times the frustrated spouse waits until the children have grown and left home before he/she will finally depart this totally frustrating triangulation. If the family's puppet has not matured enough by this point in life to make a healthy detachment from the family, the frustrated spouse may decide to find another mate. The absorbed partner may agree to stay with the family anyway since they are aging or near death.

Basic Solutions

1. The spouse with the lingering attachment to the Family of Origin needs help to learn how to make a healthy separation.

2. The couple needs to make the transition from individual positions of "Who's right?" to a marital position of "What do we want?" as a couple.

3. The couple may need to live physically farther away from that attached family.

4. The partner with the attachment needs to explore what benefits he/she is getting from staying attached and why the spouse cannot or will not meet those needs.

5. Issues of guilt, fear, low self-esteem, money (inheritance), property, or failing health may be some of the ties that perpetuate the unbreakable bond.

What the Mouse in the Corner Hears . . .

(30 year-old boyfriend comes to 26 year-old girlfriend's home before a date, meeting parents.)

John:	(to Sandy's parents) "Hi there. I've come to pick her up for the party tonight."
Sandy:	(to her parents) "We will be back rather late—not sure when."
Her Mom:	"Come on in, young man. I don't really know you very well."

Her Dad:	"What kind of a party is this? I need some specifics, young man."
John:	"It is at my friend's home—while his parents are gone for the weekend."
Sandy:	"I *trust* him—even though I don't know anybody else at this party."
Her Mom:	"Now, let's not be in such a hurry. Stay and have some cookies here."
Her Dad:	(to Sandy) "Where did you meet this guy? How long have you known him?"
John:	"We really need to get going. I promised the others."
Sandy:	(to parents) "Why can't you guys trust me for once? I know what I'm doing!"
Her Mom:	"You are not going *anywhere*, young lady, until we get to know him better."
Her Dad:	"You are *not* going to any party tonight with somebody I don't know."
John:	"We don't have time for this—I can E-mail you my life history later!"
Sandy:	"Mom! Dad! Stop it! You treat me like a baby! I *have* a brain!"
Her Mom:	(to John) "I think *you* had better leave. Come back when you have some time."
Her Dad:	(to wife) "I think I know *his* type, alright—all-night parties, alcohol, drugs, wild sex!"
John:	(to Sandy) "I don't deserve this kind of crap from them. You've got to decide whether you're going to listen to *me* or *them*."
Sandy:	(to John) "You have to understand my parents. They're just *very* cautious!"
Her Mom:	(to Sandy) "Come on, honey. Our favorite TV show just started."

| Her Dad: | (to John) "You are not allowed to see her ever again—ya *hear* me?" |

How long do you think John will keep trying to date Sandy? How many guys has she seen come and go? But why is she still home with her parents at her age of 26? Does she have financial difficulties? Is she recovering from a failed marriage? Is one of her parents in poor health? Is she actually fearful of another relationship and subconsciously glad that her parents screen each guy? Or is she just submissive to their control and afraid to anger them?

This type of emotional configuration reflects the classic "nasty triangulation" of interpersonal dynamics among three positions: Persecutor, Victim, Rescuer. Try having a conversation with two other people *at the same time.* One person is always going to excluded for at least a moment if not for many minutes. Nobody enjoys feeling like the "third wheel" or the "odd man out." How many single people look forward to hanging out with married couples? Within families, couples and groups of people, triangulation causes countless problems, hurt feelings, and misunderstandings.

Within the scenario just presented one can observe the typical shifting or rotation among the three emotional positions. Sandy's parents initially confront John, and Sandy comes to John's rescue, confronting her parents (figure A). John then confronts her parents, and Sandy somewhat defends them (figure B). Finally, John confronts Sandy, and her parents attempt to rescue her and reel her back into their secure home (figure C).

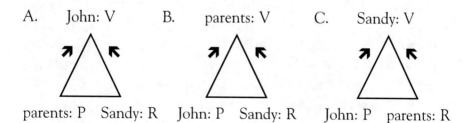

A.	John: V	B.	parents: V	C.	Sandy: V
parents: P	Sandy: R	John: P	Sandy: R	John: P	parents: R

Clinical Case Example

Often the dynamics of this configuration lie hidden and only blossom into a full dysfunctional bloom later, after this couple gets married. Just because a set of parents may accept that their child will marry does not mean that they will *ever* accept that outsider into the family. Many years of a slow poison and pervasive torture may follow.

Donna arrived in our office very depressed—tearful about her marriage woes. She stated that her husband, Randy, had chosen his mother over her. She added that his mother was even trying to turn her young children against her. She had married him years ago because she had believed that he and his family would offer a solid, stabile background for raising children. Now she was weary, disillusioned, angry, and very sad. When this "city girl" married Randy, she had moved to his home far out in the countryside. His parents lived right next door on the same tract of land which had been owned by the family for years. There were clearly no boundaries as the parents would enter their home, unannounced, without knocking, any time of the day or night. Randy's parents would even boldly enter the couple's bedroom while the couple was engaged in sex. His Mom would say hateful, sarcastic, and demeaning remarks about Donna to her face behind her son's back. When Donna would beg for her husband to support and defend her, he would deny, disbelieve, or minimize his mother's comments—suggesting that Donna was simply mistaken or overreacting to his mother's behavior.

Despite what plans the couple might decide, once Randy had told his parents, his opinion would now reflect their wishes instead. With the influence of a strong, Baptist, religious faith, Randy's parents began telling Donna what to do, how to do it, and when. And, no matter what Donna might do for her husband, his mother would competitively outdo her to stay #1 in her son's heart. Despite her desire to leave and divorce him, her damaged self esteem and lack of confidence kept her from making any definite decisions. After some individual counseling and a refusal by Randy to be involved in any marriage counseling, she decided to finally make a break from this frustrating marital situation. Had he been willing to experience marital therapy, he may have understood better how much he is tied to his parents. But Randy essentially chose his mother over his wife—probably because he did not dare anger his parents and risk losing his inheritance, property, and family possessions.

Visual Sculptures

(1) Position the couple facing each other with one hand attempting to reach out toward each other. The one set of parents grips their child from behind with two hands on each arm. Or they could tie them from behind with one or more jumpropes to symbolize a strong attachment. If the parents have any free hands, they could point a finger at the "odd-man-out."

(2) Position the attached partner *facing* his parents while in their grasp or tied to them with the jumpropes. This means that he will have his back to his partner—the "odd-man-out."

(3) Position the parents in front of their child, protectively, facing the "odd-man-out" while the attached partner peeks through from behind the protective "wall" that his parents have formed with their body positions. This makes it clear that the parents are the gatekeepers.

(4) Position the attached partner facing his parents just outside of the jumpropes, but gripping the ropes with both hands. His back is to his partner still while focused on his parents' needs.

(5) Position the attached partner seated in a chair with both parents holding him down with their hands on his shoulders. A gag (bandanna) may represent "a *lack of say* in the matter." If that partner is not allowed to see any potential mates, then blindfold him. If it is not easy to leave the home, tie his legs to the chair. This is a fairly dramatic picture—bound, gagged,

blindfolded, and held down! Yet, maybe that is exactly *how it feels* to them.

(6) Another way to illustrate the "vicious circle" or triangulation among the independent partner, attached partner, and the set of parents could look like this: Parents are chasing the intrusive partner away, the independent partner is chasing the attached partner, who is chasing after her own parents—who are chasing him away . . .

(7) Position the partner who is "torn" between his parents and his mate with his parents tugging on one arm while his mate is pulling on the other arm from the opposite direction in a true "tug of war."

Experiencing Dynamics and Changes

This couple's challenge within the "Odd-Man-Out" configuration is to expose the triangulated dynamics and the excessive, unhealthy ties to the one set of parents. The attached partner often verbally minimizes his own attachments to his parents and excuses their actions. The parents will similarly deny that their child is that attached to them. Yet they will *all* place the "odd-man-out" much farther away. Many techniques described within the "Family Feud" configuration will also work in this similar family arrangement.

One of the typical differences is that the attached partner often *likes* or *wants* his or her attachment to the parents. Find out if the attached partner actually hears manipulative cues or just senses or assumes that his parents are wanting him to stay at home. The therapist also wants to see how the parents react if their child is freed into more independence. Did they *need* those close ties (binding their child to them) to avoid their own issues and anxieties? Do the parents prefer to only connect indirectly with each other *through* the ties to their child? Once the child is pulled from their clutches, do feelings intensify when left to deal with each other *directly*? Even the "odd-man-out" may offer a healthier perspective from his detached and more objective position. It can be surprising that somebody will not be aware of how he or she was "unknowingly" rejecting a third party. With the appropriate emotional space displayed (according to *how everyone feels*) the visual awareness of the harsh effects of a triangulated situation becomes painfully clear.

Examples of Triangulated, "Odd-Man-Out" Situations

(1) Courting/Married
(new mate is intruding outsider)
"He's not good enough for you."

(2) Married/New Mate Favored
(In-laws favor new mate over own child)
"We now have the son we never had"

(3) Stepparenting
(new parent's ideas not accepted)
"We don't have to listen to YOU."

(4) Married/Live-In Parent
(Elderly parent influences his own)
"We'd better change our plans for Dad's sake—he can't be left alone."

(5) Grandparent Replaces Parent
(Live-in Grandma takes Mom's place)
"Grandma has *much more* time for us."

(6) Single Parent/Live-In Elderly
(Grandparent becomes other parent)
"*Grandpa says* it's really okay, Mom."

(7) Single Parent/New Prospect
(New boyfriend consumes Mom's time)
"I hate him. You don't care about *me!* He is just another one of your losers."

(8) Divorced Parents/Spoiled Child
(Ex-spouse spoils child, breaks rules)
"*Dad* lets me do it—on the weekends. He says I follow *his* rules at *his* house."

Sample Scenario of Interventions

1. Larry finds himself sculpted into a position where his parents have both hands on his shoulders, a scarf gagging his mouth, and a plastic chain around his waist, holding him back. His wife, Linda, is standing about eight feet away with her hands on her hips, looking at him disgustedly and shaking her head in doubt.

2. The therapist can ask Linda how much longer she feels she can tolerate this type of arrangement. The therapist then allows Linda to sculpt the situation into what she feels would possibly work better.

3. When Linda removes Larry from the bonds of his parents and positions him out and away from them, the therapist should get all of their reactions to this move. Note whether she allowed him to retain any level of physical contact or even eye contact.

4. If Larry and his family are unwilling to allow him that much freedom yet, the therapist can place Linda alongside her mate *within the same bonds* of his parents, emphasizing to the parents that they should include Linda and *not leave her out* if they want their son to stay so close. Of course, gathering all of those reactions should be interesting!

5. Assuming that Linda would not be comfortable that "tied" to his parents—even if they agreed to include her, she could demonstrate for Larry the kinds of assertive messages that could be said to his parents. Position Larry outside the "family ties" for this modeling intervention of role reversal.

6. Larry gains a unique perspective watching his mate, Linda, held and chained to his parents and trying to free herself. He can see how absurdly confining it appears as well as how difficult it is for her to work herself free—even with her best efforts. Because she has *already succeeded* in freeing herself

from her own parents, there is a good chance that he may gain some insight into watching her efforts with his own parents.

7. Because Linda is now actually dealing with *his* parents instead of her own, she may gain a better understanding, herself, as to how difficult, manipulative, guilt-producing, or insensitive his parents may actually be. Perhaps she will gain a clearer perception of what hurdles he has had to face. If two empty chairs are representing his parents, he can project what he thinks either of his parents would probably say to her or how they might react to her efforts.

8. Since the real work is his to do, Larry needs to return to the chains that bind him to his parents. Without the gag in his mouth he can now assert what he thinks he needs to say or do, having watched Linda role-model some ideas for him. But has he *earned* his voice back? Does he *believe* yet that he truly has a right to speak? Does he *fear* "talking back" to them? The therapist may need to place the gag back into his mouth until he grows weary of it and truly *wants* to change.

9. The therapist may note that he holds onto the chains or faces his parents without realizing that his back is toward Linda. Sensing that he may *not* want to let go of his close ties to his parents yet, the therapist may wish to employ a paradoxical intervention.

10. The therapist suggests that he tightly grip those plastic chains—or grab each parent with one hand each. The therapist then asks him to move around the therapy room—even down the hallway and back—and see if he can "make any move at all without his parents." If two empty chairs are representing his parents, he can attempt to drag them around in the same manner—with plastic chains or jumpropes attaching him to the chairs.

11. Hopefully, Larry will feel that constant burden or "weight" of his parents' close ties and now desire to make a change. The therapist can also ask the parents to move around, dragging Larry with them wherever they go, and see if they grow weary of that burden as well. The parents may recognize that it has been so exhausting to stay so closely connected with him. Perhaps they will encourage more independent activity on his part.

12. If Larry still wishes to maintain his close ties, the therapist can create a "tug-of-war" intervention in which the parents pull on one of his arms in one direction while Linda pulls hard on his other arm in the opposite direction. *Feeling* that constant tension and *torn* in two directions, Larry may need to make some decisions—quickly! He may need to tell each side *how* they are exerting pressure upon him. He may need to ask each side to "lighten up" or "let go" by stating good reasons for doing so. He may have to explore what he could risk losing in each decision. If he does not seem to mind losing Linda instead of his parents, then the therapist may need to have Linda move completely out of sight so that he can truly know that she may be gone forever and to *feel* what that loss would be like.

13. Linda may describe Larry's "emotional age" as that of an eight year-old. The therapist should "shrink" him down physically to appear younger (sit in a chair, kneel or sit on floor). When Linda actually sees this picture, she may understand why he cannot let go yet of his parents. Now she may also understand *why* she has had occasional thoughts that he feels just like a child looking for *another mother*—and it's HER!

Couple #3: "I am Right!"

Family Map:

The "I am Right" Family Life Cycle

This couple may not demonstrate any obvious difficulties as they move through the more superficial courting period of fun dates and occasional times together. Both Families of Origin have apparently launched their children successfully into an appropriate independence. The pair seems to be free and clear to come together as a couple. It is not until after they have married or begun living together that the hidden preferences in family beliefs and living styles erupt into conflict. Setting up house together, developing a budget, establishing a routine with chores and responsibilities, and falling into roles with potential power struggles all create many hurdles and challenges for the new couple.

Each young adult has grown up in a unique family situation with a potentially wide variety of beliefs, customs, cultural traditions, religious practices, communication styles, and unspoken expectations. No family style is entirely wrong or right—just unique and different. However, each young adult has been conditioned by their upbringing to think and believe in these ways with the assumption that this is "the correct way" to think and act. The conflicts can range from more obvious and predictable clashes such as religious preferences to the more subtle and less significant arguments over which cabinet the dinner dishes are to be stored or which direction the toilet paper is supposed to hang!

It is never a matter of "Who's right?" It is an opportunity to negotiate a new way of doing things instead of just repeating or regenerating each family's traditions. This, however, elicits the first power struggle. Will a dominant spouse emerge and seek his/her preferences with determination? Will one spouse fold, passively, "out of love" for his/her mate? Or will the couple be willing to discard old habits in order to compromise and hammer out a joint agreement with mutual satisfaction? As in comparing apples with oranges there can be no absolute "right way" to do anything because each family of origin had practiced what was "right" for them in the unique context of their own situations. It just does not mean that these old patterns are *still* "right" for the new couple. Therefore, every couple needs to sit down together and re-evaluate their wants and needs for their home life instead of blindly fighting or mechanically regurgitating old customs without question or discussion. Although the Families of Origin have actually released their children for marriage, their teachings and conditioning behaviors linger like powerful ghosts within each spouse. These ingrained parental messages haunt the minds of each spouse toward some kind of reincarnation of that family's beliefs and traditions into the new home. Failure to do so could create intense guilt, a sense of betrayal, or even failure.

If the couple continues their power struggle over "Who's right?" in an endless fashion over every new topic or challenge, then the addition of children may see a division develop among the kids with alliances forming with whomever of their parents they choose to take sides. Then, one shall hear the kids fighting with the same "Who's right?" mindset rather than a healthier attitude involving compromise and problem-solving.

After the children have grown and gone, one or both of the spouses may have had enough of the disagreements and may choose to separate. Power struggles are exhausting. If one partner does not cave in and assume a more submissive role, then the other may leave. Sometimes a spouse will become depressed, having held in much unspoken resentment and silent disagreement. Or the couple may actually thrive on the challenge and energy of the ongoing feuds, spending many years stubbornly seeking an elusive victory on numerous battlefields—each one still trying to prove that his or her family's beliefs were correct.

Basic Solutions

1. The couple must learn that neither family style is "wrong" but rather unique.

2. The couple must learn to create their own style from a fair blend of the previous two styles with which they have grown up.

3. The couple must learn to accept that a new style is okay for them to adopt.

4. The couple must become aware of the little ways in which they promote or campaign for their respective Families of Origin simply to preserve *security* and avoid family disapproval.

5. The couple needs to understand that their resistance stems from *fears* of taking a risk toward trying something new and different. Why should they want to deviate from a familiar set of customs that have *always worked well* for each of them? "*If it ain't broke, why fix it?*"

6. The couple must be ready to face comments from their families regarding their negotiated, "new style" of family life and *support each other's* position.

What the Mouse in the Corner Hears . . .

(Couple debates arrangements for holiday visits to families, parenting, and household routine)

Shawn:	"I want to have a nice family reunion at *our* house this Christmas."
Barbara:	"You *know* that my family *always* gathers at Mom's house in Topeka."
Shawn:	"Well, we don't *always* have to do that, do we?"
Barbara:	"It is a tradition that I don't intend to break! Mom would be crushed!"
Shawn:	"I have a right to have my family meet here, don't I?"
Barbara:	"Yes, you have the right—but you are being inconsiderate to my Mom!"
Shawn:	"Besides, our son, little Ricky, misbehaves at your Mom's house."
Barbara:	"Well, if you knew how to discipline him *right*, that would not happen."
Shawn:	"You just yell and scream at him. You call *that* discipline?"
Barbara:	"Well, I am NOT going to hit him like your father did to you!"
Shawn:	"What that boy needs is swift and clear punishment—*not* empty threats."
Barbara:	"*Your* way is not always the best way or the *only* way to do things."
Shawn:	"Ah-ha! And so *your* plans for Christmas cannot *always* be *your* way either!"
Barbara:	"Oh!!! You make me *so* mad! Hey . . . uh . . . *where* are the coffee mugs?"

Shawn: "You put them in the *wrong* cabinet again. They're supposed to be on the left side of the sink in the other cabinet."

Barbara: "Here we go *again* . . . Mom *always* kept them on the *right* side at home."

Who's right?

They *both* are.

And, they are both *wrong*—wrong in thinking that there is only one way to do things.

How are they *both* right, then?

Each of them grew up in nice families with clear rules, successful relationships, and rewarding traditions. This gave each of them a great deal of security and knowledge about how a family can be very successful. *Why change anything* if it produced fond memories and rewarding relationships? There is great security in familiarity. There is trust in traditions and customs *that work*. Why switch to some manner of doing things which one has no personal, first-hand experience with or clear guarantee that it will succeed? There is such a strong need to cling to the security of the *known* and avoid the anxiety-producing *unknown*. This translates down to the simplest of behaviors or details—such as where dishes are stored in kitchen cabinets. All of these little things add up toward reproducing *the known* which promotes familiar surroundings and a regeneration of comfort and security.

If one partner grows up in a Russian culture, speaking Russian, and the other partner grows up in a Spanish culture, speaking Spanish, who is right? Neither, of course, in terms of one background being *better* than the other. Both families and cultural backgrounds may be quite successful in producing warm, happy, secure homes. The solution is to blend the best of both worlds in a negotiated, flexible, compromised blend of the two successful styles of living. This may be quite a challenge and a "scary risk" to the two partners. They may both feel that the other is trying to manipulate or control them. It can be misinterpreted as a power struggle or an endless philosophical debate regarding the different family lifestyles. Each will simply defend what he has always known to work well for himself—and why *wouldn't* he?

The challenge for the therapist is to help this couple realize what their struggle is all about—and why they attack each other constantly over the smallest of differences. Each is so focused on the partner's "wrong" or "ineffective" manner of doing things instead of *what* their struggle actually concerns. Neither mate looks at himself, his own lifestyle, or any considerations about changing anything of his own. Each mate *assumes* that his lifestyle is a blueprint for happiness—and that all other claims are mistaken or misinformed. The therapist needs to state that they are *both right* and also *both wrong*. But some visual techniques may also help to clarify this couple's challenge and put in a clearer perspective.

Visual Sculptures

(1) Position the couple facing each other and pointing a finger at each other. Have each partner state repeatedly, "*I'm* always right—*you're* always wrong!" By exaggerating their claim in such a blunt and visual manner, they may back down and re-examine their actions.

(2) Position the couple facing each other but holding a jumprope, plastic chain, or long beach towel around their waists from the front. Their hands pull backward as far as they can, putting pressure on their stomach or waist. They are essentially "holding themselves back" with the memorized teachings and ingrained customs from their respective Families of Origin. Their families are not actively present in their lives, but the learned traditions persist and interfere. The more they cling to their "old way of doing things," the harder they must pull backwards. This shows that they are creating pressure upon themselves—*not* on each other. Even though their families

are not present to "pull their strings," the effect is still *felt* and *seen* through this display of "holding themselves back."

(3) Position the couple facing each other. The therapist (and possibly a co-therapist) stand behind each partner in order to act as that "voice in his head" which recites the "old traditions" of the Family of Origin. The therapist(s) whisper the "old messages and rules" behind each partner's head *to keep each of them from making any changes.* This paradox can help illuminate the absurdity of the battle and the rigidity of each partner in an exaggerated and sometimes humorous fashion (See Sample Scenario of Interventions in this chapter).

Experiencing Dynamics and Changes

The challenge facing this "I am Right" couple is to become aware of how they are projecting their own internal battles for security outward onto their partner. They blame the partner and list all the ways that the partner is "wrong." Once they become aware that the battle is actually *within* themselves between the security of the old, familiar traditions and the unfamiliar, "risky" ideas presented by their partner, the marital tension will decrease. Discussing this matter is not as clear nor memorable as it is when visualized and experienced.

Sample Scenario of Interventions

1. Robert and Laura are positioned facing each other. Each is holding a jumprope against his or her own stomach while pulling backwards.

2. The therapist states that he recognizes that they are in a conflict over "which customs" to adopt in their marriage. He acknowledges that he knows that they are not yet ready to risk any changes. The therapist asks them to *pretend* to negotiate and *pretend* to give in a little in a role-play situation. He

emphasizes that neither of them is expected to believe in his or her proposed compromises.

3. As they begin to *pretend* to yield somewhat and develop a negotiated compromise, the therapist stands behind whoever is speaking. With a co-therapist involved, each therapist can stand behind a partner and remain there. Each will serve as the familiar "inner voice" which shall advocate *that* Family of Origin's comfortable customs and trusted beliefs.

4. Here is an example of the interactions that might occur:

Robert:	"Maybe we *could* visit your Mom in Topeka first and then have a family reunion later around New Year's?"
R's therapist:	"How could you *even suggest* doing it differently?!"
Laura:	"Well, and just maybe Mom could wait for once and not always have it her way . . ."
L's therapist:	"Mom's gonna *kill you* for thinking like that!!"
Robert:	"My family *probably* would be okay with that change."
R's therapist:	"How *dare* you minimize their feelings and suggest such a change?!"
Laura:	"Mom will be upset, but she will get over it."
L's therapist:	"You're doing it *wrong!* This is just *not* right!"
Laura:	(to her therapist/herself) "You're confusing me. How is this wrong?"

Now the conflict has shifted to the internal dialogue between Laura and her own thoughts (portrayed by her therapist). As the couple attempts to actually hammer out a new plan, the old familiar voices of trustworthy traditions (spoken by the therapist(s)) interfere and confuse matters. Now the couple can realize that the real conflict is NOT *between* themselves, but actually *within* themselves as they each battle to break free from his or her own, old, dependable customs wrapped up in familiar security. And as they turn to *confront* the therapist playing this role behind them, they shall realize that *their back is now to their partner*—which underlines the idea that the conflict is *not* with him! The jumpropes further illustrate how they "hold themselves back" from taking risks and making progress.

5. The therapist(s) should emphasize or exaggerate these old, internalized voices of tradition so that the couple realizes just how rigid, stubborn, unyielding, or even absurd they can sound. If there are two co-therapists—or even just one very energetic therapist, they can start battling each other verbally, allowing the couple to hear and watch what they actually sound like—one step removed and now outside of the conflict, looking in.

6. Each partner could even try to challenge the other partner's "alter ego" or "inner voice" (played by the therapist) while the silent partner listens to how he is perceived and portrayed.

7. Role reversal is also helpful as each partner role-plays how he thinks the other partner sounds. The "inner voice" therapist(s) can remain *unchanged* so that each partner can now experience what internal pressures and conflicts the *other* partner experiences.

8. The jumpropes could also be held by the "internal voices" (therapist(s)) and pulled tighter backward and away from the other partner with each time that the partner attempts to be flexible, compromising, and sensible—yet straying away from familiar traditions.

9. The verbal battle between the partner and his conscience is very important. Here the partners have the opportunity to really confront and challenge their old thought patterns and secure little customs with the help of the role-playing thera-

pist—who shall present a tough and relentless challenge—almost to an absurdly stubborn and humorous extent! But at least the source of the conflict and confusion will be obvious and not likely forgotten any time soon!

Couple #4: "We are Right!"

Family Map:

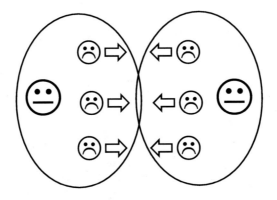

The "We are Right" Family Life Cycle

This couple faces the classic clash between two family styles which they have previously formed and are still presently in operation. Usually both of the partners have been married previously, and, for whatever reason, their previous spouses are either divorced or deceased. As this new couple decides to unite, each brings an active family style (with children attached) to the new relationship. Not only are the family styles established, but there are children who are likely to be resistant, defensive, rebellious, fearful, anxious, adamant or even depressed about changing anything. Therefore, the battlefield is set for one of the most difficult and destructive battles a couple may ever encounter.

Just becoming an accepted "new" couple to both families may be one of the toughest hurdles of all. The couple finds itself entangled in a double, triangulated situation as each partner wrestles with being the outsider to the other established family. To complicate matters, if any of the children on either side suspect that their parent is not succeeding at defending or satisfying their needs, they shall take up the sword themselves and go after the intruding adult who threatens their secure little world. Confrontations, nasty remarks, and passive-aggressive sabotage may send the new partner reeling in shock. Seeds of doubt are sown, and that partner may back away quietly, perhaps giving other excuses for his or her departure. Remember how the Von Trapp children in the movie, *The Sound of Music*, effectively scared away the baroness who was about to become their new mother?

Some of the children may decide that upsetting the kids on "the other side" may be a more effective approach, suspecting that the parent "on that side" will respond to the wishes of their own kids sooner than for anybody else. The popular television show, *The Brady Bunch*, simply does *not* portray how challenging and difficult the blending of two families actually can be! Other complicating aspects with blending two families involve teenagers at the same age, changes in the hierarchy or "pecking order," and how living space is divided, shared, and justified. Two fourteen year-old girls with contrary personalities may fight and claw like cats—and hardly be able to share a bedroom. When the nine year-old is shifted from a position of oldest child at home to a new rank of second from the bottom due to the addition of older siblings, there may be quite an emotional reaction. Setting up one home for two families coming together requires a great deal of tact, sensitivity, and communication. The organization of physical space, rules, expectations, discipline, chores, and responsibilities creates many potential battlefields. Moving into *"their* house" is not a great idea; buying or renting a third, new, neutral dwelling is a much better idea.

Assuming that the couple has survived the courtship period, actually married, and blended the families into one home (which is assuming a great deal!), the romantic idea of having a baby that will be theirs together creeps into the chaos. Perhaps against all sense or logic they indeed create one of their own to further blend with "his" and "hers" at home. This may create a mixture of feelings and responses from all the children. Some may welcome the new baby as the "missing link" which ties the family together. Others may become sour over the addition of yet another attention-consuming distraction which further divides the precious time and attention they desire from their parents. Some may eventually campaign to align the new member to their "side" or respective position. Others may take the attitude of rejecting this baby into a third category of which they do not accept or associate with. These actions may be quite subtle yet gradually effective in emotional impact and influence. Nevertheless, without any strong resolution or effective parenting from the couple, the chaos will maintain two opposing sides representing the unblended, original, two family camps.

Of course, ex-wives and ex-husbands may prey upon any dissension or chaos for various reasons or vendettas of their own. They may attempt to lure their children back to their familiar and less chaotic homes. They may add to the dissension by *agreeing* with the rebelling kids. They may tell the partners in the new couple that these actions *prove* that they don't really care about their children or put their feelings first. They may coach the children to undo positive efforts by the new couple. Or they may directly criticize, blame, or attack the new couple, claiming proof for their ineptness, immaturity, insanity, or stupidity. They may even initiate court actions, Division of Family Services' investigations, or anonymous calls to the police just to aggravate their ex-spouses.

Assuming that the couple has survived, somehow, through the years, it may be a welcome phase when all the children leave home and allow the couple to simply be themselves without the direct dissenting, demanding, and manipulating presence of all the children. Hopefully, they have maintained an identity as a couple and have not been pulled too far apart throughout the long years.

Basic Solutions

1. Each parent needs to to spend quality listening time with each one of their children so that each child can vent and express his/her fears, feelings, and needs openly.

2. Each parent needs to share openly with each child about the couple's actual plans.

3. The couple needs to be very clear with each other about their own goals so that they will give similar information to their respective children.

4. The couple needs to be strong as a unit to let the children understand that the kids are not in charge of the adult plans or adult needs.

5. The couple needs to resolve *together* the various conflicts that arise with tact, care, sensitivity, yet firmness without being dictatorial or deaf to legitimate feelings.

6. The couple may desire to hold weekly family meetings in order to vent concerns on a regular basis as long as the meetings remain constructive while expressive. This is a good method to model problem-solving and a sense of democracy while defusing potential explosions.

7. The couple has to monitor each other's parenting of the other's stepchildren as each set of kids is "not really my own" and some natural differences in attitude may occur that could add tension or create reactions.

What the Mouse in the Corner Hears . . .

(New couple introduces marriage idea to all of their children)

Dad: "Kids, these are your new siblings when we get married. They'll live here."

Mom:	"Yes, that's right. We'll be moving into their house because it is much bigger."
Dad's Son:	"Dad, she is just *not* your type! No way!"
Mom's Daughter:	"*Why* do we have to leave *our* home and live with them?"
Dad's Daughter:	"Daddy, I don't want a *new* Mommy—I miss *my* Mommy!"
Mom's Son:	"Mom, *please* don't make me share a room with *those* two little brats."
Dad's Son:	"Dad, I don't want to switch schools and leave all of my friends!"
Mom's Daughter:	"Mom, I'm scared that he could hurt me just like Daddy did."
Dad's Daughter:	"You mean we have to give away *our* dog just because she has cats?"
Mom's Son:	"Marry him—and I will *never ever* forgive you, Mom."
Dad's Son:	"If you two get together, then I'll *have to* go live with Uncle Charlie."
Mom's Daughter:	"His kid is *such a jerk* at school. *Everyone* hates him! I won't live in the same house with *him!*"
Dad's Daughter:	"I am *not* sharing a bathroom with those kids—ooh, GROSS!!"
Mom's Son:	"I have *only one* Daddy—and NOBODY's gonna take his place!"
Mom:	"Well, maybe we should take some more time to sort this out."
Dad:	"There you go again—putting your children's feelings before mine."

Similar to the "I am Right" couple's dilemma, the "We are Right" participants are battling with great anxiety against change. There is much comfort and security in preserving each family's lifestyle, activities, and present rules or familiar behavior at home. Why change *anything* if everyone is content and happy? Why take a risk in doing something new or different when there is nothing really wrong with the old familiar way? Why wreck a sure thing just because Mom *thinks* she is in love again?

The uncertain, anxious children can create a great deal of noise and chaos for this couple, which in turn can create doubt and hesitance regarding their plans for marriage. If the couple *does* hesitate, this empowers the kids to continue exerting their influence upon the couple to not bring about any changes. If the children acquire enough power (through the adults *giving it away* to them), the couple will probably fail to unite. Although children should not have this much power to control a couple's destiny, their emotions and opinions are still very important and need to be heard. Venting these feelings is an important therapeutic process. During this exploration of the children's anxieties and concerns, a *real issue* may be uncovered. In fact, many *real* issues are well hidden within the more passive children. The louder complaints are generally more likely to be anxiety-related. Only with *real* issues—such as a fear of abuse from the new stepparent—should a couple consider slowing down their plans to unite, which would bring everyone together under the same roof. This is not to say that the couple could not go ahead and get married, but the safety of that child must be fully appreciated and held as a priority.

The couple has to walk this difficult tightrope, balancing the concerns and feelings of all involved. Recognizing the difference between anxiety-driven complaints and genuine concerns is one of the important tasks for a therapist. Helping the couple stay in control without suppressing, dominating, or discounting feelings is another challenge. Basically, if the couple is not torn apart by noisy threats, manipulative claims, or behavior problems, and they can form a "united front" to deal with any real issues with sensitivity, they will prevail as strong, respectable couple.

Visual Sculptures

(1) Have the couple face each other, reach out their hands, and hold hands to form a small circle. Then ask all of their children to "get in the middle." This means that they would all get *inside* the tiny circle formed by the couple's hands. This will immediately add pressure to the hand-held bond of the couple as well as provide a very distracting presence right in front of them. If there are many kids, the couple may not be able to even see each other! The children may not want to be that close and will probably push against the arms of the couple to create distance within that small circle. The couple physically feels the tension, experiences the chaos, and sees the conflict right before their eyes. The therapist can then ease their strain by allowing them to release their hands and back up. Of course, this also demonstrates that the strain of the kids can break up the couple's relationship.

(2) Have the couple face each other about three feet apart. Have each of their children grab hold of their respective parent's arms, hands, shoulders, or even legs in order to try to pull them back and away from their partner. Meanwhile, the couple attempts to move toward each other. Not only can the couple feel their own children holding them back, but also who is pulling the hardest or making the greatest effort to do so.

(3) Have the couple stand next to each other, holding hands. Have each of her children grab hold of her free hand and pull her away from him. Have each of his children grab hold of his free hand and pull him away from her. This "tug of war" shall depict the amount of pressure felt by each partner while trying to get close to each other. Some of the children may pull at each other if (1) they disagree and do not wish for their parent to feel such pressure, or (2) some want the new union while others do not. Again, whoever exerts the

most pressure and energy may be quite revealing for the therapeutic process.

(4) Have the couple face each other, standing about six to eight feet apart. Have all of their children stand in front of them, facing the opposing partner and his/her kids. It should resemble a chess board with the children like rows of pawns in front of the opposing king and queen. Have all of the children point at each other while each parent places a hand on the shoulder of each protective pawn in front of him/her. The therapist should remember to visually represent any known influence from an ex-spouse. One end of a jumprope could be attached to an empty chair (ex-spouse) and then the other end (1) tied to the man's belt, (2) held onto by the woman, (3) tied to the partner's arm, leg, waist, neck—or whatever *feels* appropriate to that partner regarding the impact of his/her ex-spouse.

(5) Have the couple face each other about six feet apart. Have all of the children sitting on the floor in between them, probably facing their respective parent with their backs to the "intruders." Although the couple can clearly see each other and talk with each other, any movement toward each other cannot be easily taken without tripping over the children on the floor in between them. This depicts how the couple cannot forget, minimize, or deny the presence, concerns, and issues of the children. Clearly, their path toward each other is blocked with important obstacles that must be addressed. It would be interesting to see what it will take for any of the children to allow their parent to pass. What does each child need to hear or see happen before agreeing to "get out of the way?"

Experiencing Dynamics and Changes

There will be many reactions and feelings to explore and process with any of the sculpting configurations that arise from this blending of families. The challenge is to make certain that no participant is overlooked or not heard from. This couple's challenge is to walk that treacherous tightrope between either appropriately hearing all of their children's concerns or allowing their manipulative, anxiety-driven behavior to derail or destroy the couple's plans. All of these visual sculptures create unforgettable scenarios in which the children can neither be forgotten nor their concerns ignored by either parent. At the same time the children may realize how they might be unfairly pulling this couple apart and causing them great pressure, stress, and unhappiness. This may help the children to refocus on the *whole picture* and not just on *their own* wants and fears.

The therapist may need a great deal of time to carefully process all of the concerns and reactions of every participant. Each time a family member suggests a change in a sculpting scenario, that adjustment in emotional spacing will affect everyone to some extent. After a few moments of experiencing that change, each family member will need to be interviewed in order to process the emotional reactions and relative success or failure of that intervention. The key is in finding an emotional configuration that everyone is willing to try in order to get along better in this mixing of two family styles.

It is wise to begin with a family member who feels most frightened, insecure, or unsafe with the proposed blending of these two families. Let this participant sculpt the others into a picture which best depicts a safe, secure, and comfortable arrangement. Because others may feel protective toward this family member, the new arrangement suggested by this uncomfortable member will probably *feel right* to them as well. This may serve as a better core to a new configuration because it is based on the most important issues and most intense feelings. Others may base their own sculpting arrangements on selfish wants, familiar behaviors, and other factors which ease their general anxieties—yet may not be as critical as the family member who is terrified of potential physical abuse.

Often, the children will attempt to pull the parents back into a more familiar emotional configuration which includes the ex-spouse (empty chair)—and is simply a recreation of the previous family arrangement prior to a divorce. Allowing the children to *show* those wants is useful even though it cannot be a realistic option. It becomes a visual expression of their feelings for all to see and understand. The therapist will understand who is most adamant about bringing the parents back together and how it may benefit that family member. Sometimes the children may reveal that their distrust in a new blending of homes has more to do with their perceptions of that parent's emotional age and lack of responsible decision-making. Perhaps a parental child or two exist who *cannot allow* their immature parents to make this decision to unite due to perceived irresponsibility and impulsivity! Perhaps the ex-spouse's attitude has wisely enlightened or sadly poisoned the children's perceptions, depending of course upon the ex-spouse's emotional stake in all of these changes.

At some point the therapist needs to sculpt the family into the legal scenario dictated by the divorce decrees and official court decisions. Everyone needs to experience the actual reality which those legal processes indicate must take place. This includes the constant movement back and forth between the homes of each legal parent through visitation arrangements. This may actually help the anxious children remember that there will be plenty of movement, change, visits, and various family configurations in their lives as the therapist sculpts out the various changes that legally must be followed.

Sample Scenario of Interventions

1. Steve and Cindy find themselves facing each other but physically pulled in two directions by their respective children. Steve has one son wrapped around his left leg, keeping him

from moving forward. His daughter is pulling from behind by grabbing him around his waist. Cindy has one of her daughters pulling backward on her left arm while her other daughter is pulling backward on her right arm. A third child, a teenage son, has one hand on Cindy's shoulder from behind and his other hand holding the end of a jumprope which is tied to an empty chair (his father, her ex-husband). Although Steve can still reach out toward Cindy with both hands, he cannot move toward her, and she has "her hands full" with her daughters.

2. When asked how Cindy's children would rearrange this scene to *feel better*, they pulled Mom back and sat her down next to Dad's (ex-husband's) empty chair. The teenage son stood behind both chairs with one hand on each of his parents' chairs. One daughter kneeled to the left of Mom's chair while the other daughter stood between her Mom's and Dad's chairs.

3. The therapist asks Cindy how she feels about these arrangements. Cindy says she feels an "emptiness" and "unhappy loneliness" sitting next to the empty chair for her ex-husband. Ever since he divorced her she has been trying to fill that empty void. The empty chair intensifies that sense of loss—which now the children can see and understand more easily.

4. The children are then asked if they can make an adjustment based on Mom's sadness that will consider her needs as well. The children take turns rearranging the sculpting picture to allow their Mom to have a new connection with Steve without being disconnected from her, themselves. They agree that she can hold one of his hands while they form a circle around her—which still is excluding Steve. Cindy (Mom) admits that she feels less restricted, more supported, and connected with Steve, but having to focus too often on just what the

kids want as they circle around her, holding hands, and leaving Steve out.

5. While they are puzzling over how to further adjust this family scene, Steve is asked to consider his own children's hold upon him. His kids are given the opportunity to demonstrate how they wish things could be. Both the son and daughter turn Steve around to face them and *only* them. The kids hold hands with each other and each with one of Dad's hands, forming a nice cozy circle. His wife died a few years ago from cancer, and the three of them grew much closer to each other since that time. There is an empty chair nearby to represent her ghost and as a focal point for their grieving. Dad (Steve) has felt an emptiness ever since his wife's death and would love to have a new mate despite his children's preference to "just keep Dad to ourselves." They prefer not to split his attention with a new wife and *three more kids!*

6. However, as Steve's children "get their way" and see how sad their Dad appears—having to turn his back on his new love—they begin to consider a compromise. They turn him around to face Cindy, but they don't want his back toward them. They move alongside and even a bit in front of him to feel more included as he reaches out toward Cindy again.

7. Cindy's children now admit that they do not trust that their mother will make a wise decision in choosing a new mate. They claim she seems too eager and impulsive. When asked if she seems her actual age, they giggle and describe her as "much younger—maybe 14 years old." The therapist *shrinks her down* to visually appear younger by having her sit on the floor with her children still around her but standing up.

8. Cindy's son feels as if he is the main caretaker for his younger Mom, so the therapist attaches a jumprope from the son to Cindy on the floor.

9. Steve's kids suddenly remark that they have feared that their Dad's grief and eagerness to find a mate to fill the emotional void have clouded his judgment. They perceive him as younger, also, and the therapist shrinks him down to 8 years old! Both of his kids stand at his sides and hold each of his hands. Now they appear as two parents to Steve, leading him forward to meet with Cindy, who is still protectively surrounded and supported by her kids.

10. The therapist gives each family member an opportunity to adjust, validate, or perfect each sculpting picture—until it *feels right*. Then the therapist will ask each member to alter the final picture into what he or she would like to see changed. Whatever the family can negotiate must then be translated back into reality. In other words, what will it take for these connections, relations, communications, or improvements to actually occur at home? What kind of events or situations need to happen in their world so that the family *can* feel like they do in the sculpting? They *know* what would *feel right*—so what needs to change at home in order to achieve the same feeling?

11. At some point the therapist will enact the legal arrangements dictated by the court so that all movement, visitations, and therapy activities are represented realistically. If interference in the parenting of the children is perceived, then that "double message" or "mixed message" must be stated on a piece of paper that the children can carry "home" from the ex-spouse's imaginary house in the therapy session. Thereby, the interfering communication becomes a real and visible entity that the family must deal with. Should the kids accept the confusing message? Who wants to take it and deliver it to Mom? Does Mom accept it? What then does she do with it?—and she *must* do *something* with it. How does the therapist attempt to keep the children

out of the middle of two ex-spouses who continue to wage war? Can each child comfortably refuse to accept, receive, or pass on a message?

Couple #5: "No Glue"

Family Map:

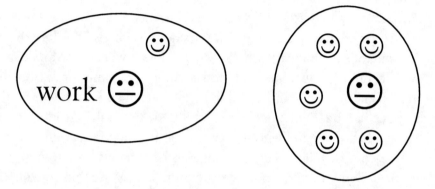

A "No Glue" Family Life Cycle Example

This couple seeks the American Dream of getting married, acquiring a home, having 2.5 kids, and living happily ever after. They were high school sweethearts; he was a football hero while she was the senior cheerleader. They have the perfect, superficial, popular connection with schoolmates, and everybody expects them to get married. They, too, expect that marriage is the next logical step in this fairy tale script. Their parents have no reason to disapprove and even help them out. His father gives them an old cottage and a section of his farmland. Her mother gives them a set of cookware and dishes so that her little girl can get a good start as a homemaker. They have a lovely wedding soon after their high school graduation, and life just seems wonderful as they fall into their expected roles on the farm.

She sets up the little house just the way her mother had done at home. She calls her daily or has her come over for consultations on the decor. Her new spouse assures her that she does not have to get a job and should stay home to manage the affairs of the house. He stays busy outside, tending the farmland with helpful assistance from his Dad while working a part-time job at a nearby factory. He is proud to be the hard-working, sole provider for the new couple. After long hours at both jobs, he comes home in the early evening for little dinners prepared by his new wife. They really do not talk very much. He then retires to watch some television while she does the dishes. And so it goes.

The couple is excited to have their first baby. While husband returns to his never-ending work outside, his wife is kept busy by all the demands of childcare. She only gets a break when her Mom comes over to help because her husband cannot take time away from his chores. As they have more children, she gets even busier with all the housework and demands of the children. Several of the children become her "little helpers"—even giving her support as well as keeping her company. His hours get longer as he expands his farming operation, and neither she nor the children hardly see him at all. He actually rather enjoys the quiet fields over the screaming chaos inside the little house. On some days he may even stop by the local bar to relax with a few of the neighbor guys. She is exhausted, overwhelmed, and beginning to wonder for the first time in her life if this "American Dream" is not that great after all. She begins to ponder her own identity, worth, and detachment from friends. She is not sure that being *his wife* and raising kids is all that she wanted to do in life. Maybe she does not need a "strong provider" anymore. But she is a good mother and loves her little helpers and hell-raisers with all her heart. They bond closely to her while her one son begins to help Dad outside with numerous chores. And so it goes.

Letting go of these children as they graduate and move out is an especially difficult time for Mom. These children have filled her everyday life. They have been her companions, helpers, and constant responsibility. She has laughed and cried with them over all the humorous and touching moments of their childhood. With each child

who leaves home, she feels a terrible emptiness and loss of her identity as "Mom." Who is she now? When the nest is finally empty, she
looks at her husband and wonders who he really is. Does she *really*
know him? Did she ever? They have no relationship as a couple. He is
like a stranger to her. She has many deep thoughts but never has
known any of his. She just wants to get out of this empty house with
its eerie silence and go find herself. She may go back to college or find
a job that gives her a sense of purpose. She may get depressed and
resent the fact that he made her stay home. There simply is no meaningful "glue" between them and the potential for divorce is great. His
endless farmwork and her consuming involvement with raising the
children were constant distractions away from their need to develop
and grow as a couple. Since they never fully achieved or maintained
that identity as a couple, they do indeed feel like distant strangers to
each other now.

Becoming grandparents does create the opportunity for a version
of the "Mom" role to be given new life as "Grandma." If this should
happen fairly soon after the last child leaves the nest, then "Mom" can
switch over to "Grandma," feel needed, and not have to deal with as
much of a loss of identity. In fact, she may insist upon baby-sitting her
grandchild every day in her home so that it is no longer empty and
silent. She now has a new distraction for years that will help her to
continue her avoidance of the marital emptiness and lack of identity
as a couple.

Basic Solutions

1. Despite workloads and the endless demands of children,
   every couple needs to maintain time for itself during the week
   so that it, too, can grow and develop. Not maintaining this
   relationship as a couple would be like buying a lovely plant
   but not watering it for many years! Fairy tales that tell of "liv-

ing happily ever after" forget to describe the many years of constantly having to work on maintaining the marriage.

2. At the time of the "Empty Nest Syndrome" the couple needs to become reacquainted and even have dates again. The assumption is that there once was a spark and a legitimate attraction, and that perhaps the "glue" can be discovered again.

3. Needs certainly change with age. What a spouse needs at age 19 may well have changed greatly by age 40. Some couples simply grow apart and want to separate.

What the Mouse in the Corner Hears . . .

(Wife presents her unhappy feelings to husband.)

Sharon:	"It's so-o-o-o lonely in the house now. I'm thinking about getting a job."
Bart:	"Why do you need that? Who will take care of the house?"
Sharon:	"Oh, I can still handle it. Might even *finally* take some college courses."
Bart:	"But I could use your help now out in the fields."
Sharon:	"You don't understand. I *never* was a country girl. I don't know who I am."
Bart:	"You are *my wife*—*that* is who you are!"
Sharon:	"I'm much *more* than that, and I intend to find out now. More to life than *this!*"
Bart:	"Maybe we could get out and go to the square dance on Saturday?"
Sharon:	"NO, that is *your* world and *your* idea of fun—not mine!"

Bart:	"I really don't have time anyway. I've got to finish plowing the fields soon."
Sharon:	"I'm not sure I *really* know you anymore—or *who* you really are either."

"NO GLUE" couples may have originally had some "glue" when they first courted and married. However, work routines, raising children, and other obligations can strain and pull these couples apart. Children can absorb every moment of one's time and attention if they are allowed to do so. Children are also very successful at "feeding on" dissension and division in a couple in order to lure one parent to their needs while encouraging that same parent to avoid his or her partner. Children often align themselves with the parent who best meets their needs, encouraging separation and avoidance of the mate who might not agree or meet those needs. Children can also sense marital tension and may choose sides to support and encourage the favored parent against the other one. They may also choose to deliberately distract the parents from each other in an attempt to diminish marital fighting and produce more harmony in the home. In fact, many couples prefer to deal with the children's needs, activities, and interests in order to avoid their own marital frustrations. They may appear for years as "the perfect family" because the parents were always so involved in their children's lives. But are they maintaining time each week for themselves as a couple?

The challenge for the therapist is to uncover what kind of "glue" or bond the couple has had, if any. If they never bonded other than in superficial and minimal ways just to simulate the appearance of a mature couple, then the odds of achieving significant progress may be rather slim. For example, if the man has *never* been empathic, warm, or openly affectionate, then the likelihood of him changing is slim. However, if the couple has had a healthy, mature courtship and has simply gone astray or "stale" with time and distractions, some quality time together to reconnect and refocus may be quite successful.

In other situations displacement onto a partner of unfinished mat-ters from childhood or prior relationships may unfairly create distance, apprehension, fear, or assumptions. For example, a female's unfinished business with her critical yet aloof father may be displaced upon her quiet and often absent husband. She might *assume* that her husband feels similarly and *expects* that he will behave the same way eventually. Therefore, she may begin reacting prematurely to her husband in the same manner she did with her father—even though her husband has not actually behaved like her father yet. But she continues to act upon her own unfinished business, *assuming* that her husband *will* act like her father soon enough.

Clinical Case Example

A forty year-old married woman came to our office feeling very depressed and suicidal. Sobbing hysterically, she stated, "Today was the day my grandchild was supposed to have been born!" Uncertain as to what she actually meant, I asked her to explain. She said that her 17 year-old daughter had become pregnant nine months ago but had obtained an abortion. We proceeded to hospitalize her to relieve her intense symptoms and explore her issues. She adapted very well to the in-patient hospital program, participating in all of the therapy groups and making many close friends over several weeks. Although we had intended to hold a family session, her quick improvement led to a decision to release her from the hospital. However, when she was informed that she would be discharged in 24 hours, she smugly announced that she was *not* going home! She was adamant about wanting to live at the hospital indefinitely. We now believed that a family session was essential.

When she learned that she and her family were going to attend a session with us, she immediately warned us that her two daughters, ages 16 and 17, were "incorrigible, arrogant, intolerable, and fiercely independent." Luckily, her husband was in town on a break from his out-of-town assignments and would be able to attend. As they entered the therapy room for the family session, Mom sat close to me, Dad sat on the opposite side of the room, and each daughter chose a chair between their parents. As I became acquainted with the daughters I soon learned that these two teenagers were very mature, responsible, sensible, attentive, and pleasant. Essentially, they were quite independent and did not really need a Mommy very often. My client was upset because they *really didn't* need her to be in the "Mom role"—the *only* identity she had practiced.

Sensing that these two young ladies were not in an obvious conflict with their mother, I suggested that—since they would be graduating and leaving home soon—they could return to the waiting room for the remainder of the session. This, of course, simulated symbolically their eventual departure from the home. The minute that they left our presence, Mom became panicked—trembling, shaking, and tearing her Styrofoam coffee cup into little bits. When I asked her what was wrong, she pointed a finger at her husband accusingly and said, "It's him! It's him! I don't really know him!!" After 18 years of marriage, she could not feel comfortable being in the same room alone with him.

I began to explore her feelings of fear and anxiety only to learn that very little if any had to do with her husband. She had much unfinished business, emotionally, with her quiet and distant father. Because her husband was also quiet and distant, she had unfairly transferred all of those old feelings onto him instead of her father. I set an empty chair beside the husband for her to focus her feelings and dump all of her father-related issues appropriately into the "Father chair." Having made that clear distinction between the two men, she soon realized that she simply did not really know her husband. She had no obvious emotional turmoil with her husband after all. They decided that they needed to spend more time together. Soon they began going out on dates, and she finally got to *really* know him. No longer did she unfairly displace her issues with her father onto him.

Part of this couple's trouble began with her becoming pregnant at such a young age and not having time to form a mature relationship with her husband. Babies were immediately in the picture; there was no time for a couple to establish an identity *as a couple*. It is interesting that eventually *both* daughters became pregnant at age 17—the same age that their Mom had first become pregnant and married. Yet, unlike Mom, both daughters had abortions performed. If the oldest daughter had *not* obtained an abortion, then Mom would have had a grandchild to fill the "empty nest" and continue her necessary "Mom role" so that she would not have to face her husband *alone* yet. But it was the daughter's abortion that led to Mom's deep depression over the realization that the nest at home *would indeed* be empty soon.

Visual Sculptures

(1) Actually, most "No Glue" couples will reveal their emotional distance in how they sit with plenty of extra chairs available. Or, if the therapist has them stand up and move to "where you feel comfortable," the emotional space should appear readily. The partners will usually be as far apart as space in the room will allow. If there are children involved, they will usually fill in the gap between the two parents. The kids may also gravitate toward the aligned adult and form two "camps" or separate clusters in the room. The therapist may find that the children on "each side" may speak for the respective adult on their "side."

(2) Assuming that the couple is initially sitting or standing far apart, have each partner experiment with moving closer or even standing right next to each other. Explore the anxieties which will most likely surface. This may be like placing two repelling magnets next to each other. Explore what would make such tension dissipate or diminish. What needs to take place so that the couple can tolerate/desire being closer to each other? What's missing?

(3) If children are present, have each partner grab onto each child who gravitates toward his or her position. Wife may be clinging to two children while husband is holding onto a third one. Have each cluster turn and face each other. Ask the children if they wish to bring the parents together or hold them apart. Ask the children what they believe would happen if they were suddenly absent from the picture. Have them move the parents in the directions they believe they would move—if they even move at all.

(4) There may a child or two who stay neutral and do not align with either parent. Those kids may just stay somewhere out in the middle. Ask them how they chose their positions. Ask them what if anything would cause them to want to change their position in any particular direction. Ask them what they believe would happen if all the children were neutral or absent.

(5) One parent may find himself alone while all the children encircle the other parent. This may be a powerful visual message to that parent who stands alone. The therapist may use jumpropes or other visual aids to add to the visual effect of the emotional sculpture. It may appear as if one parent is clinging to his three children like Teddy bears, or it might appear as if the children are protecting and taking care of that parent depending upon stance, props, positioning, and emotional age portrayal. The parent standing alone may have connections to other interests, persons, or addictions. Even though that adult may be without family members nearby, it is essential to explore what interests are occupying his time and absorbing his energy. That adult may have one hand on a computer keyboard and the other hand on a bottle of wine—and no hands free for his family.

(6) With the parents standing apart have the children visualize themselves as some kind of sticky glue that will somehow link

the parents to each other through the children. Have each of the kids show what this could look like and how they would attach to each other and their parents to demonstrate "being the glue" between the parents that holds the family together.

Experiencing Dynamics and Changes

Although the family members may all be well aware of the distance between the parents, seeing and feeling this distance in a dramatic fashion brings the issues clearly into focus for everyone. The couple may surprised at how difficult it becomes to move closer to each other without great anxiety. They may become *more aware* of how it has affected the children and their behavior. It may become more apparent that their distance has indeed shaped the destiny of this family's emotional decisions and behavior. The children need to realize that they cannot always be there to protect, defend, support, or act as a "buffer zone" for their parents' difficulties. It becomes more obvious that the adults must eventually deal with their own issues, themselves.

The couple may come to realize and accept that they may have grown apart and do not really want to continue as a married couple. Their interests and needs may have changed, and they may need to finally have an open discussion about parting. On the other hand, they may decide that they do *not* wish to split, and that they need to really spend some time closing the rift and healing any wounds or misunderstandings. These visual presentations will help bring these important discussions forward as the distance and lack of cohesion become undeniable and painfully obvious.

Sample Scenario of Interventions

1. David and Elizabeth have chosen to sit in chairs that are at opposite ends of the room. They did so, instinctively, without thinking about it. Two teenage children sit between them.

2. The therapist decides to move the children out of the middle and perhaps off to one side or even out of the therapy room. Therapist should observe any increase in tension or anxiety in the couple with this maneuver.

3. The therapist may ask the couple to sit next to each other—now that the kids have left the room—to see if they have difficulty doing so.

4. When the couple balks at moving closer, the therapist can explore "what's missing" that could help them feel comfortable. What creates tension? What produces anxiety? What needs to happen in order for them to be closer to each other again?

5. Are there influences that are pulling this couple apart? The therapist needs to explore such possibilities and visually represent these factors with symbolic props. Perhaps a bottle of wine has occupied more of David's time than Elizabeth has. Perhaps Elizabeth has an emotional attachment to her aerobics instructor, drawing her time and attention away from her family. The therapist may need to set an empty wine bottle on a chair next to David and an empty chair next to Elizabeth with the instructor's name on it.

6. The therapist may need to determine whether these outside factors *pulled* them apart or were *needed* and subconsciously *invited* by the couple to fill the emptiness in the marriage (This would clarify *where* the props would be positioned.).

7. The couple may need to explain how their respective distractions meet their needs. They need to describe what it would take for them to give them up. What would each of them need from each other to take the distraction's place?

8. The therapist may bring one child (or both) back into the room and ask him to sit wherever he wishes. If the child sits next to one of his parents, the therapist could explore how or why that child chooses that parent to be close to. Perhaps the

child senses what that parent needs or what the other parent does to push him away. In other words, is the choice due to what the child needs for himself or what he perceives that his parent needs—like protection, nurturing, companionship, or safety?

Couple #6: "The Ideal Couple"

Family Map:

The "Ideal" Couple's Family Life Cycle

It is assumed that there are "normal" people in the world—whatever that may be. It is also assumed that there are "normal" couples and families as well. Since it may be difficult to find a "perfect" couple or family, we have to hypothesize what traits such a family would have. Therefore, this couple becomes mythological or alleged to exist somewhere even if we never locate such a "perfect" family system in reality. What is probably closest to the truth is that no family can be perfect for the entire span of a family life cycle. There are too many unpredictable events, changes, losses, influences, and outside relationships that could knock this family from its ideal course in life. However, such a family is more likely to regroup or regain its healthy path in life after a period of problem-solving and coping.

This mythological couple represents the ideal actions and desired types of relations throughout the family life cycle. As the couple seeks a relationship they maintain respect for each other's individual dreams, talents, skills, and potential. They have a great time as a couple but allow each other plenty of time for individual pursuits or independent time alone without feeling possessive, controlling, jealous, clinging, or insecure. Both Families of Origin are supportive and maintain appropriate distance as they allow their kids to unite and grow. The couple communicates their hopes, dreams, goals, and expectations for their marriage and future years together. They allow each other to follow career plans or not work as either individual so chooses. They coordinate, however, as a team by creating and managing a budget as well as other shared household duties.

With the first and every child that they bring into their lives they share childcare duties and decision-making. Despite the demands upon their time, they create time every week for themselves as a couple, perhaps in activities with other couples. They also give each other breaks from childcare so that each spouse may continue to pursue individual interests. They are not reluctant to employ baby-sitters when necessary. They also plan and involve themselves in numerous family outings or events to enhance their identity as a family. Each parent also tries to spend individual time with each child alone to maintain a healthy bond with each child. Grandparents are involved occasionally and appropriately.

Emptying the nest is a happy and supportive occasion as the couple proudly applauds their children's achievements and plans for independence. They encourage, guide, and assist this transition for their children, allowing them to find themselves and pursue their dreams. The couple now has more time for themselves, both as individuals and as a couple.

The arrival of grandchildren is a fun phase for the couple as they enjoy the pleasures of spoiling the grandkids without all the work and demands that they had as parents. And they still have plenty of time for themselves in all their pursuits as individuals and as a couple. They may finally take a long trip somewhere special or downsize their home into something cozy and easy to maintain.

Basic Challenges

1. The couple supports each other regarding individual needs and interests.
2. The couple develops, grows, and maintains an identity as a couple.
3. The couple works as a team regarding the duties of the home and children.
4. Each parent spends individual time alone with each child.
5. The parents plan and initiate family gatherings and outings or events.
6. The couple involves grandparents, baby-sitters, and day care sensibly.
7. The couple deals appropriately with their own aging parents without serious disruption to their own family's needs.

What the Mouse in the Corner Hears . . .

(A "normal" day with an "ideal" couple.)

Fred:	"Hey, honey, can you take Heather to Girl Scouts today when you get home from your job?"
Gail:	"Sure, sweetheart, if you can take little Joe to soccer practice later."
Fred:	"No problem. Hey, don't forget our outing with the Harrisons Friday night."

Gail:	"Oh!—thanks for reminding me! I had forgotten. That will be fun! I'll get the babysitter lined up, okay?"
Fred:	"Great. Saturday might be a good day to take the kids to the park. They have a new Petting Zoo that just opened."
Gail:	"Good idea, but let's do that on Sunday instead."
Fred:	"Why?"
Gail:	"Because I have my pottery class on Saturday morning and your new bowling league begins that afternoon—remember?"
Fred:	"Oh, yeah. That might work better anyway because your Mom called and invited us all for dinner Saturday night."
Gail:	"Hey—if the kids want to stay overnight with my parents, we could get away to see that new movie that just came out."
Fred:	"I'll check the times just in case. If we pick up the kids on Sunday morning, maybe your parents might want to come along to the park and Petting Zoo?"
Gail:	"Well, we'll see. I would kind of like to do that just with the four of us. My parents wear out before the kids ever do!"
Fred:	"Okay, we'll just keep several options in mind and be spontaneous."
Gail:	"Sounds good. I'll see you later, my love."

This is a tough routine to keep going smoothly. It requires constant, honest communication and flexibility. It needs an understanding, unselfish, yet assertive approach to maintain effectiveness. Passivity, ambivalence, or submission will not yield honest and healthy communication. All needs and feelings must be considered and represented.

Because this couple copes well and deals with challenges and adversity effectively, they will rarely, if ever, be seen by a therapist for counseling. Therefore, there are no obvious strategies or clinical cases to describe. This couple merely represents all the couples who are doing well and do not need any coping strategies. However, this couple *must* be described in this book as another type of couple that probably exists in this world—even if they are not problematic or likely to be treated by therapists. They represent the healthy balance that we all strive for in relationships.

Couple #7: "Me First!"

Family Map:

The "Me First" Family Life Cycle

This couple is quite immature and self-centered. Each partner is more interested in what either he or she is getting out of the relationship rather than any thoughts about compromising, negotiating, or working together as a team. Basically, each spouse demands what he or she wants from the other. They are focused on finances and material goods. They will go rent movies and video games before paying their utility bill. Neither set of parents are very interested in being involved because they either have already helped to a large extent until their resources have been drained, or because they, too, are self-centered and immature. This couple is very needy and argumentative. However, they may have no problem with sexual relations because they can both use each other for mutual benefit, simultaneously. They just do not possess the maturity or common sense of most adults. If their emotional ages fall into an adolescent range, there may be much acting-out such as alcoholism, drug abuse, criminal acts, and sexual affairs. And a challenge they do not need is having children.

When the first child arrives, there will be immediate battles over who is going to take any responsibility for the care, feeding, and clothing of this child. They may argue over who is more tired, who works the hardest, who does more and how often. Neither really wants much responsibility. She will say that it is his fault that he got her pregnant. He will say that it was her fault for not taking her birth control pills. Meanwhile, the baby is screaming in the background, but neither seems to hear it over their own arguing, complaining, and demanding. The baby reacts to the tension in the house and cries even louder. Out of frustration, one of the partners may be prone to physical abuse to attempt to quiet the child. Essentially, the arrival of this baby has created a triangulated situation where somebody is going to be excluded at all times who desires attention. In essence, it may appear as if three children are fighting, and no parents exist at all. Nobody is emotionally mature enough to act as a parent.

With the addition of more children the absence of mature parenting becomes much more obvious because it is clearly needed as the family grows in size and complexity. At this point it is certainly not clear *who* does any parenting—if any! Often, one of the children becomes so frustrated that he or she decides that *someone* must assume a parental role, and, therefore, he or she attempts to do so. A Parental Child develops to meet the family need for some kind of leadership and organization. The family has become *enmeshed* with no clear boundaries between the supposed parents and their children. The child who instinctively adopts the parental role may, in fact, do a very good job. What remains sad about this role reversal is that the parents may be relieved or glad that someone else wants to perform in that capacity as they continue to squawk about their own needs to each other. However, the other children may either be relieved that someone has finally taken charge of the chaos or perhaps resentful that a sibling has become so bossy—and Mom and Dad allow it. This enmeshed family can appear as a group of unruly children wherever they go.

A child leaving home is usually a relief for the couple because it decreases the level of general chaos and number of selfish demands being voiced. However, if it is the Parental Child who is gladly departing, this will create a need for a reorganization with someone else stepping forward to take on that needed role. The adults may cling to the Parental Child and act helpless, producing guilt and concern within the Parental Child. Many times the children do not want to leave home due to insecurity and lack of proper maturing and will stick around for years—too frightened to leave this dysfunctional mess. The couple is generally relieved to be free of all the childcare demands which they never really wanted in the first place.

Basic Solutions

1. This couple would benefit from individual counseling sessions as well as marital sessions to develop some maturity and skills toward coping and communicating well.

2. Parenting skills training would be essential for this couple.

3. The couple needs to learn how to support and assist each other instead of blaming and attacking each other.

4. Family therapy would release the Parental Child from his role and restore the parents to their appropriate roles.

5. Family Therapy would also focus on monitoring the children's reactions to the parents' new efforts (to look for sabotage or rebellion that would test their parents).

6. Boundaries need to become clearly defined and maintained between the level of adults and the level with children.

7. It is essential that the couple learns to work as a team toward mature goals.

8. The Parental Child needs special attention to refocus their abilities in healthier directions.

What the Mouse in the Corner Hears . . .

Mike:	"I just saw the new Chevy truck today that I've been wanting."
Sally:	"And I saw the new washing machine that we need."
Mike:	"Well, that can wait—we already have one."
Sally:	"No, your truck can wait. You already have two in the front yard if you would just get around to fixing them!"
Mike:	"Well . . . you can just get the washer repaired more quickly."
Sally:	"I also need new make-up from Nieman-Marcus."
Mike:	"Well, that *certainly* is an *extra* expense that we can wait on."
Sally:	"I beg your pardon! You just don't understand a woman's needs!"
Mike:	"Oh, *yes I do!* If there is money in the bank, *spend* it!!"
Sally:	"You are such a jerk! You have no clue as to what is important."

Mike:	"Well, if you worked as hard as I do, you'd see I deserve these things."
Sally:	"What a spoiled brat! You have *no idea* how hard I work here at home."
Mike:	"You are *always* asking for these things that we don't need."
Sally:	"Well, at least I *ask*. You just go out and buy it without consulting me!"
Mike:	"Yeah? That's because *I* make the money—get it?"
Sally:	"Fine! From now on I will just buy what I need *without* telling you!"
Mike:	"Ha!! That's what you've *been* doing!"

(Enter the 5 year-old son who has lost his Teddy Bear and the 14 year-old daughter who wants to go out for a few hours to be with her friends . . .)

Sammy:	"Daddy, Daddy—I can't find Boo-Boo Bear!!!"
Mike:	"Go tell your Mommy!"
Aleisha:	"Hey, Dad—I am going out with my friends."
Mike:	(no response) "Where's that truck magazine?"
Sammy:	"Mommy, Mommy—I can't find Boo-Boo Bear!!"
Sally:	"Go ask Daddy to help you. Leave me alone right now!"
Sammy:	"Whaaa-aaa-aa—aaa!!!!"
Mike:	"Now look what *you* did! He's *your* responsibility."
Sally:	"Oh, thanks! *You're* the one who got me pregnant!"
Sammy:	"Whaaaa-aaa-aaa-aaa-aaa!!"
Mike:	"Shut up, kid, or I'll ground you to your room for the rest of the day!"

Sally:	"Good going, Big Shot. Why don't you just go beat him?!"
Mike:	"Go to Hell, Sally. *You're* supposed to take care of him."
Aleisha:	"I'm leaving—anybody care?" (Nobody hears her . . . again.)

With this kind of chaos and lack of mature parenting, it would be a miracle that these kids could ever grow up successfully. However, they often do cope because they begin to ignore their parents and just do whatever they want. On one hand they could act-out and misbehave to their heart's content; on the other hand they may become parental, bossy, controlling, and rigid in order to bring order to their lives. The Parental Child develops an identity to achieve some sense of order in this family. However, at school the Parental Child does not fit in well because he bosses all the kids in a controlling, arrogant fashion. In fact, he disrespects the teachers as well because he has never experienced adults as really knowing what they are talking about. Since the adults at home are "idiots," then the adults at school *probably* are, too.

However, this type of patronizing behavior may bring the Parental Child to the principal's office. The school counselor may suggest that a children's psychiatrist be consulted for possible medication or individual therapy. *The key is for the family to be seen.* Then, and perhaps *only* then, the nature of the family's observed behavior may well serve to explain the Parental Child's necessary existence, role, and purpose. Often, this Identified Patient—the Parental Child—may indeed seem the *oldest* member, *emotionally*, and quite capable of being in charge of the family. One begins to understand *why* he or she *had* to take charge at home.

The key in treating this couple is to essentially help them mature and assume responsible roles toward each other and their children. This may take months with all that they need to learn and practice. Often, this couple has never experienced healthy adult role models nor been exposed to helpful, useful information. The therapist may spend months working on listening skills, communication styles, problem-solving, teamwork building, parental education skills, non-blaming/assertive language, and self-esteem issues. They may need to attend certain parental education classes or groups. This maturing process may take months or years—but might even be required if the local Division of Family Services insists that they complete certain tasks before their children are returned from foster homes. The therapist may serve as a strong role model for them as they grow and learn.

The Parental Child may have many problems to solve and much resistance toward change because (1) this is the only identity which he has known since age eight, (2) he does not believe that the adults will *ever* act mature enough to become parents, (3) feels committed toward protecting and assisting younger siblings, (4) he is isolated at school due to his controlling, bossy behavior, (5) he distrusts all adults and authority until they prove themselves worthy, and (6) he has high esteem regarding his own effective skills of problem-solving, leadership, assertiveness, parenting, decision-making, and communication—and, now, no obvious place or role for utilizing those talents. The key for the therapist may be in helping the parents help this child to find activities, groups, clubs, and even sports in which these talents can shine, appropriately. Just telling the Parental Child to go back to being a child again is not likely to be very successful. He may not have had much experience with playing, sharing, being silly, or just "hangin' out."

Clinical Case Example

Tim and his wife Sherry brought their three young children, ages 8, 11, and 14, whom they claimed were "uncontrollable." Before the session, out in the waiting room, one could hear the children running around wildly as if no parents were present. Other adults in the waiting room were trying to gently parent these wild kids without appearing too obvious. The actual parents were busy reading magazines without any concern for what their kids were doing. The 14 year-old daughter appeared aloof and angry, sitting with her arms crossed.

When it was time for their session, the kids ran through the door and down the hall while the parents did not seem to notice or care. When they settled into the small group room, they became quite loud and noisy—sounding like a room full of unruly kindergartners. My first instinctive reaction upon entering the room was to ask, "Who's in charge here?" The 14 year-old raised her hand and yelled out, "I am." The rest of the kids and the adults all laughed out loud, but they did not disagree.

I began with an Emotional Age exercise (described later in this book) which allowed the family to privately list their impressions of each other in terms of an emotional age. All three children agreed that their parents were no more than 4-5 years of age in terms of their actions and behaviors. The two younger children were seen as near their own actual ages, but the 14 year-old was seen by everyone as in her thirties. Nobody seemed surprised by each other's impressions, but it certainly led to some useful discussions about how the 14 year-old *needs* to take charge in this family.

Visual Sculptures

(1) Having obtained an emotional age for each family member (by one of various methods), have each family member assume a position representative of that age—either in behavior or actual size. A person with a very young emotional age (0–5) should sit on the floor. One with an emotional age between 6–10 should kneel on the floor. A teenager could sit on a chair while an adult would stand up. If someone is seen as very old yet wise and active, he could stand upon a wood platform, riser, or stepstool. If someone is seen as old but feeble or helpless, they might be seated, holding a cane. With each family member portraying the family's overall impression of his own emotional age, the visual depiction of this

family will be quite interesting indeed. Roles and relations should become quite revealing and obvious.

(2) Based on emotional ages, develop a physical hierarchy with the parental role(s) "at the top," perhaps standing over others with hands placed on the shoulders of those below. Depict who is "over" another family member. Who is at the top? Who is at the very "bottom of the heap." Who are on the same level? Do they like their positions? Who has control? Who allows control or prefers to be controlled? Show this with body positioning, hand placement, and gestures that depict power, control, domination, and submission.

(3) Place the adults (who *should* be the parents) on one side of the room, the kids on the opposite side of the same room. Draw or create an actual boundary between the two subsystems to emphasize that there need to be differences and distinctions. The parents need to work as a team with clear goals and functions. The kids need not be concerned with anything in the adult world (easier said and shown than accomplished!).

(4) Position the Parental Child on a high bar stool or chair—like a "throne"—so that this child can watch over and govern the family's actions. Have the rest of the family positioned at this child's feet or sitting on regular chairs below that higher level. A crown could be worn by the Parental Child to emphasize his "ruling over" this family. This visual display can be used as a paradoxical approach to help the Parental Child feel conspicuous, very obvious, and even "alone at the top."

(5) Using the paradoxical idea presented in #4, set the higher chair (with the Parental Child) off to one side of the room while the parents play with the other children on the other side of the room. This should add to any feelings of detachment, loneliness, frustration, or fatigue in maintaining that tiresome Parental Child role. Hopefully, the child will want to

rejoin the others and enjoy some playtime. This sculpture may work best at a later date after the parents have actually begun acting more like parents, and the Parental Child role is not needed as much in order for this family to function now. The Parental Child has always secretly wished that his parents *would* act as parents and play with the kids. If he or she can finally observe this, the desire to go play and finally drop the Parental Child role should increase.

Experiencing Dynamics and Changes

This family may take a long time to believe in the changes that are needed. The kids may take a great deal of convincing before they actually trust that their parents have truly changed. The parents have much to learn and to practice, and it may be months before they make much progress. The children will undoubtedly test these new behaviors to see if their parents have *really* learned anything! The Parental Child will hold out the longest, of course, because of his protective and effective role in leading this family successfully.

By encountering visual sculptures and experiential exercises, this family will have a clearer conceptualization of what needs to be different. The parents may not like being viewed by their own children as "immature babies." The Parental Child may feel uncomfortably conspicuous in a visual sculpture which has him "ruling over" the others. These kinds of visual displays enhance the family's awareness and perhaps a deeper understanding of the need to make changes. Because of the level of immaturity usually discovered within these couples, playful and visual approaches are often much easier for them to comprehend. Who said that Play Therapy was only for children? There are plenty of adults who are non-verbal, non-expressive, and slower to understand intellectual or analytical assessments. Therefore, a visual sculpture may indeed be worth at least one thousand words.

Sample Scenario of Interventions

1. Billy and Susan participate with their two children in an exercise which reveals each family member's perception of each family member's "emotional age." The therapist displays their written perceptions on one large dry erase board (see specific exercise later in this book). Susan is perceived as being around 12 years old while her husband, Billy, is viewed as 8 years old. The 7 year-old, Ben, is seen as being 9 years of age while the 14 year-old sister, Sarah, is looked up to as 21 years old. According to their own perceptions and opinions, Sarah is the oldest and Dad is the youngest in the family.

2. The therapist suggests, "Let's see what this would look like," and places Dad and Ben on the floor together, Mom on a chair, and Sarah standing over them all with one hand on Mom's shoulder and her other hand pointing at Dad. The therapist collects their reactions to their own positions and the appearance of an apparent hierarchy or potential power structure. If they disagree and indicate that "something doesn't feel right" about this visual display, then the therapist allows each of them to reorganize the scene until it does *feel right*.

3. The therapist then suggests that each of the family members change the visual sculpture to the way he or she thinks it *ought* to be—or how it *could* work better (The therapist may comment on the idea that adults *usually* are the parents in a family).

4. The therapist may ask each family member to imagine for a moment what animal might best characterize each member of this family, writing their responses privately on paper.

5. The therapist collects all of their papers and writes the collection of responses on a dry erase board. Now the family can see everyone's impressions of what animals the family members

would become that would match their character and behavior. This safely gives this playful family an easier to describe their own behavior, roles, relations, and power struggles.

6. Billy (Dad) thought that the bear image assigned to him meant that he was seen as strong and powerful. However, the family otherwise indicates that he is seen as a "cute, little, Teddy bear who is quiet, timid, and too soft." The therapist can ask each family member what animal he or she would rather be if they are unhappy with what was suggested for them by the family. The family can react to these new ideas by suggesting *what it would take* for that family member to actually become the image which they prefer for themselves.

7. If a Parental Child stubbornly clings to his or her position, a number of creative approaches may illuminate his or her needs and feelings:

Role Reversal: Have a parent change positions with this Parental Child and promote what he or she would do if allowed to parent this family. Like politicians competing for an office, have the other parent advertise what he or she would offer as a parent. Have the Parental Child describe what fun things he feels he could do if he were truly a kid.

Superman Speech: Have the Parental Child wear a Superman cape or stand on a raised platform and provide a speech about how important his role is to protect, oversee, and guide this family. Have the family ask questions about what it feels like to be Superman and if there are any drawbacks.

Royal Throne: Have the Parental Child sit in a higher seat—like a bar stool/chair—or stand safely on a chair which shall serve as a ruling roost or throne from which to oversee the family's actions. Add a crown and give many compliments for the fine job he has been doing for years. Have the family "ham it up" as adoring subjects.

<u>Lonely Boss</u>: In an identical setup to the "Royal Throne," have the Parental Child bark commands and demand obedience. However, have each family member position himself with his back to the dictator and ignore him. Nobody listens any more.

<u>The Hero</u>: Present a gold medallion on a purple ribbon to the Parental Child, citing his or her heroics in bringing help to this family. "Like a smoke alarm going off, your behavior drew necessary attention to the fires which were burning in this family." Then, emphasize that his role has been completed successfully, and the professionals will manage the fires now and bring them under control.

8. The therapist asks Sarah to take the deserved crown and sit up high on a bar stool so that she can keep a protective eye upon this family's actions. The therapist compliments Sarah on her heroism and suggests that she maintain this role for a number of more years—perhaps 15 or more! Sarah appears proud, in control, yet puzzled or worried.

9. The therapist asks the parents to discuss plans for a fun outing this weekend with *just* Ben. As they laugh and talk about fun ideas with Ben becoming more enthused and excited, the therapist reassures Sarah that she is "doing a great job watching over everyone."

10. The therapist may enhance the level of detachment and frustration by moving the family over to another corner of the room, encouraging them to whisper about their plans so as to not upset Sarah who will not be included. Sarah strains to hear, wondering what she might be missing as well as whether the plans make sense or not.

11. Sarah throws down her crown, hops down from the bar stool, and states loudly, "This is stupid! I want to be a part of the plans, too!" The therapist allows her to join in but listens to her participation carefully. If Sarah seems to want to have fun and allows the parents to make the plans, she can stay. If Sarah starts changing the plans, overruling her parents, and bossing the others toward what she thinks would be more fun, she must return to her throne. It is clearly stated that she can participate *only* if she allows her parents to make the plans.

12. Sarah is also informed that she has the right to offer as many constructive ideas and creative thoughts as she wishes as long as it is simply information offered and not directives that must be followed without question. In this manner she can indirectly assist her parents with countless ideas and suggestions without removing them from power or grabbing the throne away from them.

Couple #8: "Bad Glue"

Family Map:

The "Bad Glue" Family Life Cycle

This couple becomes compatible in a perfectly dysfunctional manner. In other words, what they both need from each other satisfies some unhealthy need or unresolved "emotional baggage" from the past. Lopsided imbalances exist and thrive with success because of what they both need from each other. For example, the narcissistic domineering male demands an adoring wife who will submissively worship him. Simultaneously, she is very passive and dependent—desiring a strong male to take care of her and make all the important decisions. Although this may appear to be a satisfying imbalance, neither partner will grow and develop as long as each persists in meeting one's needs in this dysfunctional pattern.

They are likely to feel a very strong attraction for each other as they begin courting, not realizing that what draws them together like powerful magnets is *not romance* as much as it is the recognition by two subconscious minds that the "perfect partner" has been located to satisfy unhealthy needs and/or avoid completing "unfinished business" from the past. Their bond may become quite strong, and they may seem inseparable—yet they do not possess the mature traits of a sharing, compromising, intimate, sensitive companionship. In fact, they are actually *using each other* to fulfill subconscious needs in a self-centered fashion. Such dysfunctional imbalances reveal a hierarchy rather than a sharing, loving relationship in the following examples.

Examples:

Domineering, Controlling ⇨	needs ⇦	Submissive, Passive, Dependent
Motherly, Nurturing, Rescuing	needs	Immature, Dependent, Childlike
Perpetrator, Abuser, Mean	needs	Victim, Familiar & Secure with Abuse
Hurt, Demanding, Vengeful	needs	Rescuing, Supportive, "Rock"
Arrogant, Egocentric, Narcissistic	needs	Adoring, Loyal, Wanting to be Owned
Righteous, "Perfect," Religious	needs	Sinful, Shamed, Guilt-ridden, Flawed
"Good Guy," "I'm Okay"	needs	"Bad Guy," "I'm Not Okay"
Possessive, Jealous, Insecure	needs	Loyal, Reassuring, Dedicated, "Rock"

The introduction of children into this family system will certainly produce dramatic results as each child either emulates, rejects, or sides with one of the dysfunctional parents. Often a child will speak out for the less powerful adult while a brother or sister may actually put down the same parent, identifying with the domineering partner. If the power struggles are less visible or subdued, the children may actually play them out in a more dramatic version. Then, of course, a child may also adopt a neutral position and feel the need to intervene as a therapist, sensing the imperfections of both parents and subsequent marital imbalance. Sadly, the children do not have healthy role models and may learn to promote similar dysfunction in their lives. The greatest parent-child conflicts will often occur at the age that an immature parent became fixated or "emotionally stuck." If the emotional age of that parent is *the same age or younger* than that of one of their children, then that parent shall have the greatest difficulty with that particular child.

Instead of the parents dreading an "empty nest" situation, it is the children who may be eager to vacate this unhealthy and essentially unhappy family system. Power, control, emotional politics, and unhealthy manipulations characterize the family dynamics rather than love, trust, sharing, sensitivity, and respect. Of course, unhealthy attachments may have developed between parents and some of the children—and therefore, some of those kids feel unable to leave the family nest after all. Other children may escape and live far away with very little to no contact because they feel and recognize the unhealthy dynamics in this couple. Because love and respect was rarely an ingredient in this family system, it is not surprising that the family members often scatter to live far away from each other—simply reflecting the lack of "glue" that never ever had been present *in a healthy fashion.* Any child who chooses not to leave has probably accepted "bad glue" as a means of surviving.

As long as this couple continues to benefit from a dysfunctional imbalance that meets their needs, they will continue to stay together. However, unexpected life experiences which encourage personal growth may lead one partner toward healthier functioning, thus upsetting the dysfunctional symbiosis. For example, if the passive wife becomes bolder and more assertive over time, she may eventually decide to follow her own needs instead of putting his needs first. However, my experience with these couples suggests that the dysfunctional patterns become more entrenched with time, like ruts in a dirt road getting deeper and more pronounced.

Basic Solutions

1. The couple must become aware of how their dysfunctional union blocks growth and genuine happiness for either of them.

2. The couple must learn how to meet their important emotional needs in healthier ways.

3. The couple must admit that their behavior toward each other is a problem.

4. The couple must accept that power and control are not solutions but symptoms of an emotional struggle for security.

5. The couple needs to realize that it is not love and respect that hold them together.

What the Mouse in the Corner Hears . . . (First House)
(Control and Dominance prevail.)

George:	"Hey, Shirley—bring me my slippers."
Shirley:	"Yes, sir."
George:	"And while you're at it—grab my coffee there in the kitchen."
Shirley:	"Yes, sir."
George:	"Shirley?"

Shirley:	"Yes?"
George:	"What's taking you so long?"
Shirley:	"I was just taking the clothes out of the dryer."
George:	"Knock it off and get over here, will ya?"
Shirley:	"I'm sorry—I'll be right there!"
George:	"Damn . . . you sure as hell better be!"
Shirley:	"Here you go . . . I'm sorry."
George:	"You'd better shape up, ya know—women like you are a dime a dozen. Now go work on dinner. It's getting late."
Shirley:	"Okay . . . I'm sorry. Please forgive me—I don't know what I'd do without you."

What the Mouse in the Corner Hears . . . (Second House)

(Mothering the Immature Spouse)

Jason:	"Hey, Jen! . . . Oh, Jen—ni—fer . . . ?"
Jennifer:	"Yeah, what do you want now?"
Jason:	"Show me how this calculator works."
Jennifer:	"Jason, I'm really busy right now."
Jason:	"Jen-n-n-n?"
Jennifer:	"*Now* what do you need?!"
Jason:	"Do you know where the TV remote control is?"
Jennifer:	"NO! Why don't you get off your butt and look for it yourself?"
Jason:	"Oh—never mind. I was sitting on it."
Jennifer:	"Geez—if your head wasn't screwed on, you would lose it!"
Jason:	"Oh, Jen?"
Jennifer:	"*Now* what?"

Jason:	"The cat just threw up on the carpet. Don't worry—I'll clean it up in a little while, okay?"
Jennifer:	"No—forget it. *I'll* take care of it. You don't really know how to clean it up, and it needs to be done right away—so *I'll* do it."
Jason:	"Yeah, you do a *much* better job of that than I do. You'd *better* do it. Hey, Jen—can I have some snack crackers?"
Jennifer:	"I don't know—CAN you?"
Jason:	"Oh, alright . . . I'll just wait until you're done with the cat vomit."
Jennifer:	"Yeah—you probably couldn't even find them anyway! You are *so-o-o-o* helpless!"

What the Mouse in the Corner Hears . . . (Third House)

(Jealousy and insecurity lead one partner to possess the other.)

Bradley:	"So where do you think *you're* going, Amanda?"
Amanda:	"Just to get some groceries."
Bradley:	"Are you *sure* that's where you're going?"
Amanda:	"Yeah,—why?"
Bradley:	"How long will you take?"
Amanda:	"Why are you asking me all these questions?"
Bradley:	"I think I'd better go along with you."
Amanda:	"Why?"
Bradley:	"Last time you went to the grocery store I checked the odometer on the car when you got back, and it did NOT equal the total miles that it takes for that errand. So, *where* did you *really* go, Amanda?"
Amanda:	"That's crazy! I just went to get gas for the car and dropped by the bank, too. Why don't you trust me?"

Bradley:	"I think you might be seeing that James guy who lives down that same street."
Amanda:	"God! You are *really* losing it! (starts to cry) I just can't believe this."
Bradley:	(sly smile) "Heh, heh . . . I'll be watching you . . . or better yet—You can't leave this house unless I go with you!"
Amanda:	(sobbing) "I just want you to love me and trust me. I'll do whatever you say."

What the Mouse in the Corner Hears . . . (Fourth House)
(Mr. Can't Do Anything Wrong with Mrs. Can't Do Anything Right.)

Roberta:	"Honey, do you care if I take time to unclog this sink drain?"
Jack:	"Do we know how to do that the best way?"
Roberta:	"What do you mean? Don't you just pour the drain cleaner down the hole?"
Jack:	"Things just aren't *that* easy. It is always best to run some hot water first. This loosens the grime—don't *you* know these things?"
Roberta:	"Oh—sorry—I'm not perfect like you!"
Jack:	"Now when we have reactions like that, this just does not help matters. Don't we know how to talk with kindness rather than sarcasm?"
Roberta:	"Jack, knock it off with that attitude! You are so arrogant!"
Jack:	"You see, this is what I am talking about. We just really need to work on our little temper tantrums, don't we?"

Roberta: "You just think I can't do anything right, don't you?"

Jack: "Hey, I can't help it if you need advice for everything you do. Maybe you should just take more time to learn about what you're doing so that you will do an acceptable job. You've done a lot of things wrong in your life, ya know."

Roberta: "Oh—there you go again, dragging up *my* past to make *you* look better."

Jack: "Hey, history speaks loud and clear. We just don't like to look at ourselves, do we, honey?"

Roberta: "Don't call me 'honey!' My history is not that different from anybody else's. It's just that you had such a perfect little sheltered life, ya jerk!"

Jack: "I think you need to review your Anger Management notes, don't you?"

Roberta: "Oh!—Go to Hell."

Jack: "Not *me*—I go to church regularly. *You* should worry more about going to Hell since *you* often fail to attend church."

Roberta: "Hell's beginning to look much better if *you're* not going to be there!"

These four examples demonstrate how personality styles dominate, control, manipulate, or strongly influence the couple's relationship. At the same time the corresponding partner has an unhealthy yet strong need for this type of character in his/her life. These personality styles develop early in life and begin searching, subconsciously, for a mate who will meet their specific dysfunctional needs. The submissive mate seeks a strong partner to take charge and control his life. The partner who loves to nurture and rescue others will likely find that child-like and insecure mate who is secretly needing another Mommy. The narcissistic mate needs an adoring "fan" who, in turn, *needs* to idealize that mate anyway. The abused mate may find security in such negative behavior from an abuser because of the familiarity it creates stemming from one's own abusive childhood. The "flawed" or guilt-ridden spouse may not like hearing the "perfect" partner's lectures, but yet, he or she *needs* to be "kicked" to alleviate any guilty feelings.

It is important to keep in mind how much the weaker member of the couple needs the stronger partner to be the way he or she is. Although the weaker member may seem victimized by his mate, remember that he *allows* that pattern of interaction and helps *maintain* the dysfunctional connection. In other words, the need to *be* controlled is just as strong as the need *to* control. Although appearing lopsided or off-balance, the emotional and psychological needs are probably equal in need, strength, or intensity between the two mates.

Visual Sculptures

Type 1: Abuser with Abused

Have the abusive mate stand up and point at the partner with an accusing finger, toy gun, angry fist, boxing glove, foam bat, 12-inch ruler, or whatever symbolic prop seems most fitting and appropriate to represent the abusive stance. Have the abused mate sit on the floor or kneel before his partner and assume some type of passive, defeated, "beat-down," or other posture representing victimization. To represent the *emotional need* for this abuse have the victim open his hands toward the abuser as if welcoming or accepting the abuse. The victim could also be clinging to the perpetrator's legs, hugging him in some fashion, or praying to him—which could appear as obedience. The victim could also use a jumprope to tie himself to the abuser—the victim holding both ends while looping it around the abuser, indicating a desire to "hang on" to a bad situation. Just *feeling* these positions should raise many emotions and reactions toward enhancing awareness. Be certain to have each partner adjust the visual display to more accurately portray their relations. Then have each partner state how each NEEDS this type of arrangement between them. If one or both deny such a need, then have them state why they do NOT need such relations. Elicit the reaction of each partner regarding what is claimed by either spouse. Let each one have the opportunity to change the visual sculpture to a happier or more acceptable picture. This allows each to visualize what changes need to take place, if any. Also, allow each mate to experience the other partner's position with a role reversal demonstration.

Type 2: Dominator with Controlled

One could make use of many of the above visual ideas if they seem appropriate. However, *control* or *possession* might be shown more effectively by using some other props. One could actually obtain a large dog's collar and leash to indicate ownership and control. Toy handcuffs might feel more correct in some displays. The use of jumpropes could sufficiently restrain or tie up a mate very well. The *emotional need* to be controlled can be seen in the partner's acceptance of a collar being placed around his neck, no straining or resistance to the leash, and obedience to the master's commands. A bandanna or scarf tied around the head as a gag might represent the lack of a voice or opinion concerning issues. The dominating spouse might wear a crown, hold a whip, toy gun, or royal scepter. The submissive partner may even be smothered or covered up with a blanket—literally "in the dark." A role reversal with all of these props could be a powerful experience to enhance awareness in each partner.

Type 3: Parent with Child

The nurturing, rescuing, motherly-type of mate would be standing up while the immature or emotionally-needy mate would take a child's position in a chair or on the floor. The parental figure would be reassuring, loving and supportive—probably with both hands on the mate's shoulders or patting him on the head. A blanket might serve well to encompass the childlike partner, wrapping him toward the parental partner who holds both ends of the blanket. This could also become "smothering" at times! The childlike mate could also be hanging on, clinging, hugging the parental mate's legs, or roped into the parent's grasp. The use of an apron with apronstrings could play out several metaphors well. Jumpropes could show the "ties that bind" with the parental mate looping the jumprope(s) around the mate's body and holding both ends of the rope(s). The childlike mate could be clinging at the same time. The motherly mate might also wear a nurse's cap to suggest how rescuing that partner represents her desire to "fix everyone" around her. These roles should also reflect the negative aspects of parenting as well—such as a critical, opinionated, judgmental parent with the rebellious, acting-out child—if this is occurring. Finger-pointing, pouting, resistance, alienation, and needing attention could all be displayed visually.

Type 4: Perfect Mate with Defective Mate

The use of signs may be more effective with this pair so that particular messages can be *seen* as well as heard. Printed on signs could be the titles of:

(1) "I'M OKAY" with "I'M NOT OK"

(2) "GOOD SPOUSE" with "BAD SPOUSE"

(3) "PERFECT MATE" with "FLAWED MATE"

(4) "TO BE ADMIRED" with "TO BE SHUNNED"

(5) "GOING TO HEAVEN" with "GOING TO HELL"

(6) "ALWAYS RIGHT" with "ALWAYS WRONG"

(7) "SUPERIOR" with "INFERIOR"

(8) "BRILLIANT" with "STUPID"

Visual or pictorial cues could include (1) an angel's halo and devil's horns, (2) Happy Face symbol and a Frowning Face symbol, (3) picture of a religious cross and a Red X (scorned, sinful), (4) the grade "A+" and the grade "F", or (5) "100% Best" and "Big Zero." Wearing these signs or symbolic props should elicit feelings, reactions, and awareness of their positions. Role reversals can add much to their insight and understanding of how each position can feel. Explore with each partner how each role benefits him and also what would be lost without that position. Low self-esteem and/or guilt often keep the "inferior" mate into accepting his "one-down" position. Each position needs to realize how powerful BOTH of them are—and that there is actually a surprising *balance* of power in their dysfunctional dance. Remember that each *needs* the other to be dysfunctional in order to acquire his/her respective needs!

Sample Scenario of Interventions (Type 2)

1. Archie and Edith are both asked how they envision their relationship with regard to any issues of power or control. Archie sees himself as a king who rules with wisdom and experience "for the benefit of everyone." Edith sees herself as a dog on a leash, subservient to her husband—the "master"—who she feels does not know her feelings.

2. The therapist gives Archie a crown and a bar stool for a throne. Edith receives a large dog's collar with a long chain attached. Archie sits on his throne "for the good of everyone" and holds the chain while Edith sits nearby "at his feet."

3. The therapist asks each of them how they *feel* in their positions with an emphasis on their likes and dislikes. The therapist also asks them *how they appear* to each other.

4. The therapist asks each of them to guess how it might feel to be in the other mate's role. Then, the therapist directs a role reversal; each mate trades positions and props with the other.

5. Now that Archie is on the leash with his wife Edith on the throne, many strong feelings arise in both of them. Edith decides she likes this feeling of power and control over him finally. Archie is becoming bitter, grumpy, and impatient at feeling out of control. He wants his old position back, but she

is unwilling to relinquish control just yet. The therapist asks each of them to *be* the other mate—talking and acting like him/her as they appear to each other. The therapist helps each of them process their new feelings—exploring why they prefer and even cling to certain roles. Archie has to admit that neither of them likes being "on the leash." Now he understands her reactions toward him recently.

6. The therapist has them return to their original positions. Edith now becomes aware of another aspect—"feeling smothered" and "kept in the dark"—as well as chained to her husband. The therapist brings that feeling to life, visually, by tossing a blanket over Edith. Now she feels both "smothered" and "in the dark" as well as "on the leash."

7. When Archie observes his wife's visual portrayal of her emotions in this manner, he starts to feel sad. It reminds him of someone being buried alive. He can no longer see or experience his wife's presence. He then begins to realize that this *detachment* is exactly what she has been trying to communicate to him for months.

8. The therapist has Archie join her under the blanket so that they can be together and see each other. But they both realize that this would not be a healthy relationship as both feel cut off from the world. However, they like being together on the same level, so the therapist explores with this couple how they could finally "meet on common ground."

Couple #9: "Us First"

Family Map:

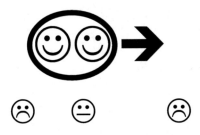

The "Us First" Family Life Cycle

Everyone has known a couple like this one. This couple seems to have every common interest and share nearly every activity together. They are *always* together. One hardly ever sees one partner without the other. They own a business together, go to the fitness center together, dine out at restaurants together, go shopping together, and go with other couples to clubs or parties together. They operate and function as a *single unit* as if each partner has a symbiotic need for the other in order to feel complete. They are impressive as a team and rarely seem to disagree. Basically, one does *not* exist without the other. But they seem *so normal* because they are intelligent, productive, charming, entertaining, humorous, and successful as a couple. And when they bring their troubled child to a therapist, that therapist may feel relieved to have such wonderful parents to work with.

Although it may have actually been an "accident" because this couple has been inseparable, the couple knows that having children is the expected "thing to do" in this society. Questions might be asked of them if they did *not* produce children! Although they may work well as a team with the duties of parenting, they will often both need to be gone together for various reasons and require a live-in nanny or regular Day Care service. It may seem as if their children are being raised by everybody else. Of course the couple will have their traditional pictures of the kids in the wallet or purse. There is just not much of a connection or relationship between the parents and the children as a result. The reactions on the children's part may be (1) grow up quickly and act like adults so that they can access the parents' world more successfully, (2) experience self-doubt and low self-esteem because it does not seem that the parents are really interested or loving, (3) express anger and resentment at feeling ignored, alienated, or forgotten, (4) become independent and detached, possibly resentful, defiant, and often in trouble.

Emptying the nest may be a welcome yet bittersweet event as the symbiotic couple launches their children into the world. They may suddenly recognize that they really missed out on their growing up. They have been so busy that they are actually surprised that the kids are suddenly of an age to leave home. Yet, there is relief that the couple is finally on their own, independent, and not requiring any more attention. It is likely that there will be little contact among the family members as they all carry out independent careers, probably scattering to various parts of the country. This family shall remain *disengaged* from each other.

With this particular couple the death of a partner creates significant issues. First of all, the surviving partner is devastated by the loss of his symbiotic mate. He or she does not know how to think, act, or behave on his/her own. As strange as this may sound, this couple was "too close" and did not preserve their individual identities well. Deep depression and suicidal feelings may result as the partner may wish to join his deceased mate. One of the children may feel this emotional impact, sympathize, and come to the rescue. The silent yet deafening call for a new partner may be felt deeply by one of the children. A son responding to his mother or a daughter coming to live with her father may create some serious emotional traps. The child may feel that he/she can never ever abandon the parent. If pulled into a similar, symbiotic relationship, some boundaries may be crossed inappropriately and even incest could result, simply as a means of preserving the family foundation. Then, there is always the chance that Dad could find a new, adult female to court, and daughter is rejected and ousted AGAIN.

Basic Solutions

1. The couple needs to develop healthier times apart, practicing individual activity to decrease the symbiotic nature of their connection.

2. The couple needs to develop closer relations with each child.

3. Individual therapy would help each partner to learn more about his or her need for such a symbiotic relationship.

4. Family outings and events must be developed to enhance family identity and relations.

5. The couple may feel uncertain, insecure, or afraid of actual parenting, playfulness, or disciplining with children and may need therapy for such unexplored feelings.

6. Children may need intense individual therapy to release frustrations, enhance self-esteem, decrease depression, and eliminate acting-out impulses.

What the Mouse in the Corner Hears . . .

(The couple announces yet another upcoming absence.)

Frank: "Wanted to let you know, Jerry, that your Mother and I will be gone for the next three weeks on the Caribbean cruise we earned from our bonus sales promotions at our company."

Stephanie:	"Yes! We are so excited to be going away again. After all, we have not been anywhere for at least six weeks now!"
Jerry (age 13):	"Who do we contact this time for meals and help?"
Stephanie:	"We hired Virginia to watch after you all. Here is her phone number."
Jerry:	"Why can't we ever go along on your trips?"
Frank:	"These are business trips that we have earned. When you get older and join the company, you can begin earning your own points toward a trip."
Stephanie:	"Besides, Jerry, these are *adult* trips for *adults* and not *really* for young people."
Jerry:	"We have *never* had a *real* family vacation like other families do!"
Frank:	"Stop your whining, Jerry! We have always provided *everything* that you have needed—(to wife) right, honey?"
Stephanie:	"Yes! Jerry, you are acting like a spoiled child!!"
Jerry:	"YOU'RE the ones who are spoiled! You always get whatever YOU want."
Stephanie:	"Oh, Frank—I just don't know *why* he acts this way."
Jerry:	"Why did you guys *ever* have kids anyway?"
Frank:	"Well . . . it had *not* been part of our plan, but it *did* happen, didn't it?"

This couple is so wrapped up in themselves and their shared activities that they seem deaf to their own insensitive comments made toward their own children. The most difficult aspect with this type of couple is that they seem so healthy and successful and would have great difficulty accepting that they are part of any serious problem. They do not understand that their children's reactive behavior could be at all connected to their own actions. Very few friends or associates would be likely to believe that either. This couple can be so convincing to many therapists as well. Some therapists might start thinking instead that there are such possibilities as bad genetics or children possessed by demons! Any therapist who begins to suggest that it *might* be a *family* problem may find himself with one less client. This couple will quickly fire any counselor who proposes such a "ridiculous" idea and take their child somewhere else.

The only chance of enhancing the awareness within this couple or uncovering these hidden issues lies in experiential approaches in the very first session. Otherwise, after this couple has offered *their* version of their child's history, they may leave him with you "to be fixed" and vanish back into their busy world. It would be like dropping off a car for repairs and then returning several weeks later to retrieve it. Efforts to bring this couple into therapy will be very likely met with many excuses related to busy schedules, job demands, and out-of-town travels. Each excuse sounds logical, reasonable, and believable—yet, this couple is placing more importance upon everything *other than* their child. This should be a strong clue for the therapist that this couple has very different priorities that might serve to explain their troubled child's emotions.

Much work will occur in individual therapy with the child who quite likely will be suffering from depression, rejection, alienation, poor self-esteem, no self-confidence, and anger. This young client will need much help with anger release, development of self-esteem and a healthy identity. He may be confused about childhood and why his parents have little interest in "kid matters." He may feel strongly compelled to "grow up quick" and enter the only world which seems acceptable—the adult world. He may be obsessed with finding ways to get their attention—even to the extremes of criminal actions, outrageous behavior, dramatic claims, or suicidal attempts. Whatever he attempts to do only confirms this couple's belief that their child just needs serious psychiatric treatment.

The only chance for one of their children to become close to one of the parents would probably happen if one of the parents should die. The intense symbiotic needs of that adult mixed with the lifelong desire of the alienated child could bring them together rather quickly. Despite resentments and uncertainties, that inner dream and longing for love and connection may drive that child to that desperate parent. This does not mean that the adult needs to be obvious or openly inviting. Subtle comments, looks, and quiet moments may communicate more than any words might. A child may do *anything* to preserve this family or soothe that lonely parent's pain. This includes many inappropriate crossings of the natural boundary between adults and their children—such as psychological affairs and incestual sexual relations. However, this emotional bond may also prevent healthier relations with same age mates. Will guilt over leaving her father alone keep the daughter from getting very close to male partners? Will father give subtle hints that he cannot survive without her? Or will father find a new businesswoman to become his new wife—and the daughter is *rejected again?!*

Clinical Case Example

A wealthy couple presented their depressed, 13 year-old son as being unruly and rude toward them, undermining their authority and challenging their rules. It was stated that he was "not really their son" because he had been adopted. The mother explained that she had suffered seven miscarriages before they decided that adoption was probably the only means for them to acquire children. This boy was actually dressed in a suit and tie and acted much more mature than his age of 13. He reported that his parents did not ever play with him but took him to many "boring" adult functions. He added that he did not really have any peers or close friends because his parents kept him busy with so many of *their* activities. However, in no way did he feel close, emotionally, to his parents despite the many shared activities.

At one point he became so frustrated with his parents' controlling attitude and comments that he blurted out, "Why did you both go to so much trouble to have me for a son?" Without hesitation his mother replied, "Well, when we are at the country club with other couples, they would share pictures of all their children—and we just did not have *any* pictures to share and just felt so uncomfortable." Their son groaned loudly, and it was certainly clear how this couple was so self-absorbed in themselves. I worked for a long time with this son to help build his self-esteem and confidence toward appropriate confrontation and expression of feelings toward his parents. Luckily, his parents were willing to be involved to an extent in his therapy, and they began to painfully accept how they *do push* him away.

Visual Sculptures

(1) Have the troubled child stand facing his parents about two feet away. Ask him how this position feels for him. Most likely he will state that he feels outnumbered 2:1 and intimidated by their united stance opposing him. They may feel that he is "in their way" or "blocking their path"—yet they may be surprised at *his* discomfort.

(2) Have the couple stand, one arm around each other, while the identified patient (their child) is positioned facing into one of the corners of the room. The couple will probably be puzzled over his specific position at such a distance while never really noticing how they present themselves in such an inseparable manner.

(3) Place the child or children gently (and with apologies!) between the parents as they stand next to each other. Note any resistance, anxiety, discomfort, or reactions. Often the parents will ask how long they have to maintain this position in the session. Ask any uneasy children if they wish to move to a more comfortable position.

(4) Have the children sit on the floor in front of the standing, inseparable parents. Have the couple point at the children on the floor while their other arm is around each other. This sculpture should emphasize, visually, the powerful stance of this couple.

(5) Have the couple stand back-to-back, locking their arms so that they cannot move forward. Have the children attempt to pry them apart and get in-between them. See if the couple makes any effort to accommodate the children. Note how hard the children actually try to pull them apart, because they may not even try or believe that it is worth the effort. Relate this to how they feel at home.

(6) Have the couple stand either back-to-back as in #5 or side by side as in #2 and begin to discuss possible individual activities for each of them. Maybe he could join a bowling league (without her). Maybe she would enjoy a pottery class (without him). Can they even conceive of enjoying time apart from each other? Can they physically (in the sculpture) make a single move without the other? Does that *ever* bother either one of them?

(7) Have each partner stand or sit as far apart in the room as possible and *stay there* for the entire session. Note what they each begin to feel at such a distance. Note if one of them becomes more anxious or restless before the other one does. If any children are present, they may sit wherever they choose—and by whomever they wish to be near, if anyone. Learn from the children what they think would happen if the parents continue to be so far apart. Also attempt to discuss individual activities with the couple as in #6.

(8) Have each partner take a turn experiencing a role reversal with one of the distanced children. Let that partner experience the loneliness, distance, and detachment of that child's

former position while now observing the child in his new position, very attached to the partner's mate.

Experiencing Dynamics and Changes

Experiential learning is most significant for this particular couple as it may be their only effective opportunity to gain insight into how their behavior may indeed be part of the problem. They may be surprised at both their own and their children's emotional reactions as the therapist attempts various emotional configurations. They may be stunned at how difficult it actually becomes to attempt certain changes in emotional spacing. This sudden change in awareness (since the couple is usually so wrapped up in themselves) may be a helpful breakthrough. Then, again, *nothing* may get through this couple's impenetrable defense and persistent need to see themselves as "okay"—*only as a couple.*

Perhaps, this couple may also gain a better understanding for the loneliness, rejection, alienation, or sadness of each child by *observing* and *feeling* the physical distance in each emotional configuration that is experienced in the session. Role reversals may really add to this awareness. Because neither partner likes being disconnected from each other, experiencing the distant position of a detached child may be quite revealing and emotionally unforgettable. It may serve to explain why the original need to unite in this symbiotic fashion was so crucial—but are they now creating the same intense need in their own alienated child?

Sample Scenario of Interventions

1. Jack and Jillian with their daughter Janice are asked to stand wherever they feel comfortable in the therapy room. As Jack and Jillian stand, they move closer and put one arm around each other, looking into each other's eyes and smiling. Janice

rises from her chair and stands with her back against the far corner of the room.

2. The therapist asks Jack or Jillian to attempt to draw their daughter closer. Nothing which either of them can say makes one bit of difference. They seem puzzled and even a bit angry because they have given her "everything that money could buy."

3. Feeling more frustrated with her parents, Janice turns and now faces *into* the corner.

4. As the couple is about to comment on how much trouble Janice has become, the therapist moves her out of the corner and positions her facing directly in front of the couple.

5. Although she is encouraged to express what she is feeling to her parents, she turns around, putting her back toward them, and becomes tearful. She states that she is "always outnumbered" and tired of trying because she can "never win."

6. The therapist allows Janice to return to a more comfortable position again—back in the corner. But then, the therapist moves the couple apart with each partner being placed in a different corner of the room. Now everyone can have the same experience of being distant, detached, and disconnected from everyone else.

7. The therapist then allows one of the adult partners to join with Janice in her corner. The other partner is now able to see and experience what it feels like to be the *only one* not connected.

8. The therapist then switches the adult partners in their positions so that the other partner can now experience the "odd man out" role as Janice now aligns with her other parent in her corner.

9. The therapist then allows the couple to reunite (happily) but now realizing how their daughter Janice may actually feel, _always_ being in the detached isolated position.

10. The therapist may attempt to have them "pose for a family portrait" with their daughter standing right in between her parents. Note how much anxiety is created by Janice's position right between her inseparable parents.

11. Individual activities or hobbies may be suggested for the couple and portrayed by each partner moving several steps away from each other while Janice remains right in the middle. The couple may be surprised at how difficult some of these moves are for them.

Cultural, Generational, and Sexual Identity Considerations

Questions have been asked about other types of living situations— possibly other types of couples. It should be noted that these eight basic types of couples can overlap or co-exist. For example, a couple may have the lack of desire to yield on family traditions (as in the "I am Right" couple) while having an immature, self-centered focus (as in the "Me First!" couple). One may also find a "Me First!" couple with an "Odd Man Out" configuration. Another couple could act immaturely ("Me First!") and plan to get married again ("We're Right!") with a great deal of opinion and interference still coming from their Families of Origin ("Family Feud"). Therefore, these eight types of couple configurations are describing the kinds of conflicts and dynamics that can occur, but are not always exclusive or independent of each other. These kinds of dynamics are presented to assist the clinician in identifying the types of couple's issues needing to be addressed with specific ideas on how to work with each kind of problem.

CULTURAL: Within a specific culture and its deeply-rooted traditions and customs, a therapist must understand and respect what is "the expected norm" for families. There may be unspoken yet expected forms of behavior that have been passed down for generations. What may appear to be unhealthy or dysfunctional for that culture may, in fact, be widely accepted and functional. Therapists need to listen closely for what the complaints or issues *actually are* instead of becoming distracted or misled by assumptions regarding the differing cultural beliefs and customs. Although a therapist might assume that a certain out-dated custom may be contributing to the problems, the dynamics of the couple may instead actually reflect one of the eight couple dilemmas already described in this book.

Mixing cultural backgrounds in a marriage may present the most difficult challenges. Imagine: Spanish with Indian, Russian with Swedish, Korean with German, Italian with Irish, or South African with Chinese? Perhaps a submissive Korean woman would blend well with the strong-willed German man. But which traditions or customs would be presented to the children? Which religion would predominate? The bottom line in any case is that the couple needs to blend their backgrounds and identify which traditions shall be maintained and to what extent, depth, and frequency. Certainly, this is at the central core of the "I am Right" or "We are Right" couple's challenge. Some couples will not survive these attempts to blend. In other families, one partner may give in to keep the other mate happy, yet build resentment over the years for having abandoned his own traditions and customs.

GENERATIONAL: Questions also arise regarding elderly couples and their challenges. As some older couples lose their ability to function physically or mentally, their children often feel obligated to care for them. This can lead to situations in which the elderly pair will be moving in with one of their children's families. This may lead to a challenging blending of two quite different living styles—similar to a "We are Right!" conflict. Should the younger couple's living style have to change drastically just to accommodate and enhance the comfort level of the older parents? Should the ailing, elderly parents be expected to give up their living habits and customs because of this move into the child's home? Even though all the adults may agree upon a plan, will this prevent the young children in the home from acting-out or exhibiting anxiety?

If one of the elderly parents has died and just the surviving parent needs assistance, this may create an "Odd Man Out" configuration as the one older parent moves into the young couple's home. It could also set up an "I am Right" dilemma between the one parent and his child regarding how the home should be run. The solution resides in the family's ability to communicate, negotiate, and compromise some form of agreement that adequately meets the needs of everyone involved.

Many older couples have difficulty around the time of retirement. For years the housewife has ruled the quiet home and operated a consistent routine to accomplish all her tasks without her husband's approval, interference, or presence. Now she may find a restless, bored, needy husband who has just retired and plopped himself right into the center of her routine at home. It becomes more frustrating if he begins criticizing how she does things or making new suggestions to *improve* her routine. He, himself, has lost a sense of identity and role as well as no longer feeling productive or useful. As he begins to try to become useful in her world, she may react as if he is trying to control her and disrupt her established routine. They actually face a similar blending challenge as when they first married ("I am Right") because he is bringing his work role home now to face her established routine.

They need to negotiate a *new* routine based upon their *new* situation.

Another challenge at retirement age involves a sudden change in lifestyle when the elderly couple decides to sell their home, buy a large motorized camper, and begin traveling wherever their hearts lead them. This ("Us First") action may bewilder or disrupt their grown children's lives who counted on their presence for holidays, babysitting, weekend visits, and traditional gatherings, etc. The couple certainly has the right to do so, and it may be a long-anticipated, well-deserved, and healthy course of action. It is the rest of their family who may have to cope with this sudden change in their own routines.

SEXUAL IDENTITY: Many people have questioned whether Lesbian or Gay couples are another type of couple. My response has typically been that the main difference that I find is simply their sexual preference, itself—*not* their dynamics, relations, emotional distance or configuration. They can experience any of the challenges of the eight couple types already presented in this book without their sexual preference making much of a difference at all. It has been my experience that their sexual preference does not create a different or significant type of emotional configuration than that of any heterosexual couple. As I have traveled around the country providing these lectures, I have asked whether other professionals agree or disagree with that conclusion. Thus far, nobody has expressed disagreement with this conclusion.

DUAL CAREER COUPLES: Some therapists have pondered if the modern, two-career, hard-working couples are a new form of yet another couple type. However, their ties to many activities, hobbies, and job-related obligations may reflect either (1) another version of a "No Glue" couple who have become distant due to many time-consuming activities and duties, or (2) a modern version of a "Me First!" couple who seek many gratifying outlets and independent activities for themselves with little interest in running the family home, or (3) an "Us First!" couple who agree to be overinvolved away from the family home in particular pursuits—often together. Their insight is easily enhanced by visual depictions of all their ties to their many pursuits and duties.

Metaphoric and Projective Assessments

6

Emotional Age Exercise

No matter what the actual chronological age is for any person, his behavior and mood may suggest the actions of someone of a different age. Whether older or younger, the emotional age of any person will more accurately portray their emotional position, needs, and quality of relations with another person. In *any* type of relationship the examination of emotional ages will illuminate the true nature of the relations and explain why certain behaviors and problems occur. Comprehending this kind of perspective may provide helpful insight and invaluable awareness for everyone involved. For example, when the boundaries in a family system seem vague, weak, or possibly crossed, there may be ineffective or immature parenting along with the presence of a Parental Child. When a therapist suspects this may be happening in the family, this exercise which determines emotional ages can be very revealing.

"Every member of the family shall participate in this exercise. Each of you take a piece of paper and write everybody's name down in a column on the left side of the paper. Make a column in the center of the page and write each family member's exact age in years. Now think for a moment about each family member and how each one behaves. Does he or she act like his/her actual age? Does he act older? Younger? Pick the exact age which represents how they *really act* and behave and write that number in a column on the right. I will keep your answers confidential."

This is each family member's *emotional age*. Collect the papers from everybody and then make a master list on a chalkboard or simply discuss the collective perceptions for each family member. Some therapists like to average all the numerical responses to get a composite number which truly represents a family consensus and removes the attention from any individual response. However, if the responses are quite different, it would be wise to explore these variations in perception, giving family members an opportunity to openly share their perspectives. Differences may suggest that the family is recalling *different moods* of that family member.

What is convenient about this exercise is that an opinion about everybody's behavior is collected from each family member in a relatively innocent fashion in just a matter of minutes—without anybody having to utter a single word. This is especially helpful with non-verbal families or families who are timid about expressing perceptions openly. What is often amazing is how the family just *knows* these unspoken emotional ages and usually agrees upon the perceptions without any prior discussion. This is significant when the kids describe their parents as much younger and at least one of the siblings as much older. This revealing exercise can promote much discussion and some important feelings about how the family perceives its members. For the therapist it provides a unique, quick, and easy method to assess potential problems with family roles and boundaries.

	actual age	averaged emotional age	family's actual responses for each
Mom	36	23.2 **(23)**	20, 24, 18, 22, 25, 30
Dad	40	52.8 **(53)**	46, 60, 56, 55, 48, 52
Thomas	16	25.3 **(25)**	28, 18, 29, 26, 19, 32
Susan	13	7.5 **(8)**	8, 6, 7, 8, 9, 7
Becky	8	9.8 **(10)**	10, 10, 9, 11, 9, 10
Joey	4	4.3 **(4)**	4, 5, 4, 3, 6, 4

The therapist could actually write all of these responses on a chalk-board or dry erase board, giving the family time to absorb the answers. It helps the discussion if they can continue to refer back to the information visually. Although one might assume this exercise may only take a few minutes, the therapist should be prepared for what might become an hour or more of discussion!

When Dad asks why everybody thinks he is "so old," he has opened the door finally for the family to reveal and share impressions which may have been perceived for years but never openly expressed. No family members *have to* reveal which response was theirs, but they can certainly join into the discussion easily because that particular family member has asked for opinions. The therapist should observe *how* each family member reacts to the discussion about himself— because his *emotional reaction* may actually validate the family's perceptions regarding his *emotional age!*

In the above example, the therapist could predict some problems in that Mom is viewed as 13 years *younger* while Dad is seen as 13 years *older*. Their 16-year old son actually has an averaged emotional age **(25)** which is two years *older* than his Mom's **(23)**! One can also note that 8 year-old Becky is seen as more mature **(10)** than her 13 year-old sister **(8)**. The relations in this family are now becoming predictable. The discussion could focus on *what makes* each family member seem those ages and what *needs to be different* for each family member to become his/her actual age again.

The therapist may wish to sculpt the family into emotional postures and positions based upon their information from this exercise.

Family members who are emotionally age 0–6 would sit on the floor. Family members emotionally acting ages 7–12 could kneel on the floor. Family members displaying adolescent emotions (ages 13–19) could sit in chairs. Members of the family who seem like mature adults could stand up. Those who act elderly or much older than their adult age could lean on a chair, against a wall, or on a cane. The therapist can be creative to achieve the visual arrangement which *feels right* to everyone and produces the most helpful, colorful, or dynamic visual results.

Kinetic Family Drawings Group Activity

The Kinetic Family Drawing (K-F-D) is one clever way to elicit a family member's perception of family roles, relations, power, and politics in the family. Although it is usually given to the one "identified patient" who was brought to a clinic for therapy, this exercise gives the *whole* family the opportunity to present *all* perspectives at the same time in a group drawing activity. There are several ways that this can be accomplished.

(1) Have each family member create a Kinetic Family Drawing individually at the same time. Tell each member to, "Draw the family doing something." In this manner the drawings contain some kind of action or activity which can reveal relationships, dominance, passivity, competition, isolation, cooperation, conflict, alliances, and emotional space. This becomes a form of "sculpting on paper." When each member has finished, hold up each drawing and have that member describe the action and what each member is doing. This can be quite interesting in terms of how they perceive their family and what words they select to describe them. Look for pat-

terns of agreement or similarity as well as differences among all the drawings.

(2) Have one family member volunteer to depict the family in a K-F-D on a chalkboard. Then ask him to describe the action and what role each member is taking on in this drawing. Check with the other family members to see if they either agree with this drawing or whether they see it any differently. If someone does have a different viewpoint, have him come up to the chalkboard and change the drawing to his perspective. Then see if the family agrees with that viewpoint. Keep allowing changes in the drawing until the family agrees that it is "close enough" to the truth. If they cannot agree about how they see themselves behaving in the family, then this becomes a topic in itself for further exploration.

(3) The therapist can ask for individual K-F-D's from each family member and then have the family assume the roles and actions in each drawing. One drawing at a time, the family poses in the positions depicted and may begin to *feel* the patterns that they are acting out. The family may notice that one member is always in charge, another one always left out, or, perhaps another member is usually upset. By bringing each drawing to life, the family may begin to connect with memories, emotions, and their own dynamics in first-hand experiential recreations of their own lives.

A Family of Animals

This imagery exercise can capture powerful descriptions of family behavior, roles, dynamics, and personalities in a seemingly innocent and easy fashion.

"Each family member shall make a list of the names in your family in a column on the left side of your paper. Think about each family member, one at a time, and think about how they behave most of the time. What animal do they remind you of? Is it a big or little animal? Loud or quiet? Friendly or unfriendly? Don't tell anybody what you are thinking! Write the kind of animal you are thinking about beside that family member's name. We will list all the answers up here when everybody is finished."

Although the imagined animals may be different, look for similarities in the power, nature, and character of each image. Be careful as the therapist not to *assume* that you know what each image means. Someone's idea of a bear may quite different from your own! In a safe and innocent fashion, each family member is truly characterizing each other's role and behavior in the family. Aggressive and passive positions become obvious. Who has power and authority becomes clear. Roles can now be seen as appropriate or not; boundaries clear, vague, or intruded across. Here is an example that a therapist listed on a dry erase board.

Dad	grizzly bear, lion, tiger, bear, wolf	(powerful, dominant)
Mom	goat, lamb, pony, sheep, kitten	(passive, harmless)
Tommy (15)	gerbil, raccoon, snake, lizard, weasel	(sneaky, rambunctious)
Susie (13)	squirrel, eagle, raccoon, owl, lioness	(wise, clever, watchful)
Bob (9)	shark, wolf, hyena, wild dog, bobcat	(wild, angry, hurtful)

In this example there is a certain emotional tone to each group of perceived images. Mom may be surprised that her set of animals seems so powerless or passive while Susie's group seems more protective, wise, and motherly (Parental Child?). If Mom is not effective as a parent, then this may explain all three of her kids' reactive behaviors. Tommy feels he can get away with things; Bob is angry that his sister is "in control" instead of Mom; Susie feels the need to help with parenting while Dad is away at work so much of the time. And all of these hidden dynamics were safely exposed in a playful manner with this simple exercise.

Each family member should have an opportunity to react to what the others have perceived. Does that person agree or disagree with their perceptions? Why or why not?

> How does each person see himself?
>
> What does this suggest about his own insight or view of himself?
>
> Does someone have an entirely different view of himself other than what the family sees? How does that seem to happen?
>
> What does he think about the others seeing him so differently? (Note *how* the family members react in this discussion because it may reflect the animals that were chosen for their behavior.)
>
> What roles, conflicts, and dynamics are likely to occur among these animals? (This can be acted out in an upcoming exercise.)
>
> Does someone model after another member?
>
> Who would be likely to form alliances?
>
> Who sounds troubled, detached, or isolated?
>
> Is this actually happening in the family now?
>
> Which other animal would seem most likely to be able to help or effect a positive change?
>
> Which other animal might be influencing or perpetuating this trouble?

One can just imagine how many real issues can be indirectly and safely discussed with the seemingly unrelated images of animals. In the same manner that Play Therapy works well with children, these indirect methods offer a form of useful Play Therapy for adults.

The therapist can then suggest that a sculpture or visual portrayal of this family of animals be created to see how these characters would mix and relate. Each family member should select the one animal that he believes best represents his personality and then act it out. In the playful mode of role-playing the "animals" will feel free to act out their roles with little resistance or conscious defensiveness. The therapist can observe and comment on how the various animals relate, coordinate, protect, defend, come into conflict, or negotiate solutions. The family will just feel that they are playing around while actually revealing much more of their character and typical behavior because of the innocent and playful manner that the animal roles create and inspire.

If small children are present in the family, it may be easier for them to select a toy animal for each family member from a collection in the therapy room that contains a wide variety of choices for that child. They may have more trouble *thinking* of animal choices without being able to see them—as a nice toy collection of animal figures would provide. It is just much easier for the younger child to pick and choose rather than to sit and think!

Shopkeepers at the Mall

This exercise allows the family to reveal much about their likes, dislikes, style of interaction, roles, character, personal world, and political moves. Perhaps this particular family is more oriented toward business, productivity, or achievement.

> "Pretend that your family and all your relatives own stores at a large shopping Mall. You can own the shop of your dreams and can have whatever *you want* in it. This is *your* store to run in any way that you wish. What would you call it? What items would you have in it? Would you just manage it and hire workers? Or would you run it all by yourself? Would you specialize in a particular product, a line of products, or a variety of departments? Would your goal be to have fun or to make lots of money?"

Have the family think about this for a few minutes and then share their different visions. On a piece of paper or dry erase board draw an empty map of this Mall, outlining places for shops. Ask each family member, one at a time, to indicate where their shop would be located on the map. Each one can draw it in to show size, shape, and location. The family will unknowingly create another "sculpting on paper," depicting emotional space by how they position their stores in proximity to each other. Would any of the shops be likely to cooperate, trade, sell to each other, or be in competition with each other with sales gimmicks? Would any of the family members be interested in shopping at any of the other stores? Why or why not? (Does this indicate a lack of interest in that member's life?)

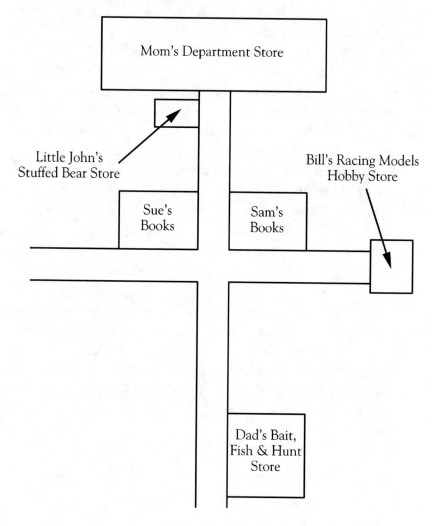

Who placed his store next to another family member's store? Whose stores are at the greatest distance from each other or "off the beaten path" and detached? Which stores are the largest or in prominent positions? Does the large size of a store reflect power, self-esteem, confidence, or control? Does a smaller size store suggest lower self-esteem, passivity, dependence, or poor confidence? Are the two book stores in the example into a fierce competition for somebody's attention? Or are they cooperative and very friendly? How would each family member react if the therapist would suggest moving stores around, limiting space, or possible mergers? (Is that not like the same kinds of emotional space changes in a family sculpting?)

What each family selects for their store describes their personal likes, interests, and hobbies. Although it may be no surprise at all regarding what some family members select, it may be quite revealing about other family members and their dreams that they have been quietly contemplating. How they run their store is revealing in terms of their style of organizing, delegating, and distributing power. Who *wants* to visit their store and *who doesn't* can reveal much about relationships within the family system. Types of products, variety (or lack of it), the name of the store, and stated goals can all be rather revealing about that member's attitude, creativity, and character. Which stores seem backed by enthusiasm and a winning attitude? Which ones, if any, feel destined for disappointment and loss? Who doesn't even seem to care?

The therapist can become quite creative with this exercise as it develops. He can encourage much family interaction to enhance interest in each other's dreams and desires. It provides yet another opportunity for the therapist to view the dynamics of this family's roles and communication patterns while they work on this project, revealing much about themselves and their relationships in a creative, playful, and indirect fashion.

Departments of Government

This exercise allows the family another safe way to explore their perceptions of roles and dynamics among themselves. Perhaps other exercises just would not draw their interest like this one might. Perhaps this family is more educated - like a college professor's family who might share a greater interest in current events. The therapist may decide to list the following departments of government on a chalkboard or provide a printed hand-out. It works well to hand the family members a list of these offices so that they can designate how many of them they feel that they operate within the family while also indicating which office(s) they see the other family members being involved with. Again, an incredible amount of information is obtained quickly and easily regarding their perceptions of each other in the family.

Department of Defense	Department of the Interior
Department of Economy	Department of Education
Department of Transportation	Department of Internal Affairs
Department of Communication	Department of International Affairs
Department of Finance	Department of Health & Welfare
Department of National Security	Department of Commerce
Department of the Environment	Department of Justice
Supreme Court	F.B.I. or C.I.A.
Library of Congress	The Pentagon
The U.S. Mint	The National Archives
U.S. Congress or Senate	The White House
Department of War	United Nations ambassador
The Federal Reserve	National Parks Service
Department of Labor	Homeland Security
Smithsonian Museum	Armed Forces
U.S. Post Office	Speaker of the House

As each department or service depicts a different level of power, responsibility, and authority, it is interesting to see what each family member selects as their role(s) in the family. Have each family member describe how he sees his department(s) operating and what kind of services it provides. As the therapist lists all of the responses on a chalkboard, see how these various departments may cooperate, be in conflict, or possibly duplicate services. Note whether anybody feels overloaded with duties and obligations from multiple roles.

Ask the family which of the chosen departments seems most powerful, harmless, helpful, useful, important, busy, or least useful. Do these responses reflect the same dynamics for those particular family members?

What does this exercise reveal about the hierarchy of power and responsibility in this family? What does it reveal about roles and hidden power?

Do the family members agree with and understand why each family member selected his/her choices? Have them talk about *why* those selections do or do not make sense to them. What have *they* selected for the roles of the other family members?

Example: (what they selected for themselves)

Dad	The Pentagon U.S. Mint	(in charge of operations)
Mom	Department of the Interior Dept. of Transportation Dept. of Health & Welfare Dept. of Education	(runs the home)
Bob (19)	Department of Defense	(protective role)
Susan (14)	Department of Communication	(gossip central)
Billy (9)	The F.B.I.	(sneaky snitch)
Johnny (5)	National Parks Service	(loves outdoors)

An entirely different list would be developed for their collective impressions of each other's roles and duties.

Dad:	Supreme Court, U.S. Mint, Senate, Dept. of War, Speaker of the House
Mom:	Dept. of Labor, Transportation, Education, Environment, Security

Bob (19)	Congress, Senate, Dept. of Defense, Armed Forces, United Nations
Susan (14)	C.I.A., Library Congress, National Archives, Smithsonian, Post Office
Billy (9)	F.B.I., Dept. of War, C.I.A., Dept. of Defense, Dept. of Interior
Johnny (5)	Smithsonian, National Parks, Library of Congress, National Zoo

All of these additional perspectives add greater depth and detail to the roles and character of each member in the family. Sometimes the self-perceptions will not match those opinions of everybody else in the family. The discussion and processing of this abundance of information may take quite some time, but it can be well worth the journey.

Magic Wands, Wishes, and Miracles

A therapist will often ask a client what he really *wishes* could happen in his life or what he *wants* to have happen for himself. A client will often respond with, "I don't know," when actually he *does* have *some* idea. He just does not have any faith or belief that it could ever be, so therefore, he does not even wish to mention it. In fact, he may not ever mention his dream because he is so discouraged over the probability of it never happening. Therefore, it is the therapist's chore to elicit these doubted and hidden desires so that true feelings and hopes can be understood and discussed. On many occasions the client was wrong about the unlikely potential of his dream and was actually helped to find ways to make it happen after all.

Some members in a family may doubt that what they wish could change in the family will ever likely occur, and so, they withhold declaring their hopes for such changes. The family therapist may benefit from using these fantasy techniques which help to *suspend reality* and allow their fantasies and wishes to be finally spoken and realized.

The Magic Wand

"Pretend that I have a powerful magic wand in my hand which can grant you any wish. Ask yourself what you really wish could be different in your family. What would you want to have different at home? It does not matter whether or not you think it could actually happen in reality. Just know that I can make *any* desired change happen in your family with just the wave of this magic wand! Now, what do each of you wish or want to see happen differently at home? And know that nobody will get in trouble for just stating what they want during this exercise."

The Magic Dust

"In this magic vase (bottle, jar, etc.) is a powerful dust (glitter) which can grant you three secret wishes that you never believed could happen for you. Granting these wishes would mean more to you in your life at home than anything else. Be advised that desires for money, wealth, or material things are not likely to be granted. Think about how you wish your life could be better with others. After I sprinkle this magic dust (glitter) over you, then you can safely share what your three wishes are."

It is good for the family to hear what each member truly desires and needs. Often, another family member may have an idea or be able to assist that member toward their hopeful wish. The family's new awareness of all the desires, needs, and dreams of its members may actually serve to promote change because everyone is more cognizant of each other's true feelings. Awareness is a huge step toward any change because then we all know what it is that people truly want and need to do.

Examples:

"I wish Dad would not work so many hours and could be home more."

"I wish Mom would give me chances to show that I can be trusted."

"I wish Dad would stop drinking."

"I wish Mom would take time to listen when I need to talk."

"I want Bob to quit hitting me every day."

"I wish Susan would quit borrowing my clothes without telling me."

"I wish everyone would quit yelling so much at home!"

"I wish we could take a family vacation all together for once."

"I just wish our family would actually do something together."

"I just want somebody to notice me."

Another technique called, "The Miracle Morning," has been floating around the therapy field for years, but I am unaware of who should get the proper credit. This is how it would be used.

The Miracle Morning

"When you go to sleep tonight, something magical will happen while you are sleeping. When you awake in the morning, something miraculous and wonderful will have changed in your world. What would you want this miracle to be?"

Fantasy techniques like these help to free a client or family from the perceived painful and depressing reality of their life and experience a vision of their own hopes and dreams that had been buried, suppressed, or nearly abandoned. Bringing these wishes to the surface for open discussion may lead to new paths, possible solutions, different behavior, or constructive brainstorming instead of pessimistic hopelessness. But it seems as though it requires a fantasy approach to get near these dreams and unearth these hidden hopes.

The Inkblot Party

Everybody knows that an inkblot is *just* an inkblot. Yet, people will constantly see many other shapes, forms, and images that each of their minds will uniquely construct—based upon that person's life experiences, personality, and emotions. These projections of our own thoughts and feelings into those inkblots are like looking through windows into ourselves. Yet, people do not typically suspect that this kind of a playful exercise is going to reveal anything significant or obvious from a silly inkblot. However, every single word, image, and impression is as unique to one's personality as a fingerprint. Therefore, in an indirect manner, much is being learned from every impression and perception expressed. The context remains playful, innocent, and relaxed—which encourages free expression and less resistance.

This exercise works well for groups, families, couples, and even individuals in therapy. Set up a table to work on with at least four colors of paint in squirt tubes. Each person receives a piece of paper and folds it in half. Opening up the paper and laying it out flat, each person drips, dabs, dribbles, or streaks paint from different squirt tubes. <u>Not much is needed</u>! Then each person folds his paper back together, squishing the paint inside against a flat surface. After doing so, re-open the paper and have each person follow these directions.

> "As you open your paper and gaze for the first time upon your colorful creation, allow your first impression of what you are seeing to come to you. Write that down, and then look at your picture again. When you get another impression, write that down as well. List as many impressions as you perceive as you turn your picture upside down and view it from different angles. Be sure to get *at least* two different impressions."

Have each person present in the room take a turn holding up his own inkblot. Others present will look at that person's inkblot and take turns offering their own first impressions of what they see in his inkblot. Only after everyone else has shared their perceptions, have that person finally reveal his own impressions that were written down. The therapist can note differences in responses and how those impressions may reflect upon each person's present attitude, mood, and situation.

For example, Betty may look at Steve's inkblot and see a beautiful peacock with a colorful spread of tail feathers. Betty has been feeling better about herself recently and more confident about her life. George sees Steve's inkblot as a huge ocean wave with lots of debris crashing down over him. George has been feeling overwhelmed and "drowning" under the pressures at work recently. Steve sees his own inkblot as a peaceful waterfall plunging into a deep canyon. Steve feels as if his life is flowing forward again but facing some dark, unknown pitfalls somewhere up ahead. The therapist can comment on the mood and emotional tone of each reaction and how it may reflect on current feelings in one's life. This is another easy way to access emotional issues with couples and families as well as with therapy groups.

7

Metaphoric Imagery and Therapy

Metaphoric Imagery and Sculpting

Relations within Couples

First described in 1979 by family therapist, Peggy Papp, metaphoric sculpting with couples is a dynamic, fun, and extremely helpful technique in assessing and treating the issues with couples. This approach sidesteps conscious, verbal defenses and goes beneath the surface to the subconscious emotions and politics which are operating in the dyad. Instead of blaming, talking, and hearing words, the couple moves into a mode of *seeing* and *feeling* their dilemma in a relatively harmless and fun fashion. The metaphoric images and descriptive characteristics reveal the psychological nature of the relations and the emotional tone of the dynamics. However, because this is achieved through metaphors, it remains indirect and safely distant from reality despite the intuitive truth and genuine emotion that the metaphors clearly represent.

This technique is so quick and easy to present, while appearing playful and irrelevant, that it bypasses most defenses and typical resistance before the couple realizes what it is revealing about themselves and their relationship. Here is exactly how it should be presented by the therapist.

> "Let's take a break and do something here just for fun. Close your eyes (optional) and imagine for a moment that your partner takes on the form of an animal, or an object, or a famous person or place. Imagine what image would *feel right* to you as you think about how they act or behave. Take time to get the image clearly in your mind with as much detail as you can imagine. Do not say *anything* yet. Just say, 'okay' when you are ready. (After they say, 'okay':) Now imagine a second image which represents what animal, object, famous person or place **you** would become *in relation to* the first image you created. As you get *that* image, reflect on how the two would interact or relate to each other. Let me know when you are ready."

Note that the partner's image is *always* created first *before* one's self-image. People present themselves in many different ways depending upon whom they are in a relationship with. Susan will behave one way when dealing with her priest, another way when talking with her mother, and another way when cuddling with her new boyfriend. How she sees herself in a relationship is greatly dependent upon *whom* she is with. Therefore, the partner *must* be metaphorically imaged first so that the client knows *which* of his many "selves" is the right one for that particular relationship. Susan might be a "Girl Scout" with her priest, a "sharp-tongued snake" with her Mom, and a "cuddly kitten" with her boyfriend. That is why the mate or significant other must be envisioned first. Despite the emphasis on couples, this imagery exercise works just as well with *any* relations: employer/employee, parent/child, co-worker/co-worker, schoolchild/teacher, brother/sister, wife/mother-in-law, etc.

Encourage each person to stick with the first image that comes to his mind—even though it may seem confusing, irrelevant, silly, weird, or stupid. There is usually a very good reason why that image came forth—even though the person does not understand this yet. Their conscious minds will try to edit, delete, or alter those first impressions into something more acceptable, pleasing, or logical if the therapist allows them to do so. For example, a therapist at one of my seminars *knew* that his pair of images *felt right* but could not understand the connection between himself and his wife. He saw her as "Leonardo Da Vinci" and himself as "a bear in the woods." These seemingly detached images began to make perfect sense as he described more details.

> "Leonardo Da Vinci was a brilliant artist and inventor. My wife is a very talented artist, and she is constantly doing innovative things at home. In fact, she rearranges the furniture and redecorates the home so often that it frustrates me. I go outside and stomp around in the woods like a bear over the frustration of the house constantly being turned upside down. Hey—wait a minute . . . She's an artist—and the whole house is her canvas! She has a right to express her talents in that fashion. I should respect that artistic creativity and quit grumbling around in the woods. Wow!!"

Some clients may insist that they cannot be creative or imaginative. One or both partners may clam that they cannot think of anything. I have found that with more time and encouragement one or both will think of *something*. If only one partner has a pair of images, proceed with that one set and allow the other partner to react, agree, or disagree by providing his own images if he feels that his partner's images are "incorrect." The therapist may have to just state, bluntly, "What does your partner remind you of when under stress? A big aggressive animal? A small harmless creature? A solid or fragile object? A famous character?" The therapist does not want to lead the client at all, but he may have to ask these further questions to trigger or jump-start their imagination.

A number of therapists have wondered if the partners might change their responses as they hear each other talk. It has been my experience for over 24 years that they do *not* alter their responses at all. Each person seems to stick to their own images because it was what *felt right* for them. If anything, they adamantly defend their impressions and continue to develop more detail with time. However, it is not a bad idea to simply have them write down their impressions before any discussion so that everybody can be certain that nothing was altered, copied, diluted, or edited in some fashion.

If a person comes up with two or three images for his partner (or himself) and feels that all of them are accurate in some manner, then he is probably contemplating various moods or situations in which he experiences that partner in a variety of ways. In this case, have that person stick with either his *first* impression or the image which best fits his partner *most* of the time. All of the images are important, but selecting the most prominent one is what is preferred at this point in the session. Images specific to moods and various situations are indeed useful and important—and will be discussed later in this chapter.

After the couple has indicated that they each have a pair of images, have each one begin to describe what he imagined—first for the partner, then for himself. It is critical that the therapist **not assume** that he knows what these images mean. Just because a client may say that his spouse is "Shirley Temple" or "Mount Rushmore" or "a grizzly bear" or "an ocean wave" does *not* mean that the therapist actually understands the image yet. "Shirley Temple" could be a "sickening-sweet, spoiled brat" or a "talented child star" or "innocent, cute, and charming." "Mount Rushmore" could be a "famous, prominent land-mark" or a "cold wall with a phony set of faces" or a "solid, depend-able rock." A "grizzly bear" could be aggressive and dangerous or strong and protective. Therefore, each partner must describe each image in as much detail as possible with the therapist facilitating this discovery process. The therapist needs to ask:

> What *kind* of grizzly bear?
>
> What is the grizzly bear *doing?*
>
> What is the *mood* of the grizzly bear?
>
> What *size, color, or shape* of grizzly bear?

How does the grizzly bear *relate* to others?

How does the grizzly bear *relate* to the (other image)?

How is the grizzly bear *important*?

How could the grizzly bear be a *better* grizzly bear?

How could you imagine the grizzly bear and the (other image) *getting along* better?

What do you wish could be *different* between the grizzly bear and (other image)?

How would you *miss* the grizzly bear if it were not around any longer?

These kinds of questions develop the detail of the image and enhance the understanding for each partner and the therapist. The more detail that can be elicited, the more personal and relevant the images become. Each partner keeps projecting more information about their relationship into the safer images, making it much easier to share their feelings, frustrations, and perceptions about each other in this indirect way.

A "big tiger" could be:

(1) a handsome, magnificent, and powerful leader, or

(2) a snarling, dangerous, menacing, stalking beast, or

(3) a dominant, controlling, overprotective creature, or

(4) a strong, silent provider with a big, gentle heart

As one can observe, the more specific descriptions which elaborate on the original metaphor of "a big tiger" can certainly produce quite different meanings and role definitions. The therapist *must always* elicit "*what kind* of big tiger" this is! Likewise, the therapist cannot assume that he knows what the relationship would be like between the partners just because a "big tiger" is involved. The therapist needs to ask *how* this big tiger interacts with the other metaphoric image and what kind of contact, conflict, communication, exchanges, or cooperation would occur.

Sample responses regarding the "big tiger" character:

> "He is silent and powerful but *he gives mean looks* that make me obey."
>
> "He is snarling and dangerous, but *he never ever strikes.*"
>
> "*I feel trapped and guarded* by his controlling behavior."
>
> "*I don't see him often,* but I know he is out there working and providing well."
>
> "He is a big old cuddly cat who *holds me safely* in his strong paws at night."

One time a client told me that her husband was a "panther." My own mind conjured up this impressive image of a powerful, sleek animal with strong muscles and shiny black fur. When I commented on this image forming in my own mind, she laughed and said, "No—*not* a black panther! A Pink Panther—like Peter Sellers!" (Her reference was to the bumbling detective played by the actor Peter Sellers in the movie, *The Pink Panther*) That taught me quickly *not* to assume that I understand *any image* that is mentioned by clients.

Clinical Case Examples
Matching Metaphors

This is an example of how these pairs of metaphoric images can be so matching or emotionally synchronized. The wife described herself as a bubbling, rushing, active, sparkling mountain stream that is constantly in motion, keeping very busy. She saw her husband as a large swamp. Initially, this sounds negative, stagnant, and somewhat humorous. However, she quickly explained that he has distinct boundaries, a definite location where she can always find him, much depth, and from that depth grow beautiful new things that rise above the surface. He is a grounding force in her busy world, and she admires and loves him *deeply.*

The husband saw his wife as an orchestra conductor on the podium, waving her arms wildly as she actively conducts the symphonic orchestra with her baton and elicits beautiful music. It is an active, busy, productive image—just like the rushing mountain stream. The husband saw himself as the orchestra pit which supports the conductor by containing the musicians who produce the music. The orchestra pit has definite boundaries and a location that the conductor can always depend upon. From the depths of this pit rises beautiful music which has been produced by the orchestra contained within. Both sets of images reflect the same kind of relations, actions, and feelings in this couple. These emotionally synchronized images allow the therapist to believe that this couple has a healthy understanding and open communication with each other. There are clear indications of loving support and respect for each other's role.

A Picture Worth 1,000 Words

The old saying, "A picture is worth a thousand words," rings true with this case example. For weeks I had been working closely with this couple, but we had a great deal of difficulty achieving a clear understanding for each partner's position. It seemed as if the harder we tried to work things out, the worse things were becoming. It was confusing and frustrating until this imagery exercise clarified matters in a matter of minutes. An image can capture an emotional position or psychological perspective far better than words may ever achieve. And this exercise was clearly the turning point in their therapy process.

The wife described her husband as a stubborn bull who would never take action, listen, or make any effort to move from his entrenched position. As a result she was becoming more frustrated and angry with him. She saw herself as a snarling tiger who is circling the immovable bull, getting louder and snarling more viciously with every day that passes. The husband saw his wife as an erupting volcano who scares him to death with her intense anger. As a consequence he saw himself as cowering and hiding in a cave from her frequent eruptions. This response astounded his wife who thought he was being a stubborn jerk with his passivity. Yet, his passivity was now seen as a coping strategy for his own survival. She had no idea that it was her own "snarling" which was causing the retreat and lack of action on his part.

As a result of this imagery exercise, she backed away from "snarling" at him, and he felt more comfortable to "come out of hiding in his cave" to actually deal with her. What had become a negative, vicious circle of non-productive behavior was now transformed into an open, comfortable, and productive line of communication again. Neither had been able to see each other's position until these sets of powerful images clarified their confusing and baffling stalemate. Therapists should remember that an image may capture that elusive perspective much more quickly and easily than countless efforts with words might ever do.

Similar Feeling, Different Intensity

This couple basically shared a similar perspective with each other but demonstrated a difference in the intensity of their descriptions. This is not unusual and can be expected frequently. This serves as another example of how a couple can view themselves.

The husband saw himself as a loyal, obedient, predictable, compliant, faithful dog who would jump to please his Master and do anything for her out of his undying love for her. He saw his wife as a cat with two distinct moods. At times she could be soft, cuddly, loving, nurturing—and a very sexy kitten. At other times she would be aloof, independent, self-sufficient, assertive, and untouchable with her claws out to keep others at a distance. He admired both "sides" of her, but was sometimes unsure which one would be greeting him!

She saw her husband as the dearest, sweetest, most lovable, elderly lady who works in a public library. The lady has everything quiet and neatly organized around her. She views her as a very special lady. However, the wife saw herself as a wild tornado that comes right through the library creating havoc, chaos, and disorganization. Nobody is hurt—just thrown off track. It is true that she kept life interesting and unpredictable for him!

An Important Difference in Perspective

Sometimes the differences between a couple's pairs of images may be subtle or slight, yet carry a significant difference in meaning. That may correlate directly with the significant difference in their views and account for their difficulty in resolving issues. Though images may be similar, look for the difference in their emotional tone.

The wife reported that she saw herself as a very busy little bee, always buzzing around everywhere, taking care of everything. She was very happy in her busy little "zipping around" to manage everything. However, she saw her husband as a coiled Cobra snake that was about to strike out at her, and she could not understand why that would be. Her husband was indeed ready to tell her to "buzz off" as he viewed her as a "nagging mosquito" who was driving him crazy with her hypomanic behavior. He saw himself as a "large flyswatter," ready to swat her if she did not slow down to a reasonable, manageable pace. Not until she had experienced this imagery exercise had she had a clue what the conflict was actually about. This led to a healthy and open discussion about their concerns.

The Frozen Musician

Many times when clients become "stuck" in their lives, they will blame others or look to others for the missing initiative within themselves. This kind of exercise can quickly reveal such a dilemma in easy-to-understand images. The client in this case was a middle-aged woman who had been a professional musician before she got married. She left the music field to raise her three children and filled her world with their activities. Now that they had grown and left home, she faced an "empty nest" and no career in music at the same time. This woman was miserably depressed and entered the hospital for treatment.

She blamed her husband for a number of things, claiming that he was not supportive or encouraging to her. We invited him to the hospital for a marital session and included this imagery exercise. She saw herself as a beautiful golden statue of a musician with his baton held high in the air, poised and ready to conduct the symphonic orchestra . . . but no music, no sounds, no movement—just frozen in that position. She saw her husband as a dog that was sniffing around the base of this splendid golden statue and then lifting his leg to pee on the statue. Despite this perception of a demeaning behavior, the statue *still* did not move.

Her husband saw his depressed wife as a massive boulder of granite with all kinds of gems, crystals, and glittery pieces contained within it. He saw himself as a curious cat, circling around this boulder, marveling at its beauty, but wondering *why it never moves or does anything*. With those remarks his wife suddenly realized that he was *not* "pissing on her," but just pondering her own lack of action. It finally dawned on her that *she* is the one who needs to motivate herself to return to a music career—*not* him. She was criticizing and blaming him for her own lack of initiative. This new awareness was extremely helpful to her, and she began to work harder on herself in individual and group therapy.

She left the hospital feeling much better and with some realistic plans for herself. No longer did she blame her husband for anything. That marital tension was gone. Two weeks after her discharge from the hospital, she called me to offer me a report on her progress. She said, "Guess where those images are now? I am a drum major leading the band in a parade down the main street of town. There is lots of music, drums drumming, and people cheering." I asked where her husband was in this picture. She added quickly, "Oh, he's right there, too. He's marching along behind me, beating on his bass drum!" So, she had returned happily to her field of music and was also experiencing her husband's loving support.

Two Victims

As therapists work with relations between any two people, it is not unusual for both partners to feel as if they are *both* being victimized by the other. Because both feel unhappy and focused on their own misery, they want to blame their partner. This imagery exercise helps clarify those emotional positions and offer insight to this couple through vivid images that capture this notion of *both* partners feeling victimized.

This young couple showed up at my office on an "emergency visit," having found my name in the Yellow Pages of the phone book. They were intensely angry with each other and could barely speak or look at each other. He claimed that she was crazy and needed to be locked up in the State Hospital. She claimed that he was delusional and needed a psychiatric evaluation. I concluded right away that discussing anything rationally was not likely to happen at this moment in time. Imagery might be a safer, indirect, and clearer method to assess their issues and work around their deadlocked communication. It is also true that when emotions are that close to the surface, imagery is rather easy to produce. When actively experiencing emotions, most people know exactly "*what* that feels like."

She saw herself as a beautiful horse locked in a huge metal cage. She saw her husband as the jailer who is holding the keys to the big cage. He is standing just outside the cage and taunting and teasing her with the keys (Interesting that he had wanted to lock her up in the State Hospital!). He stated that she is the Roman emperor, Augustus Caesar. He saw himself as "a group of persecuted Christians about to be fed to the lions." When she heard him describe his pair of images, her mouth fell open, and she exclaimed, "*YOU* can't be the victim! **I am!** How do *you* feel persecuted?"

This sudden awareness that *he*, too, felt persecuted intrigued her, motivating her to *want* to hear his view of things. He calmly explained to her how her anger and various remarks of hers had led to his feeling that way. As she listened with interest to his perspective it suddenly dawned on her that most of what she had "dumped" on him was more of a reaction regarding her frustrations with her father—*not* her husband. With this new ingredient added in to the mix, I set a chair for the deceased father with whom she had alleged unresolved issues. As she used the empty "Dad chair" to focus her frustrations and vent her feelings, her husband became quite interested and supportive. This removed him from the "hot seat" and his feelings of being persecuted. It soon became obvious that almost all of her anger was actually directed at the "Dad chair," and that she had been unfairly displacing her frustrations onto her husband. It was *her father* who held the keys to the locked cage with her inside.

They left the session that day in a calm, reflective mood. Throughout the next week her husband would stop her whenever she began "dumping" on him, setting out an empty chair, and then asking her if the anger belonged to him or her father (the empty chair). Most often, it was anger directed toward her father. In no way did the husband *want* to return to the feelings of being persecuted for things he had not done. However, when they returned a week later for their second session, she announced that it was not her father holding the keys to her cage after all. *She* had herself locked within this cage! It was *she* who held the keys outside the cage. We processed these feelings and perceptions using the metaphoric imagery as a tool.

They were supposed to return again two weeks later, but she called me on the phone to report that they would have to reschedule due to his work hours. While she had me on the phone, she added that "the cage door has opened." I asked her how that had happened and if she had galloped out of her cage yet. She replied that she had unlocked the cage herself and that the door was standing wide open. She was *not ready* to go out of the cage yet, but she knew that she *could* whenever she wanted to. And then, as quickly as this couple came into my life, they disappeared. The intensity of their struggle had passed, and much insight and positive progress had already been gained, thanks to the usefulness of the imagery.

Ten years later I received an unexpected phone call from this same young woman! She said, "Hi—remember me? I was the horse in the cage, and my husband was the group of persecuted Christians." Because imagery is so memorable, I had no difficulty recalling their situation—even though it had been ten years and hundreds of patients later! She said that she just wanted me to know *where those images were now!* She described her and her husband as two beautiful horses, galloping along together through the pastures and jumping over fences together. She said that they were having a great time and were very happy together. Then she quickly said goodbye, and I have not heard from them again. This case certainly demonstrates the usefulness of this exercise as well as the powerful retention of such images in one's mind.

The Elderly Leech

There will be times when a therapist may doubt that a particular pair of people may be able to perform this creative and imaginary process. For example, somewhere within this author resided a quirky notion that elderly couples would have more trouble with this exercise— either because they would not feel as openly expressive, or perhaps, just because they are old! As I experienced this lovely, older couple in their 70's, I noted her prim and proper, "churchlady" posture along with her perfect white hair (and bluish tint). He had trouble with his hearing aide squealing and leaned forward on his cane to try to hear me better. I finally decided to try this imagery exercise despite my own peculiar hesitations.

I introduced the exercise and gave them the instructions. I waited patiently as they both took a good five minutes to contemplate their images. Then she announced with confidence that she knew what she would be. She said, "I would be a blood-sucking leech on his nasty little ass!" (My mouth fell open, and I never doubted again that older people would have difficulty with this exercise.) She added that his "ass" belonged to a grumpy old dog. He *claimed* that he didn't hear her response as he continued to fiddle with his hearing aide. He saw her as a "mousetrap" and himself as a "sneaky rat." We had plenty to work with at this point, and I was quite appreciative of how much clarity this exercise provides so quickly!

The Thrill of the Chase

This imagery exercise can also reveal positive, humorous, and happier elements in a couple's relationship. In this case both are in agreement that there is a thrill to their actions, and this led to a productive and interesting discussion about their dynamics. She saw herself as a "cute little red fox" being chased by her husband, "an elegant hunting dog." He saw himself as the mythical giant ape, "King Kong", and she was his obsession as the human lover, played by actress "Fay Wray." These fun images led to a most colorful discussion about power, control, dominance, thrill of being chased, submission if captured, sexual excitement, romantic adventures, etc.

Hidden Dangers

Because these metaphoric images derive from subconscious feelings and bypass conscious defenses more easily, this exercise may reveal aspects of a relationship that neither person had meant to reveal or had not discussed openly yet. This may include certain fears, jealousies, doubts, insecurities, or potential dangerousness. In this clinical case example neither partner had discussed the tensions at home which were approaching a level of potential abuse. Verbal abuse had been escalating toward physical abuse, but neither partner had felt comfortable sharing "just how bad it really was."

The wife saw herself as a gorgeous antique wedding dress laden with lace and pearls. It was a very expensive outfit. She saw her husband as a "nasty, black mud puddle" that might "soil her" and ruin the priceless gown. The level of tension became even clearer in her husband's pair of images. He saw his wife as an expensive, ornate, antique lamp with teardrop crystals encircling the rim of the lampshade. It was absolutely stunning as well as quite fragile. The husband saw himself as a baseball bat, poised and ready to swing.

After feeling my own surprise at these responses, my first reaction was, "It sounds as though something might get broken. Is this possible? Is there a way that the lamp can *stay safe*? *Where* does the bat do its swinging? How can the dress *avoid* getting soiled? Does the lamp or the dress ever *put itself* in harm's way? Does the lamp *do* anything that might make the bat *want* to swing at it? Does the dress become careless about getting dirty?" Each question was asked slowly and carefully so as to keep the discussion in this indirect mode that would help this couple discuss these difficult concerns safely. Although they appeared uneasy and surprised at what the images were suggesting, they were able to discuss the situation in this indirect metaphoric fashion without feeling directly confronted or "on the hot seat."

By discussing how these images might work together more comfortably and avoid danger or harm, the couple was able to work through their escalation at home without having to directly talk about it. After this session, the wife pulled me aside and admitted that the danger had indeed been real, but that she was so relieved that they had been able to deal with this effectively without direct confrontation or blaming. Tensions at home remained manageable after this session. The therapist can expect that such hidden dynamics will indeed surface with these imagery techniques.

The Truth Shall Set You Free

There are many times when a therapist will wonder if the couple's relationship is going as well as one or both of them may claim. (This can be relevant to negative claims as well.) This imagery exercise may help reveal the actual nature of their present behavior and genuine emotions—often betraying what they had just been reporting verbally. In this case example the couple was headed for divorce, but the husband insisted on a final effort through counseling in the desperate hope that the marriage could still be salvaged. His wife openly claimed that she had no feelings left for him and could care less what he did with his life. She described him as having a bad temper and an abusive nature that she no longer wanted to be near. She claimed that fifteen years of marriage to him was enough, and that she was ready to stand on her own.

Her husband admitted that he *did* have a problem with expressing anger appropriately—but that he was reading many self-help books and making great progress. He begged his wife to give him a chance because he knew that he would be "a better man toward her real soon." Bottom line: she could care less. She agreed to try some traditional strategies such as taking some quality time together—like out for a quiet dinner or a weekend retreat. Despite going through these activities, she remained unchanged in her feelings or desires. He continued to claim that he was dealing with his anger much better and that he was a changed man. I had my doubts that just reading these self-help books would elicit such quick progress.

I decided to use this imagery exercise like a thermometer—to take a temperature reading of this couple's emotional positions—so that I could know what they actually felt about their relationship. He betrayed his own verbal claims immediately with his pair of images. He saw himself as a Big Game hunter, armed with expensive hunting equipment, crossbows, and rifles with telescopic scopes. He saw her as the "elusive prey" that he is *tracking*. He expressed confidence that he will eventually *hunt her down* and capture her. He did not indicate "dead or alive." She bluntly stated that she saw him as a huge, seven-foot, hideous alien creature that has "sucked everything of worth out of my mind, body, and soul." With these images clarifying their emotional positions, they proceeded to quietly divorce.

Sculpting Metaphoric Images

Peggy Papp, MSW, originally designed this exercise for use in a weekly couples group therapy setting. After extracting two pairs of metaphoric images from each couple and having them describe their impressions, she would have them act out each pair of images. This added the experiential element to these powerful pairs of images. Now the couple could *feel* their metaphors and *experience* the relations between the images. For example, a wife, who sees herself as a "whipped puppy," might choose to sit on the floor cowering, while she has her husband pace around her in a circle, snarling and griping at her as her image for him of a "vicious wolf." The therapist can then check with each partner to see if this does *feel right* to them somehow. Then they could switch to his pair of images and see how that *feels* when those images are played out. Do both pairs of images achieve a similar picture or emotional reaction? What is different?

The therapist can work with these powerful images which contain much useful information toward effecting some important changes. The therapist may use some creative questions to challenge the scenario into some role reversals, changes, or new directions.

"Do you wish to continue cowering like this for much longer?"

"Do you enjoy circling around her and snarling at her? What would you *rather* do?"

"Let's trade places. (to wife:) Snarl, gripe, and circle him now. How does *that* feel?"

(to husband:) "Does this trapped position feel good? Isn't this how *she* may feel?"

"What could you *both* do differently, now, at home?"

"What would help you *not want* to snarl at her any more?"

"Do you do anything as the puppy to make the wolf mad?"

"How could the puppy 'grow up' and be as strong as the wolf?"

"What makes the wolf snarl the loudest?"

"What makes the whipped puppy whimper and cry most often?"

"Having experienced both roles, which one did you like the best? Why?"

231

Within a couples' group therapy setting this kind of activity can be playful, revealing, and useful to the other couples who are observing. They can contribute their own constructive feedback, suggestions, insights, and helpful notions as they *see and feel* each couple's unique relationship. Often it may indirectly provide help for their own issues and conflicts. Regardless of the therapeutic setting, this form of experiential learning goes beyond the imagery and adds another important aspect to this discovery process that enhances understanding and perspective in any relationship.

Situation and Mood-Specific Imagery

Once the couple has achieved a general sense of how they view each other with the imagery exercise just described, the therapist can delve more deeply into their relations with a more specific examination of how they relate in different situations and various moods. The pairs of images can change drastically from situation to situation and from mood to mood. For example, imagine how any couple might respond when asked to find images for:

> How you relate during sexual intimacy . . .
>
> How you see each other while parenting the children . . .
>
> How you each behave when under stress . . .
>
> How you relate when discussing finances . . .
>
> How you act when your own parents are around . . .
>
> How you each seem when the in-laws visit . . .
>
> How you see each other when you both are trying to communicate . . .
>
> How you both behave when out with other couples or in social groups . . .

The results that the therapist can obtain from a couple when going into this kind of specific detail with powerful imagery will certainly add more depth and understanding to all aspects of their relationship. Obtaining and processing all of this emotional information may take weeks or months, but it would be well worth the journey. This can be especially effective with couples who seem to prefer and even enjoy this safer method of exploration. It just seems easier to describe their relationship indirectly through metaphors of animals and objects rather than to speak directly about oneself. It seems to free the person to describe the relationship with more detail and candor because of the indirect nature of the metaphors.

Reviewing Families of Origin

As each couple works with these metaphoric perceptions of each other, it is extremely revealing and helpful to include their own metaphoric impressions of both their own parents and their in-laws. The couple may learn just how similar the imagery may be between themselves and their own parents. Perhaps Sharon sees herself as a "shy lamb" and her husband as a "grouchy bear." When she explored images for her parents, she was astounded to learn that her mother had been a "timid lamb" while her father had been a "gruff bear." It may also serve to explain how that partner was raised to become a "grizzly bear" or a "lamb." The emotional perceptions each partner has of his own parents may shed a great deal of insight into the present conflict or issues within this couple. Unresolved issues with parents may be affecting the couple in a similar fashion with a similar scenario being repeated again. It can also be interesting to see if the spouse will also view his in-laws in the same manner as his partner did when imaging her own parents. The therapist can use all of the above, previously-described techniques to elicit these metaphoric images for each Family of Origin.

Current Family Perspectives

This same exercise can be expanded to include *all* family members with *all* of their impressions of *all* the other family members. This can take much time and require careful work, but it can be quite memorable and powerful. It gives the whole family a new way to talk about themselves in a way that children can participate and discuss easily. To visualize this complex set of images and relations, the therapist can position them according to *each* set of responses and implied relations according to the metaphors. The family can always correct the therapist if it "just doesn't *feel right*," and change their own positions to what does *feel right*. In this sculptured arrangement the family can *see* and *feel* their relationships according to the metaphoric imagery. It may take several sessions to explore all the images, combinations, and possible interactions among the metaphoric representations of *all* the family members.

Group Therapy Option

This same exercise could also be used in a group therapy context if it is typically a closed and regular group where the members know each other fairly well. They have become emotionally close to each other—like a family—through their therapy hours together. They will have interesting perceptions and images for each other that can be extremely insightful and useful. Each group member could have a turn sculpting the entire group into the metaphoric images he imagines for all of them. This could greatly enhance the self-awareness of each and every group participant. The group therapist could develop hours of insightful processing for his group from such an imagery exercise.

Specific Therapeutic Processes

8

The Magic Shop

Variations of this exercise have been used for over 30 years. Its origin is unknown to this author, and many professionals report that they have never heard of it. With this approach family members, couples, group therapy members, and others are able to express their needs, wants, and strengths in a fun, creative, and clever context. Here are the directions.

> "Welcome to the Magic Shop. On the shelves of my shop you will find unique items that cannot be found anywhere else. These items are in great demand but are not for sale. I will only barter or trade for what items you bring with you. Because I only have a limited supply of these greatly desired items, I will protect my products and will not trade for just anything and *not* for just any given reason. You must convince me that you *really have a need* for this product, and that what you are trading is of good quality and of worth for another customer. Now, take a look at my items up for trade today."

Anger	Despair	Happiness
Loneliness	Humor	Caring / Empathy
Love (romance)	Love (security)	Love (companionship)
Fear	Responsibility	Nurturing
Calm mood	Hope	Friendliness
Acceptance	Passion	Sobriety
Guilt / Shame	Loyalty	Trust
Energy	Assertiveness	Confidence
Social Comfort	Security	Reassurance

Each person thinks of one trait which he possesses, which is either a good quality that he has plenty of, or is a less desirable quality that he wants to be rid of. He then asks the therapist if he can trade for one or more of the items listed above. The therapist can pose a number of creative questions for this family member to challenge his needs.

"Can you explain why you *really need* this particular item?"

"Have you had this item before? How did you run out of it?"

"How do I know that you will take proper care of it and not waste it?"

"Explain your plan for managing this item better this time."

"*When* did you decide that you needed this item?"

"How can I be sure that *your* _____ is of good quality and in good condition?"

"I cannot spare much. How much do you *really need*? What is it for?"

"I could use all of your _____. Are you *sure* you don't need to keep some?"

"How will you make use of this new _____ you are receiving from me?"

"How do I know that you will use it in the proper manner for the right reasons?"

"How much do you need? How do you know if that is all that you need?"

These kinds of questions elicit the frequently unspoken feelings and needs of the different participants. This can enhance the overall awareness in a family, couple, adolescent group, supervision group, church group, or even just with individuals. This process can shed light on the reasoning behind particular behaviors and reactions. Presented as a "fun" activity with the challenge of haggling, bartering, and competing for what you desire, this exercise indirectly reveals the dreams, needs, wants, and frustrations of the participants.

This process is visually aided by bringing these invisible concepts and traits to life. First of all, it help to place the quantity of the item next to it in some form of physical measurement—such as pounds, liters, cups, stones, sticks, rods, beads, beans, fluid ounces, or certificates. The idea is simply to make such items tangible and real—so that a participant can actually feel as if he is taking this trait home with him. In the movie, *The Wizard of Oz*, the great and powerful Oz granted their wishes for Courage, a Heart, and a Brain with *only* symbolic props: a Hero's medal, a ticking mechanical heart, and a Diploma. Yet, they *immediately* felt better due to this symbolic ceremony and process. If the items are visually represented by some form of quantity or measurement, then the participants will be able to see when the Magic Shop is running low or out of a particular item.

5 lbs	HOPE		3 stones	RESPONSIBILITY
8 lbs	HUMOR		8 stones	LOYALTY
6 lbs	PASSION		5 stones	TRUST
10 lbs	LOVE		12 stones	NURTURING
2 lbs	CONFIDENCE		1 stone	CARING
-out-	ENERGY		2 stones	ACCEPTANCE

The therapist can increase the stress level of the situation by "running out" of certain items, refusing to barter with poorly-stated requests and forcing certain family members to compete—perhaps rewarding the "highest bidder" because of his clearly-stated reasoning. The therapist should only do this instinctively as the dynamics of the family suggest. This technique can be a clever approach toward learning a great deal more about a family's emotional needs and their unique methods of getting those needs met.

The therapist could make use of a dry erase board to list whatever items he wants to present to a particular family, group, or couple. Or the therapist could present a printed handout with 50 items listed just to see what their overall needs may be. The therapist could also limit the choices to a small selection of highly relevant items specific to those participants present in the room (example: "sobriety" for an alcoholic family). Items such as "fear," "despair," and "loneliness" might seem negative or undesirable. Yet, someone who is reckless may need "fear" to develop caution. Someone who cannot grieve may need a few pounds of "despair." And someone else, who is too busy with too many people and projects, may need some "loneliness" to acquire some time alone for himself.

Defusing Emotional Bombs

Many family members just have too much difficulty expressing themselves openly or safely with a feeling of security. They feel trapped with intense feelings of anger, hurt, sadness, guilt, shame, or grief. There is often no reasonable or logical place to release such feelings. The human target for these feelings may be deceased, living at a great distance, or "whereabouts unknown." Other appropriate "targets" may still live in the home but may be too volatile, dangerous, intimidating, or fragile to approach.

> "He will *kill* me if he knows how I really feel!"
>
> "I am afraid she will have a heart attack if I lay this guilt trip on her."
>
> "I am so mad, but I don't want to scare my spouse away."
>
> "I need to get these feelings out, but I don't want to *ever* hurt anybody's feelings."

"I will go to my grave before he ever finds out about this!"

"I cannot be mad at him—my God, he's dead. I feel guilty for feeling this rage."

"I've never met my real father, so I will probably never get to say what I need to."

Nevertheless, the family member still feels stuck with intense feelings but with no easy outlet. As the therapist becomes aware of such needs, he can recommend writing a letter to that person, dead or alive, near or far, volatile or fragile, because *that letter will **not** be actually mailed.* With that reassurance and understanding the family member is finally free to say whatever they wish to say in writing, knowing that there can be no reprisals, reactions, turmoil, or ugly comebacks.

"Write this letter using any language, cuss words, emotional tone, etc. that you wish so that your feelings are free-flowing. Imagine that this person is sitting right in front of you, but he or she *has to listen* to every word—even if it means that they are tied to a chair, handcuffed, or bound and gagged! This is your chance, *finally*, to say exactly what you have been wanting to express—in any way that you wish to do so! Don't hold back—don't edit or worry about what anybody might think, because *nobody* will ever see or read this—not even me (unless they want feedback). Write out these feelings, but *don't try to do so all at once.* That could be overwhelming. You may get on a roll and write 30 pages, or you may only be able to muster a small paragraph at first. Work on this over a period of days or even weeks—as you *feel* things, and as you begin to get in touch with *all* of your thoughts and emotions. Read it over each day and see if you have said all that you need to say. Eventually, you will **just know** when you have emptied out all of your pent-up, held-in feelings."

When the family member has accomplished this well, the therapist shall usually see a great relief with this safe, silent, and private emotional release. Often the member sees no need to say or do anything further. But, if he *does* still wish to do something openly and directly, he now has "taken the edge off" of his intense feelings. *Now* he can sort through his thoughts more clearly (no longer clouded by intense emotion) and decide what *really* needs to be communicated—if anything at all.

This process sometimes helps the client realize that whom he was originally targeting may not be the true source of his woes. For example, one woman targeted her mother, but after writing her feelings out, she realized that it was her father whom she was furious with. But, after writing a letter to him, she learned that she was actually angry with herself. If she had actually "dumped" all her feelings on her mother or father in person, she would have then learned from her process that those actions would have been unfortunate mistakes. Therefore, writing provides a private and safe alternative method of working through intense feelings with others who are not present.

Another consideration is to allow family members to "unload" on each other between sessions *on paper only* so as to "defuse" intense emotions and not waste time in the next therapy session with unnecessary "dumping." The same would be true for a couple—that they could practice releasing intense feelings and gripes toward each other on paper first, between sessions, and then they could use the actual therapy time to process what they learned, experienced, or clarified for themselves. Having released the intensity on paper *first* also helps each of them make certain what their issues and feelings truly are *before* a session. All of this processing through written release between sessions certainly saves "wear and tear" on the therapy hour by "defusing the bombs" and avoiding wasting precious therapy time with endless "dumping."

Nonsense Team Activities to Elicit Dynamics

Encouraging family teamwork with various fantasy exercises will almost immediately reveal the dysfunctional dynamics in the family system. Adding time limits or greater complexity to the task increases the stress and pressure upon the family to work faster with better communication, coordination, and cooperation—ingredients which are often absent or deficient. The therapist can watch for the following roles and dynamics.

> Who takes charge?
>
> Who initiates a plan?
>
> Who is quick to participate?
>
> Who argues or competes in creating the plan?
>
> Who balks or sabotages?
>
> Who is silent or withdrawn?
>
> Who is powerful in a passive manner by *not* assisting—which may lead to the family's failure in completing the task?
>
> Who is the best little helper?
>
> Who seems deaf or plays dumb?
>
> Who gets stressed?
>
> Who seems to play the peacemaker or negotiator?
>
> Who seems intent on success and winning?
>
> Who is just having fun?
>
> Where is the authority, hierarchy of power, and dominating forces?

The nonsense activity becomes a metaphor for how the family tries to do *anything*. The same politics are in effect with all other issues. It is the **process** the therapist is observing because the **content** is actually fictitious and meaningless. There are families who can hide many of their dysfunctional behaviors while sitting sweetly in front of the therapist. Giving them teamwork challenges will lead to their usual behavior and common interactions as they forget to hide their dynamics. Asking a dysfunctioning family to do *anything* as a "team" will elicit their usual "at home" behavior. The challenge of the task, the competition among members, and the increased pressure from stressful twists that the therapist introduces will distract the family from maintaining their "sweet" or phony facade.

The therapist wants the families to experience success upon their first trial because he wants them to have confidence that they *can* do the silly task. Having hooked them into the activity with an initial success, the therapist raises the stress level a bit and challenges the family again with an added element such as reducing the time allowed, adding handicaps, etc. Now the family will begin to show their true colors. With more stress will come more dynamics. The therapist will begin to observe the actual roles and behavioral issues develop. From those clues he can redesign the task to challenge the roles and typical behaviors. For example, if Mom always gives directions, the therapist can take away her voice by asking her to be silent. At the same time he might ask Dad or somebody else in the family to now be the new person to offer directions. This rebalancing of roles can be an interesting challenge. There may be much resistance toward any changes the therapist proposes, but since it is *just* a "nonsense activity," the family may be less resistant toward experiencing something different.

Pretzels

Have the family stand in a close circle. If there is not an even number of participants, then the therapist could join in or have an assistant do so in order to create an even number. Another option for evening the number of participants would be for the odd-numbered family member to stand just outside of the activity and even direct it. Have each participant put his right hand out in front of him and grab hold of one other person's right hand. Then reach out with the left hand and connect in the same way with somebody different. This creates a tangled, interwoven web of hands and arms called a "human pretzel." The family's task is to untangle this mess without letting go of anybody's hand. They may have to climb under or over others to do so. With more people it becomes much more complex and stressful. With fewer members the therapist may wish to increase the difficulty by (1) giving them a very short amount of time to finish, (2) not allowing them to communicate verbally, (3) putting the youngest or most passive person completely in charge. If Dad always directs, take his voice away. If Mom always helps and rescues, blindfold her. If the ten year-old son does not feel he gets any credit or voice in matters, let him lead the action. The family completes the task when they have untangled themselves into either one full circle or two interlocking rings. Because of the stressful intrusion into personal space with physical contact and the need for clear communication and decision-making, this can be a frustrating challenge for dysfunctioning families. The therapist can encourage various family members to accept new roles and try new behaviors in this metaphoric process. Perhaps the family will see that their usual way of organizing and attacking a problem does not work, and new ideas may bring better results.

Towers

This simple exercise with wooden blocks gives the family another challenging activity to reveal their process of attempting to work as a team. The therapist looks for all the same kinds of dynamics as previously suggested.

> "You must work together as a team with each member of the family adding one block at a time to create a tower. The more blocks you use, the more points you will be awarded. The higher and more complex the tower, the greater will be your overall score. You have just one minute to do this. Go."

As time is reduced stress levels are raised, and each family member will begin to show how he reacts to stress and to the behavior of other family members. A discussion following this activity can compare their actions with how they relate at home.

Crocodiles

This exercise gives the family the opportunity to choose its members to perform certain duties toward helping the family survive the threat of "intruding crocodiles." Although the threat is fictitious, the therapist can observe how this family organizes its own survival against a perceived threat. Here are some of the roles that could be assigned.

Leader—organizes a plan and directs the action
Spotter—watches through binoculars for crocodiles
Messenger—relays the information of impending harm
Protector—stays behind and guards helpless members or home
Helpless—one who seems most vulnerable and needs protection
Warrior—actually will fight the crocodiles

The family can discuss how they decided who is to fill each role. Each family member can state how well he likes or dislikes his assigned role. The family can act out a scene to see how their plan works or fails. The therapist can be quite creative with this kind of scenario. Different kinds of threats can be substituted: bear, flood, fire, tornado, gang, drug dealer.

Grief Sculpting for Losses

Losses create a unique situation for a family. Every person can grieve differently. Each family member may therefore behave differently but not accept or understand each other's style of grieving if it does not resemble his own. Everyone will deal with some degree of denial, anger, depression, guilt, fear, existential anxiety, and spirituality. Many people have difficulty expressing emotions, accepting intense feelings, and "saying goodbyes." Some missed the funeral or refused to go, often leaving themselves with a sense of incompletion and unresolved feelings. Some members never got a chance to say goodbye or discuss any unfinished business with the deceased person. Although the letter-writing described in the "Defusing Emotional Bombs" section can help, others find relief through *doing something* physically or *experientially* to alleviate their pent-up feelings.

The therapist should first assess *how* each family member grieves. Are they grieving presently? Have they ever begun? Are they blocked by some situation, person, or set of mixed emotions? If explored during a family session, other members can assist, verify, challenge, or confront each other in order for the truth to be realized. Regardless of how much the therapist is able to learn or have time to assess, the following sculpting scenario can elicit much information and emotional release. This is an important and powerful type of session emotionally and should be reserved for times when more traditional methods have failed. It is the belief of this author that a experiential encounter with visual props will always bring clients closer to their blocked feelings. (Allow two hours.)

If the client is an individual, then family or close friends may be invited just for this specific session. The therapist lets everyone involved know about this upcoming "Memorial Service" about two weeks in advance (When they arrive, one may note their somber mood from the suggestive hypnotic effect from knowing in advance and mentally preparing for this event). The therapist should arrange for an 8 × 10 framed picture of the deceased person to be brought to this session so that the family has a visual focal point. The therapist can provide silk funeral flowers from his prop closet. The therapist should arrange for a co-therapist or knowledgeable associate to assist in this session by playing the role of the body. The "body" of the deceased person can lie on the floor or on a couch. If it is impossible to obtain an assistant, then the therapist could place a blanket over pillows on a couch to simulate the form and presence of a body (Other therapists have acquired CPR dolls or actual mannequins.). Each member attending this special session should be asked to bring a special memento or item with emotional significance and connection with the deceased person. They can place these items next to the framed photo or on the "altar." Have chairs arranged to simulate a few rows in a church—or at least facing the body, picture, and flowers.

"Funerals are for the living survivors to honor and reflect upon the life of the deceased. Some of you may not have had that opportunity or simply were not ready at the time. Today we are holding a memorial service to continue the process of dealing with this significant loss."

(1) With the photo and body in the foreground, have each family member deliver a short talk or eulogy about the deceased person to the other family members, who are arranged in an audience setting. The focus should center on that member's relationship with the deceased, recalling special times, humorous moments, and beloved traits. These comments about the deceased person may help trigger emotions from other members. Give everyone enough time.

(2) Have every participant stand in line to file past the "body" so that each member is given an opportunity to say what they need to—directly to the deceased person. The therapist may have certain members get in line again if the therapist doubts that they are finished and suspects that they need to say or release more. A particular client may have to get back in line six or seven times before he really begins to face his own difficult task.

(3) Similar to the line filing past the "body", each family member may kneel next to the "body" and say their remarks. However, the person playing the corpse can respond to each

246

family member according to how the "corpse" believes the deceased person would have responded. In this fashion a dialogue can occur. Challenges, confrontations, or nurturing, validating and reassuring responses can now enhance the ability to bring closure for that family member. Other family members can whisper ideas to the "corpse" to help coach that person in the direction that *feels right* or at least seems plausible. If played by a co-therapist, the "corpse" can be pre-programmed by the therapist to produce certain reactions or trigger specific emotions. For example, if the therapist knows that his client dreads an unforgiving response from the corpse, he may inform the co-therapist to "be sure to *not* forgive him." Another example would be when the therapist knows that the client is likely to attempt a quick, easy resolution instead of releasing anger. The co-therapist would be instructed to trigger his anger or confront his "quick, easy solution."

(4) Following the example in #3, the therapist can also have the family member respond to his own remarks, playing the parts of *both* the mourner and the corpse. This is based upon the belief that the family member *knows* how his deceased relative would *probably* respond and can play out his own thoughts and beliefs in this dialogue arrangement. Other family members can validate whether or not the deceased person would have been likely to have responded in that manner. Someone may wish to jump in and play the part of the corpse to enhance or challenge the process. The therapist shall have to decide which direction seems most therapeutic at that point in time. The therapist can also whisper suggestions into his client's ear toward resolution and emotional release. This Gestalt approach of playing *both* roles is extremely powerful and productive in enhancing awareness.

(5) Follow the procedures for sculpting emotional distance by placing the different family members in a spatial arrangement to the corpse based solely on the emotional relations that had existed with that deceased person *prior* to his death. With other family members verifying the suggested arrangement, the therapist can clearly see who was closest / farthest in relations, and who may be most likely affected by the death (*whether or not they show this openly*). *Seeing and feeling* the distance may trigger strong reactions.

(6) Some family members may cling to the idea that they do not *have* to let go of this deceased person and can just *keep talking* with them, endlessly. *Seeing* him again and *being able to speak* with him again may be quite satisfying but at some point *not* therapeutic or realistic. Saying goodbye allows each family member to bring closure and move forward again. The corpse will need to rise up and leave the room "to go to Heaven," but not before each family member has his chance to say his goodbyes. The corpse may need to remind them that he will always be with them in each of their minds and in spirit forever, and that they can talk to his spirit at any time and in any place if that is helpful. But the corpse should add that each member needs to *be alive* and go forward with *living* his/her life. If utilizing jumpropes as props, the client will *feel* the loss of that dependent attachment when the corpse rises up, lets go of the rope (which the therapist had looped around his arm), and leaves the room to "go to Heaven." The corpse could even take the framed photo, holding it in front of his face, as he leaves their presence. *Seeing* the body and photo leave, *feeling* the loss of a physical connection, and *hearing* the door shut with finality—or "the thud of reality"—will typically bring a flood of overdue emotions.

Other Types of Losses

Although the discussion has centered on death and dying, there are grief reactions for many other kinds of situations. Divorce, romantic break-ups, employment layoffs, drug relapses, drastic health changes, forced retirement, disabilities, "falling off the wagon," sudden financial loss, or loss of status can all throw an individual or family into a grief process. All of the same phases of denial, anger, depression, bargaining, and acceptance will occur with these kinds of losses. The therapist can hold a memorial service for that loss and have that loss symbolically represented with props. Both children and adults benefit from taking a symbolic object and (1) digging a small hole and burying it outside, (2) throwing it away in a large trash can, or (3) burying it under a pile of pillows. A mock funeral can also be held for the individual who *almost died* through a suicide attempt or reckless behavior. Imagine the adolescent who lies there "dead," listening to how his family loved and appreciated him as well as what tearful "goodbyes" would be spoken. The therapist should avoid this type of session for a character-disordered client who may enjoy the attention his actions created. One does not want to reinforce or reward attention-seeking behavior and the notion that "dying is cool."

Grief Play Therapy for Children

Because some of these described experiential approaches may be too intense for children, a more indirect play therapy technique may be preferable. A child could use play therapy figures to carry out a memorial service. The child would choose *who* would be there, *where* they would be positioned, *what* they would say, and *how* they would act. The child should have himself represented by a toy figure so that he can depict what he, himself, would say and do at the memorial service. It especially becomes interesting to hear what kind of "goodbyes" the child would create for each family figure involved in the memorial service. In this manner the child can actively participate in an indirect and less intense fashion. Many of the same ideas already presented could be brought into this play therapy context (Some resistant adults may prefer this approach as it offers more safety and less intensity.)

Making Communication Visible in Couples

Based on the model of Transactional Analysis (Eric Berne) from the 1970's, each partner can be split into three basic mindsets or "ego states." The "Parent", "Child", and "Adult" frames of reference can help a couple understand the dynamics within themselves and between each other. When *any* interaction occurs, each partner is communicating from one of these three mindsets and influencing reactions from ego states within the other partner. Studying this process helps to explain *why* certain reactions and behaviors occur during the couple's attempts to communicate. For example, if one partner is acting childish, the other may feel a strong need to respond from a parental mindset. In a similar manner when one partner becomes critical or patronizing, the other partner may feel reduced to a child's insecure feelings and less confident behavior.

Examples of interactions from each ego state:

PARENT	critical, nurturing, domineering, directive, supportive, opinionated, judgmental, controlling, overprotective, helpful, patronizing, preaches rules, morals, ethics, leadership, etiquette, religion
ADULT	factual, informative, business-like, assertive, decision-making, logical, rational, realistic, sensible, fair, level-headed, open-minded
CHILD	curious, fun-loving, happy, sad, mad, scared, nervous, anxious, lonely, inventive, creative, artistic, musical, outgoing, silly, prankish, dependent, cowering, abused, insecure, compliant, obedient, brave

This model helps the couple to realize *what* they are actually doing to each other by *seeing* this process. Just *talking* about these dynamics with the couple can be too academic and cerebral for them. They would benefit more effectively from *seeing* and *feeling* this transactional model in order to understand what they are doing and how often they do it. There are two basic ways to accomplish this visual display.

(1) Place three chairs in a line opposing three chairs in another line across from each other. The left chair in each line will contain all interactions coming from the "Child" state of mind. The middle chairs contain the "Adult" interactions, and the right chairs will represent all remarks made from the "Parent" frame of reference. The therapist will help the couple learn which remarks belong to which ego state so that they can move to the corresponding chair. Then they shall learn in which mindset they may be spending more of their time when trying to communicate.

(2) It is also visually effective to use one chair for each partner, facing each other. The three positions of Parent, Adult, and Child are represented by different positions taken by each partner. The "Parent" role stands behind his chair, pointing at the other partner or standing with his hands on his hips. The "Adult" role sits "on the level" in his chair and deals in a direct and mature manner with the other partner—perhaps with hands held out in an open, accepting manner. The "Child" role sits on the floor in front of his own chair in a variety of postures depending upon his particular mood. If angry, he might sit cross-legged with arms crossed as well. If sad or hurting, he might curl up in a fetal position. If abused, demeaned, belittled, or acting submissive, he can assume a defeated posture with head bowed. If playful or teasing, he can appear alert, happy, and unaffected by anything that the partner is doing. The therapist will assist each partner to find a visual position that matches his mindset and emotions.

The therapist will observe their process as he helps them learn the various positions or chairs to sit in. The therapist will find that a couple will quickly learn which chair is for what mood or which position is for which mindset. This is because they are *feeling* their positions and therefore learning this technique much faster. For example, once Susan experiences her own anger in the "Child" chair, she will not soon forget in which chair she felt that feeling! Typically, a couple will become deadlocked in their communications. However, now they can *see where* they became stuck.

For example, Susan finds that she is always sitting on the floor in an sad "Child" position while her husband is towering over her from behind his chair in a "Parent" mindset, pointing a critical finger at her. Either she is being too sensitive and submissive, or perhaps he is just that dominating and demeaning. *Experiencing* these positions can bring about a quicker desire to change things. Susan would rather sit in her chair and "grow up" a bit. Maybe if she chooses to react differently, her husband might not feel as if he has to parent her. Maybe he will join her by sitting in his own chair and talking "on the same level." Because they could *see* their roles and comprehend their dysfunctional positions, they found it easier to try a different role and experience a healthier mindset.

This becomes an exercise which they can utilize at home on their own just to *see* where they get stuck whenever they need to discuss various issues. This form of visual feedback helps them to *feel* their dilemma and develop insight for what could facilitate healthy changes.

Chairs for Ghosts and Missing Persons

Setting an empty chair in a therapy session always draws attention because everybody wonders whom that chair represents. It becomes an extremely useful focal point for overdue communications, untapped emotional release, or as a reminder of somebody's influence or impact still being experienced by the other participants. Because there are many different uses for empty chairs, here are a variety of ideas for consideration.

THE GHOST: After the loss of a loved one and during a period of bereavement, an empty chair should be included in therapy sessions to represent the recently departed family member who is *emotionally still present* in the minds of the surviving others. At certain times during any session a family member may need to share tearful words, angry feelings, an apology, love note, nagging question, or goodbye message—and will have the chair as an essential focal point for those interactions toward the deceased. The therapist could place a framed photo of the departed family member on the chair or tape his/her name to the upper part of that chair for all to see. Later on, the family may choose to finally eliminate the ghost by letting go, dismissing it, or holding a final burial for that person. At that time the chair is symbolically removed. Each and every family member should feel positive and ready to move forward if the removal of the chair was a healthy step of progress for them.

MISSING PERSONS: An empty chair may need to represent other persons either related or directly influencing a family's emotions. It could be a father who abandoned the family by walking away from them all and disappearing to an unknown destination. It might be a parent whom the children have never met or known. It could be the birthmother who terminated her parental rights and relinquished this child for an adoption. It might be the daughter who has run away, and nobody is quite sure where she is. It sadly might be the son who was mysteriously abducted six months ago. For each of these situations and others, the empty chair depicts an important influence and emotional impact upon the family that needs to be present for them to deal with.

UNDESIRABLE "MEMBERS": This category includes those influences which have intruded into the family so often that they begin to *feel like members* of the family. This includes alcoholism, drug abuse, a sexual affair, an eating disorder, gambling addiction, abortion, unwanted pregnancy, rape trauma, or war flashbacks. The family needs to be able to speak to these problems, so they require a focal point. Props placed on this chair are especially useful in these situations—such as a wine bottle, pill bottle, plate of food, name or photo of extramarital sexual partner, baby doll, and war relic, cap or medal. *Feeling* that presence may certainly trigger strong emotional responses that have never had a chance to be vented previously. By having those issues take form and occupy a chair opens the door for important therapeutic work. (Imagine the alcoholic being able to confront his bottle and attempt to tell it goodbye.)

ABSENTEES: It is certainly not unusual for a therapist to experience less than the expected number of family members showing up for a therapy session. It becomes frustrating for a counselor to prepare for a family discussion with five family members—and then only two members are able to attend. Bob had soccer practice; Dad had to go into work early; John had to finish an important homework project. Mom and Brenda were the only two that could attend. The therapist may be tempted to simply reschedule this family session until a time when all members can attend. However, that time may not happen anytime soon, and valuable opportunities could be lost in the flow of therapy.

The therapist can proceed with a family session, setting out eight chairs for the five family members even though only two actually arrived. Those two members can still indicate where every family member would probably sit in those eight chairs. Between Mom's opinions and Brenda's perspective they will probably be very accurate regarding seating, comments and reactions to discussions, placement in sculptings, and emotional issues. The therapist can probe their perspectives by asking, "What would Dad say about that if he were here?" or, "What would John do about that?" If Mom is not sure (a rare likelihood), then Brenda may very well know. The absent family members may be more likely to be present for the next session when the others tell them about what they "said" at the session that they could *not* attend! However, a busy family may typically have *somebody* absent every week, so this approach will be certain to include the absent member *through the perceptions* of all the others. In this fashion the momentum and flow of therapy is less disrupted and kept intact. The absent members can always validate or deny reported comments at the next session that they can attend.

Clinical Case Example

A fourteen year-old boy was referred by school authorities for truancy, opposing authorities, and rebellious behavior. His mother clearly had a negative and sarcastic attitude toward her son from the first time I encountered them. Then I learned that the father had abandoned this family just months earlier. This adolescent son has a strong physical resemblance to his father, and Mom had no obvious or logical target for her frustrations and anger. I placed an empty chair in the first family session for the husband (and father) who had abandoned them. When Mom realized who the chair was for, I asked her if she needed to say anything to her missing husband. She finally vented much anger toward that chair with my support and encouragement. Then I had her son sit right next to that empty chair so that his mother and I could differentiate between Dad and son. We determined how they were different in many aspects, which helped the mother to distinctly distinguish between what feelings belonged to her husband or to her son. With those emotional matters clarified and settled, the mother was noticeably calmer and more pleasant. Her bitterness was gone, and her relations with her son were kind and loving again. The son was clearly relieved and "glowing"—as if he had gone through the release of an exorcism. His behavior was respectful and thoughtful. The empty chair had served its purpose very well as a necessary focal point.

The Silent Movie

The use of a video camera can be quite effective as a means of feedback for the family. They are able to observe their own behavior and *see* how they interact with each other. However, they may still get caught up in the verbal discussions and be blind to many dynamics which are occurring visually. Think about how many sessions are dependent on what was discussed, shared, described, or what problems, topics, goals, and issues were verbalized. What would the session be like *without* any of those typical ingredients? After filming a family therapy (or marital therapy) session, the therapist invites the family to view the previous videotaped session with him. To accomplish the most enlightening results the therapist turns down the volume on the television monitor so that family cannot get lost among the words. Then each family member *has* to rely on watching the facial expressions, body posturing, body movements, gestures, signs of anxiety, seating changes, restlessness, motionless withdrawal, emotional distance, and physical spacing. They have no other way to review the session other than visually. This heightens their awareness regarding their own behavior as well as what dynamics are truly occurring within the family system.

The therapist can also point out his own observations as well and rewind particular scenes so that the family can clearly observe what the therapist has noted. The therapist can certainly stimulate discussions by questioning each family member on what he or she "sees" in the "silent movie" version of the session. Most family members get so caught up in the verbal discussions that they completely miss many of the telltale dynamics that were occurring throughout the discussions.

Hopefully, the family can learn from this visual training and observe more about themselves more often.

The therapist should attempt to put himself within the camera's view as well. Although most therapists will probably avoid doing this for a variety of excuses, it is helpful for the therapist to also see his own nervous habits, visual reactions to the family, and shifts in his own behavior. The therapist should be willing to learn about himself as well.

Clinical Case Example

When forced to just *see* themselves interacting with each other, a family was astounded at how they appeared on the videotape. Mom looked like an exotic bird, waving her arms constantly like a bird flapping its wings. Dad never moved, appearing like a statue or corpse. The kids were caught on film pinching, touching, and kicking each other when the parents were looking elsewhere. It was easy to see who initiated conflicts and who maintained the battles. Occasionally, several family members would react simultaneously (to something discussed) with facial grimaces, body shifts, and chairs turning away. At those moments we would first guess what had been said and then, we would rewind the tape to see what had actually been stated. This new visual awareness was so intense that many behaviors began to change. Therapists may not realize that families rarely get this opportunity to watch themselves. Self-awareness for each family member can be memorably enhanced.

Happier Endings

This is a great self-esteem building activity that leaves virtually everybody smiling and feeling loved and appreciated. When a session has been especially intense or difficult, this exercise can help the couple, family, or group leave on a positive note. Too frequently the emphasis during sessions has been on problems and deficiencies. This brings the focus back around to positive qualities, strengths, verbal compliments, and reassuring words of support and hope. The therapist can attempt to regain a balance in difficult sessions by ending with this positive exercise.

With couples the therapist can close the regular work about ten minutes before the end of the session and ask the couple to close their eyes for a moment. Having them reflect back in time to when they first met, courted, and fell in love, the therapist asks them to find three things they really liked about that time or about each other. When they each have three things, they can open their eyes and share them *directly* with each other—not with the therapist. This exercise took them away, mentally, from the negativity of the present and reconnected them with some positive memories and feelings from the past. Although this does not *solve* the problems of the present, it at least reminds them that it has not *always* been a tough time and that they have had a *mixture* of experiences. The mental trip back through time helps relieve the pressures of the present as well. In a hypnotic fashion the couple can attach themselves to positive feelings from years ago and bring that mood back with them to the present moment. This has the effect of balancing the mood of the session and have them leave on a more positive note.

With families and groups the therapist places one chair in a central location with everyone else basically facing that one seat. One at a time each family or group member will get his turn in that chair. While that particular member is sitting in the special chair, all the other family or group members will each take a turn, giving the targeted member at least one compliment, words of support, encouragement, or messages of love and nurturing. The therapist can utilize this opportunity in a number of ways.

> "Each of you think of two things you really like and appreciate about Susan."

> "Each of you express one positive feeling toward Bill."

"Each family member shall give Robert three supportive statements."

"Every one of you shall find a way to tell or show Mom how you love her."

"Each of you find two ways to express support or encouragement for Billy."

"Think of *at least one* simple thing about Sam that you *really* like."

"If you cannot think of anything to say, then offer a hug, kiss, backrub, or handshake."

It is wise to pick one approach and use the same words for each person's turn. This keeps the exercise consistent and fair. It also gives the other family members time to think while each member is taking his turn. For families who are less verbal, they may prefer to show their love and appreciation with hugs, kisses, or backrubs. For families who are both less verbal *and* less likely to show emotions, they can write their compliments or words of love on paper and pass them to the special chair's occupant. However, it is preferable to hear what each member says to another in front of the others—as it acquires a powerfully supporting group effect. When somebody receives an award, it feels more special when given in front of an audience rather than when given to that person, alone, in private.

By the time each family member has had his turn in the special "Happy Chair," everybody now has been positively stroked and complimented or told how they are loved and appreciated—even those who had been feeling excluded, persecuted, neglected, or withdrawn. It is not surprising that everyone feels somewhat better as they leave the session after this exercise! Again, this *does not solve* the problems of the present, but it does help everybody to feel somewhat better after a difficult and emotionally draining therapy hour. Children enjoy the positive feedback so much that they may often insist on ending *every* therapy session after this one with the same "Happy Chair" exercise.

Therefore, this particular exercise also works very well at home at the conclusion of weekly family meetings. In the same manner everybody can leave the family meeting feeling positive and loved. It serves to help family members *remember* the positive aspects and traits of each other as well as allowing some time to *practice* giving *and receiving* such compliments or messages of love and support. This is a great thing to rehearse on a weekly basis!

A Final Word

Reading about this type of therapy is different from actually *trying* this kind of work. To perform a different kind of therapy requires the therapist to be different. This is where the biggest problems develop. The therapist runs head-on into himself. Complacency, security, old habits, and routine just lure counselors into not making any changes.

Resistance wins.

Many therapists *know* about these kinds of techniques but *still* are not using them.

They do not trust that their eyes will really see new ideas and solutions.

They do not trust that they will be successful with difficult families.

They are afraid of appearing foolish or silly.

They do not accept that they will know what to do next—once a visual display is underway.

They would just as soon believe misleading words—which a client's conscious defenses control well—instead of an impromptu, spontaneous, and genuine emotional picture or portrayal that easily bypasses resistance.

In my opinion this kind of visual and metaphorical therapy is clearer and easier. It removes the guesswork and unclouds the vision. It reveals dynamics innocently and cleverly. It presents an honest emotional picture. The therapy hour flies by because the therapist often sees *too much* rather than not enough—and there is not enough time to pursue everything that was observed. It is faster, to the point, and more efficient.

And, perhaps, most of all, clients *remember* the results of these techniques for years—far longer than most words have succeeded in being recalled. After all, a picture *is worth* a thousand words!

My motto in life has always been:

"IF YOU DON'T TRY, YOU'LL NEVER KNOW . . ."

Make the effort to be more effective.

Just *try* it. That's all.

Bibliography

Berne, M.D., Eric (1964), *Games People Play*, New York: Grove Press, Inc., 192 pages.

Burns, Robert C. (1982), *Self-Growth in Families: Kinetic Family Drawings, Research and Application*, New York: Brunner-Mazel, Inc., 277 pages.

Carter, Elizabeth A., and McGoldrick, Monica (1980), *The Family Life Cycle: A Framework for Family Therapy*, New York: Gardner Press, Inc., 468 pages.

Hammond, PhD., D. Corydon, editor (1990), *Handbook of Hypnotic Suggestions and Metaphors*, New York/London: W.W.Norton & Company, 602 pages.

Helmering, Doris Wild (1976), *Group Therapy—Who Needs It?*, Millbrae, California: Celestial Arts, 211 pages.

Mills, Joyce C. and Crowley, Richard J. (1986), *Therapeutic Metaphors for Children and the Child Within*, New York: Brunner-Mazel, Inc., 261 pages.

Bibliography

Minuchin, Salvador (1974), *Families and Family Therapy*, Cambridge, Massachusetts: Harvard University Press, 268 pages.

Minuchin, Salvador, and Fishman, H. Charles (1981), *Family Therapy Techniques*, Cambridge, Massachusetts: Harvard University Press, 303 pages.

Oaklander, PhD., Violet (1978), *Windows to Our Children*, Utah: Real People Press, 335 pages.

Papp, MSW, Peggy, editor (1977), *Family Therapy: Full Length Case Studies*, New York: Gardner Press, Inc., 210 pages.

Satir, Virginia (1967), *Conjoint Family Therapy*, Palo Alto, California: Science and Behavior Books, Inc., 208 pages.

Satir, Virginia (1972), *Peoplemaking*, Palo Alto, California: Science and Behavior Books, Inc., 304 pages.

Satir, Virginia, and Stachowiak, James, and Taschman, Harvey (1975), *Helping Families to Change*, New York: Jason Aronson, Inc., 296 pages.

Starr Adaline (1977), *Psychodrama: Rehearsal for Living*, Chicago: Nelson Hall, 379 pages.

Wiener, PhD., Daniel (1994), *Rehearsals for Growth: Theater Improvisation for Psychotherapists*, New York/London: W. W. Norton & Company, 269 pages.

EFFECTIVE STRATEGIES FOR HELPING COUPLES AND FAMILIES

Thank you for choosing PESI, LLC as your continuing education provider. Our goal is to provide you with current, accurate and practical information from the most experienced and knowledgeable speakers and authors.

Listed below are the continuing education credit(s) currently available for this self-study package. ***Please note, your state licensing board dictates whether self study is an acceptable form of continuing education. Please refer to your state rules and regulations.*

Counselors: PESI, LLC is recognized by the National Board for Certified Counselors to offer continuing education for National Certified Counselors. Provider #: 5896. We adhere to NBCC Continuing Education Guidelines. These self-study materials qualify for 8.75 contact hours.

Psychologists: PESI, LLC is approved by the American Psychological Association to sponsor continuing education for psychologists. PESI, LLC maintains responsibility for this program and its content. PESI is offering this activity for 6 hours of continuing education credit.

Social Workers: PESI, LLC, 1030, is approved as a provider for social work continuing education by the Association of Social Work Boards (ASWB), (540-829-6880) through the Approved Continuing Education (ACE) program. Licensed Social Workers should contact their individual state boards to determine self-study approval and to review continuing education requirements for licensure renewal. Social Workers will receive 8.75 continuing education clock hours for completing this self-study material.

Addiction Counselors: PESI, LLC is a Provider approved by NAADAC Approved Education Provider Program. Provider #: 366. These self-study materials qualify for 10.5 contact hours.

Nurses: PESI, LLC, Eau Claire is an approved provider of continuing nursing education by the Wisconsin Nurses Association Continuing Education Approval Program Committee, an accredited approver by the American Nurses Credentialing Center's Commission on Accreditation. This approval is accepted and/or recognized by all state nurses associations that adhere to the ANA criteria for accreditation. This learner directed educational activity qualifies for 10.5 contact hours. PESI Healthcare certification: CA #06538.

California Nurses: PESI, LLC is a provider approved by the California Board of Registered Nursing, Provider Number 6538 for 10.5 contact hours.

Iowa Nurses: PESI, LLC, is an approved provider by the Iowa Board of Nursing. Provider #: 346. This learner directed educational activity qualifies for 10.5 contact hours.

Procedures:
1. Read book.
2. Complete the post-test/evaluation form and mail it along with payment to the address on the form.

Your completed test/evaluation will be graded. If you receive a passing score (80% and above), you will be mailed a certificate of successful completion with earned continuing education credits. If you do not pass the post-test, you will be sent a letter indicating areas of deficiency, references to the appropriate sections of the manual for review and your post-test. The post-test must be resubmitted and receive a passing grade before credit can be awarded.

If you have any questions, please feel free to contact our customer service department at 1-800-843-7763.

PESI, LLC
200 SPRING ST. STE B, P.O. BOX 1000
EAU CLAIRE, WI 54702-1000

Product Number: ZHS007185   **CE Release Date:** 04/18/06

PESI®
P.O. Box 1000
Eau Claire, WI 54702
(800) 843-7763

Effective Strategies for Helping
Couples and Families
Evaluation/Post-test

ZNT005645

This home study package includes CONTINUING EDUCATION FOR ONE PERSON: complete & return this original post/test evaluation form.

ADDITIONAL PERSONS interested in receiving credit may photocopy this form, complete and return with a payment of $49.00 per person CE fee. A certificate of successful completion will be mailed to you.

For office use only
Rcvd. _____
Graded _____
Cert. mld. _____

C.E. Fee: **$49**   Credit card # _____

Exp. Date _____

Signature _____

V-Code* _____ (*MC/VISA/Discover: last 3-digit # on signature panel on back of card.) (*American Express: 4-digit # above account # on face of card.)

Mail to: PESI, PO Box 1000, Eau Claire, WI 54702, or
Fax to: PESI (800) 675-5026 (fax all pages)

Name (please print): _____ _____ _____
                            LAST   FIRST   M.I.

Address: _____

City: _____ State: _____ Zip: _____

Daytime Phone: _____

Signature: _____

• Date you completed the PESI Tape/Manual Independent Package: _____

• Actual time (# of hours) taken to complete this offering: _____ hours

PROGRAM OBJECTIVES

Please evaluate this book's effectiveness in communicating the following objectives:

	Excellent				**Poor**
Describe nine different styles of emotional positioning within couples.	5	4	3	2	1
Describe how nine types of couples create various family issues over generations.	5	4	3	2	1
Identify the essential treatment issues & strategies within each of the nine couple styles.	5	4	3	2	1
Demonstrate how to uncover and assess emotional positions in couples and families with clear, visual approaches.	5	4	3	2	1
Utilize a variety of non-threatening strategies to "go beyond words" safely and find underlying issues, unresolved feelings, and political motives.	5	4	3	2	1
Help families release unresolved feelings effectively through safe forms of expression.	5	4	3	2	1
Help families identify problems through powerful imagery and playful exercises.	5	4	3	2	1
Sample from a rich assortment of time-tested, successful, non-threatening strategies	5	4	3	2	1

POST-TEST QUESTIONS

1. The nine types of couples discussed were based upon
   a. Their ages in the family cycle
   b. Their family of origin backgrounds
   c. Emotional bonding and distance
   d. Their compatibility and similarities

2. Lack of cohesion in couples can be disguised by
   a. Attention to children in the home
   b. Activities as a whole family
   c. Over involvement with hobbies or work
   d. All of the above

3. Metaphoric sculpting refers to
   a. Creative story telling for couples
   b. Play therapy utilizing clay
   c. An imagery exercise to reveal dynamics
   d. A fantasy game in family therapy

4. Why is imagery work preferred over verbal discussions?
   a. Clients can "see" the problems and solutions
   b. One can often recall images more easily than words
   c. Images elicit genuine and unexpected emotions
   d. Imagery work seems more fun, safe, and indirect
   e. All of the above

5. The "Ghost Chair" refers to
   a. A fantasy tale read to families
   b. A chair used for absent members
   c. A scary position in the family dynamics
   d. Examining emotional space in the family

6. Emotional age is important because
   a. Families and couples act and react on that level
   b. Chronological age is too hard to remember
   c. All parents can act like kids
   d. It can be determined when anger developed

For additional forms and information on other PESI products, contact:
**Customer Service; PESI; P.O. Box 1000; Eau Claire, WI 54702
(Toll Free, 7 a.m.-5 p.m. central time, 800-843-7763).
www.pesi.com**

**Thank you for your comments.
We strive for excellence and we value your opinion.**